Britain's Invisible Earnings

NICHOLAS SOWELS

With contributions by

DUNCAN JAMES
IAN HUNTER

A HUDSON RESEARCH INTERNATIONAL REPORT

Gower

Aldershot · Brookfield USA · Hong Kong · Singapore · Sydney

Published by :

Gower Publishing Company Limited
Gower House
Croft Road
Aldershot
Hants GU11 3HR
England

Gower Publishing Company
Old Post Road
Brookfield
Vermont 05036
USA

ISBN 0 566 05787 5

Printed and bound in Great Britain by
Anchor Press Ltd, Tiptree, Essex

Contents

Figures and tables

PART 1

1 Introduction

Since 1973, the British economy has undergone a remarkable transition. Structural changes in the world economy have brought about a profound evolution throughout the developed West. But there can be little doubt that Britain's economic experience has been unique in many ways. The key to this lies in the shift of resources out of industry, or more specifically manufacturing industry, and into other areas. Of course, this has been taking place over a long time and is common to all industrialized countries. Since World War II, in particular, they have witnessed a fundamental and sustained migration of labour and capital away from agriculture and industry to the service sector. In some ways, this parallels the move out of agriculture and into industry which occurred during the 19th century as the Industrial Revolution swept across Western Europe and North America.

In Britain the retrenchment of industry was already comparatively advanced before the first oil-shock. It was a phenomenon variously interpreted as a sign of economic maturity, competitive failure, or some inevitable and unchangeable combination of the two. Some observers argued that having been the first to industrialize, Britain would naturally lead the world into the next phase of development. Instead of being detrimental to the long term health of the economy, such change was actually positive and should not be resisted. Others feared the consequences for Britain's long term prosperity and pleaded that the erosion had to be stopped at all cost. Between these schools of thought lay a more fatalist approach: one that lamented the poor performance but saw little real possibility of combating it.

After the 1973/4 oil-shock the gradual, relative decline of the British manufacturing has turned abruptly into one of absolute contraction. Within two years output fell by 8 percent. Though it subsequently recovered somewhat during the boom of the late 1970s, the revival was to be short lived. Numerous factors combined to cause a dramatic fall of 14.3 percent in manufacturing output between 1979 and 1982.[1] These have been extensively detailed elsewhere, but a brief outline will be given here because their subsequent evolution remains significant to the British economy.

Most generally, the second oil-shock, beside battering British manufacturing industry, affected the entire world economy. In the OECD as a whole, growth slumped from an average rate of 3.6 percent between 1977 and 1979, to a feeble 1.0 percent from 1980 through to the end of 1982.[2]   This slowdown was accompanied by a drop in trade growth, which halved to about 3 to 4 percent per annum.   Given that Britain exports roughly one third of its GNP, the consequences for domestic growth are obvious enough.

At the same time, there can be little doubt that the new Conservative government's monetarist economic policy played a significant part in squeezing economic activity. Whatever the theoretical merits of monetarism — and its broad adoption in the developed world has undoubtedly helped to end demise of spiraling inflation — its application proved considerably more difficult than the government had expected.   Despite the introduction of an apparently rigorous Medium Term Financial Strategy (MTFS), with its targets for sterling M3, the step by step reduction of the money supply remained an elusive goal.   Far from falling, inflation, the object of the government's exertions, actually rose.   This was partly due to pent-up pressures inherited from the previous Labour government.   But Mrs Thatcher's own policies did much to add fuel to the fire.   The switch to greater indirect taxation through VAT, combined with the wage explosion following the Government's acceptance of the Clegg Commission's findings on public sector pay, helped to boost the consumer price index to 20 percent in 1980.   In reaction the government encouraged interest rates to rise rapidly, as a move to assuage public opinion and especially money-market scepticism.

Although high inflation held down the real cost of money, high nominal interest rates in the upper teens had a marked effect on activity.   Companies in all sectors set about slashing stocks, pushing the economy into deeper recession.   In addition, the climb in interest rates helped enforce a rapid rise in the sterling exchange rate.   The pound was already experiencing upward pressure, given its newly acquired status as an oil-backed currency.   When interest rates then shot up, sterling rose vertiginously.   This had a catastrophic impact on the competitiveness of British industry, both at home and abroad. Last, but by no means least, the government introduced a series of deflationary budgets as the fiscal component of its MTFS.   This policy culminated in the 1981 budget, which administered a third dose of deflationary "medicine", while the economy was still in severe recession.

The combined impact of these factors had to be felt to be believed.   By early 1982 Britain had become a society stricken by mass unemployment unseen in 50 years.   To be sure, this was mirrored in nearly all developed countries, but Britain's record was worse than most.   The surge in unemployment came largely through the contraction of Britain's manufacturing workforce. In a desperate battle to survive, British manufacturing cut its labour requirements by 20 percent in the three years to 1983. It was a brutal and bitter rationalization, but one which industry often had little option but to pursue. Astounding too, was the crash into a trade deficit on manufacturing goods. For the first time ever, the former "workshop of the world" chalked up a deficit on manufactures in 1983. Nor was it a marginal adjustment. From a surplus of £2.4 billion in 1982 (on semi-manufactures and finished goods) the sector careered into a deficit of £2.3 billion a year later.[3]

Since this dramatic turn of events, manufacturing has succeeded in reversing its decline. There have been notable advances in productivity over the last years, which have done much to propel output and profitability back to pre-recession levels. In addition to such quantifiable improvements, much qualitative and anecdotal evidence suggests that there has been a considerable evolution in Britain's industrial culture. An important, some would say fundamental, shift in attitudes has occurred in those industries and enterprises which have survived the recession. Repeatedly, management surveys, opinion polls, and industrial reportage have commented on such recent trends as "management asserting its right to manage", a "new realism on the shop floor", and even a growing "co-operation" between the "two sides of industry".

It remains to be seen how universal and permanent these apparent changes in behaviour are. When they were first observed in the early 1980s many sceptics, not unjustifiably, queried their foundations. In particular, it was thought that the shift in working values was overwhelmingly connected with rising unemployment. Once it ceased to accelerate, or even contracted, labour relations would revert back to the normal confrontation. In this context, much concern has been voiced about the persistence of high wage increases — especially as the gap between Britain's wage inflation and those of its main competitors has remained. But, even here the outlook may now be less pessimistic than was once thought. If pay rises continue to push ahead of inflation, at least they have kept fairly constant. Contrary to previous opinion, they have not accelerated markedly as people got used to high unemployment or even as the level of joblessness has fallen.

Furthermore, there has so far been little sign of a revival of the confrontationist labour relations that so marked the 1970s. To be sure, industrial action has not disappeared altogether. The strikes in the motor industry in early 1988, combined with other action by nurses and seamen indicate that the potential for industrial conflict still exists. Yet, at the same time, there can be no doubting the radical transition undergone by the labour movement over the last decade. The miners' strike of 1984/5 and the subsequent breakup of the NUM — that unassailable vanguard of British trade unionism — were only the most, brutal manifestations of change. They revealed dramatically the general problems facing organized labour, coming to grips with a rapid economic transformation and the attendant evolution of social and political conditions.

Nevertheless, despite such developments, the total volume of manufacturing production in the UK was still lagging behind its 1973 peak at the end of 1987, and only seems set to recover its former level during the course of 1988. In this crucial respect, Britain's record is unique among the major industrial powers, and raises fundamental questions about the future of manufacturing.

The first centres on employment. After five years of output recovery the sector has yet to produce a turnaround in its employment levels. Despite the return to profitability and the consolidation of investment, British manufacturing as a whole is still rationalizing its demand for labour. Put another way, productivity in the sector continues to outpace output, with the effect of squeezing out employment. Unless there is a major change in the overall economic and political environment, it must be seriously doubted whether manufacturing will be able to play more than a marginal role in generating future employment.

This immediate concern overlaps with the long term structural position of the sector in the British economy. Of the major industrialized economies, Britain and the United States are alone in having a manufacturing sector that now employs less than one in four of the working population. This has led to much heart-searching on both sides of the Atlantic. In the US fear has been expressed that the sector may never again recover its former strength — although its performance since the beginning of is leading to re-found optimism. Concern has focused not only on the "smokestack" industries, but also on high-technology activities where the US traditionally has had a commanding world position. In the UK such doubts over "de-industrialization" have a longer history, but intensified since the start of the 1980s.

To promote employment, many politicians, labour leaders, businessmen, and economists have repeatedly vaunted the virtues of the service sector. It has not gone unnoticed that employment in services has tended to weather recession better than in industry. After

6

some decline, service sector employment in the UK was up 9.5 percent between 1980 and beginning of 1987. But even this relatively strong performance pales when compared with the expansion of service sector employment in the US. Incredibly, the sector generated over 11 million jobs during the same period, at a time when industrial employment in the US showed no net growth and unemployment was hammering the rest of the OECD.[4]

For America's industrial partners in Europe the achievement has provided an enviable example. Saddled with an average unemployment rate that refuses to fall back into single digits, many European governments have tried to foster service sector growth. In particular, it is widely hoped that the sector could mop up youth and unskilled unemployment through boosting the supply of "no-tech, not low-tech", low-paid jobs. This drive has gone hand in hand with the promotion of more pro-market and American business ethics and practices, as part of the political shift to the right across the Western world since the late 1970s. By trying to stimulate private and especially small business enterprise, greater labour market flexibility, a reduction of state involvement etc., the hope is that some of America's success will rub off. This is an ideological objective clearly pursued by Mrs Thatcher's government.

Yet, whatever the merits and feasibility of trying to Americanize Britain's economic culture, it is becoming increasingly clear that Reaganomics is considerably, even fundamentally, flawed. While the benefits of lower unemployment cannot be denied, services-led job creation in the US has been facilitated and accompanied by major financial problems. In cutting taxes and permitting a colossal federal budget deficit to emerge, the Reagan administration did much to stimulate US growth and employment at a time when the world economy was floundering in recession. But, such a Keynesian expansion has directly contributed to a series of unparalleled trade deficits. As in the UK, a sharply appreciating exchange rate, brought about by a tight monetary policy, played a key role in catalyzing the shift in the trade picture. By undermining US manufacturing competitiveness, the strong dollar permitted producers across the globe to undertake a massive export drive to the US. To some extent, these trade developments are the natural corollary of the shift of labour and resources into domestic services. The reason for this lies in the asymmetric developments of production and of consumption. Whereas most industries, and especially manufacturing, are "tradeable" by nature, many services are not. Thus, while domestic production in the US has shifted into services — in part to seek refuge from foreign competition in those activities which cannot be imported — overall demand has risen less. As a result, the markets for manufactured goods have

7

been increasingly left open to imports while competition in services has become more pronounced.

Britain has some important lessons to learn from this experience, lessons which link up directly with the second major problem caused by the retrenchment of manufacturing. Through much of its post-war history, Britain has been subject to a growth constraint from its current account (the difference between earnings from the export of goods and services and the payment for imports). Broadly speaking, this constraint stems from the greater propensity of the UK to import goods from the rest of the world, at any given level of growth, than it is able to export when the rest of the world is growing at the same rate. Consequently, if the current account is to remain in balance, growth in the UK has to be slower than in the rest of the world. In practical terms, this has meant that governments of both political persuasions have been hampered in pursuing faster growth strategies. Strenuous efforts to boost expansion have invariably been followed by equally strenuous efforts to curb the subsequent current account deficits, (as well as the inflation which accompanies overheating).

GRAPH 1: BRITAIN'S CURRENT ACCOUNT PERFORMANCE 1975-1987.

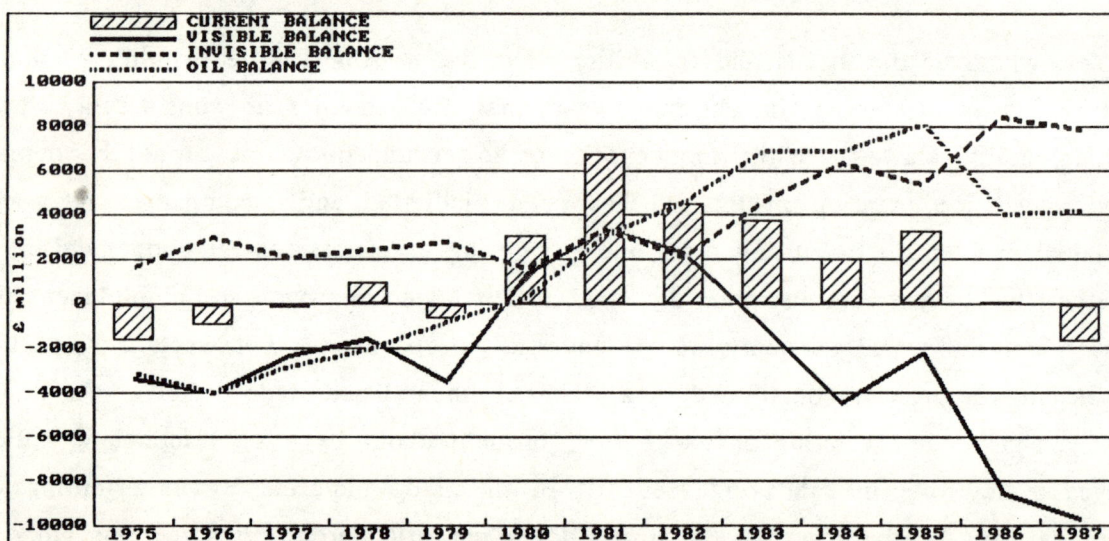

The UK is has not been alone in facing this situation, but it is a factor that has affected Britain more strongly than most of its economic partners.[5] Furthermore, it is a constraint on growth (and hence employment) which has strongly reasserted itself since the beginning of 1986. Until then, Britain's trade position and the dramatic shift into manufacturing deficit had been shored up by North Sea oil revenues. The almost-overnight slump in oil prices in January 1986 cut these from £8.1 billion in 1985 to £4.2

8

billion in 1986. As a result, Britain's current account surplus virtually fell to zero in 1987, and went into a £1.7 billion deficit in 1987 (see Graph I above).[6]

Before the collapse in oil prices, many economists (including some in the Treasury) were arguing that a gradual run down of oil revenues during the second half of the 1980s could be feasibly met through a structural change in the economy. Britain's comparative advantage would shift away from primary production back to manufacturing and service industries. This would effectively reverse the relative movements which had occurred between the oil and manufacturing sectors at the turn of the decade.[7] Whether or not such an automatic readjustment would have occurred, or was indeed even theoretically possible, is now immaterial. Instead of progressively acclimatizing itself to the post-oil era over a period of five to ten years, Britain is having to come to grips with a greatly reduced oil sector much more quickly.

It must therefore seem doubly unlikely that manufacturing industry, especially, will recoup its former trade position. As was highlighted by a House of Lords report on overseas trade, the switch into a manufacturing trade deficit was led by a deterioration in a relatively small number of key industries, notably: electrical and electronic engineering; motor vehicles; food, drink, and tobacco; textiles; footware and clothing; timber and wooden furniture; and paper, printing and publishing.[8] Due to such concentrated retrenchment, the ability of manufacturing industry to reverse its trade deficit within the foreseeable future must be seen as questionable.

Consequently, there are really only two ways in which Britain's current account can be returned to balance — assuming that oil earnings do not recover substantially.

The first involves substantial devaluation of the pound. Sooner or later it will bring about a balance as the relative competitive position of British and foreign industry changes. To some extent this has already occurred. Although, sterling was rising during the first half of 1988, its value against against most major currencies (with the exception of the dollar) has fallen considerably since early 1986. Furthermore, the pound is expected to resume its fall towards the end of 1988 and into 1989, as current account pressure continues to build up, and the bullish speculation in the currency markets of the first half of 1988, gives way to trading that reflects sterling's "fundamentals" more accurately. But devaluation also carries a price. It poses the severe threat of inflation, as imports become more expensive. At the same time, though often less noticed, devaluation

9

effectively entails a relative impoverishment of those holding the devalued currency. In other words, Britain is poorer relative to its competitors.

The second alternative is for invisible earnings to rise. These invisibles comprise the the exports of services, income earned on overseas investment, and transfer payments (in Britain's case the latter are largely inter-governmental and connected with international obligations to the EC, NATO, and other institutions, as well as overseas aid). It has long been received wisdom that if Britain's post-war industrial performance has been weak, then at least the record in services has been generally quite good. If the future of the developed world increasingly lies in the service industries, Britain should be well placed to capitalize on its comparative advantages. Most symbolic, perhaps, has been the surge in international financial activity over recent years; a surge which the government and the British banking establishment have tried to capitalize on, through the reform of Britain's financial institutions. It is hoped that long experience in international finance will ensure Britain a major role in the world financial boom, and so help raise invisible export earnings.

This report examines the scope of earnings generated by the private sector (ie. excluding government transactions). In doing so, it begins with a broad description of the nature of services and how they are likely to evolve within the Western market economies. This is followed by a general discussion of the changing structure of trade over the last two decades, in the developed world, and the role which services are playing in it.

Thereafter, the report will examine Britain's major export services, on an industry-by-industry basis (using the classification provided by the Central Statistical Office on the UK Balance of Payments, henceforth simply referred to as the "Pink Book"). Given the wide-ranging nature of services, such an analysis clearly cannot be exhaustive. But, by covering the main sources of invisible earnings, the investigation here will provide an extensive understanding of the industries involved and thus of the sector as a whole. The study uses largely qualitative techniques, outlining the major factors affecting each particular industry, backed up by quantitative material derived from official sources and trade-specific literature.

In conclusion, forecasts are made for the future developments of Britain's service exports, within the world economy. These are based on the perceived course of international service trade, combined with the specific future of Britain's individual industries.   Again, the analysis is qualitative in the first instance, although it is accompanied by a tentative quantitative prediction of the various sectors and aggregated earnings over the next five to ten years.

Notes and references:

1.   OECD: *Economic Surveys*, of the UK, annual series.
2.   OECD: *Economic Outlook*, half-yearly series.
3.   Central Statistical Office (CSO: *United Kingdom Balance of Payments, the "Pink Book"*, annual series.
4.   OECD: *Labour Force Statistics*, annual series.
5.   A.P. Thirlwall: *The Balance of Payments Constraint as an Explanation of International Growth Rate Differences*, Banca Nazionale del Lavoro, Quarterly Review, 1978.
6.   CSO Pink Book
7.   P.J. Forsyth and J.A. Kay: *The Economic Implications of North Sea Oil*, Fiscal Studies, July 1980
8.   House of Lords, *Report from the Select Committee on Overseas Trade, Vol 1*, HMSO 1985.

Other general references include:

W. Keegan, *Mrs Thatcher's Economic Experiment*, Penguin Books, 1984.
_____, *Britain Without Oil*, Penguin Books, 1985.
P. Riddel, *The Thatcher Government*, Basil Blackwell, 1985.
K. Smith, *The British Economic Crisis*, Pelican Books, 1986.

2 The nature of services and their development

The idea of a service economy has long evoked a degree of schizophrenia in economists and socio-political experts. It is variously seen as a stepping stone to a more humane post-industrial society, or as a block to the growth and development of advanced capitalism. Post-industrial theorists and prophets have frequently seized upon the relative decline of large scale industry as holding the (non-Marxist) key to fundamental social change. In place of the strident, individualistic materialism of the consumer, they see the development of a less competitive and more collectivist civil society. The shift away from conspicuous consumption and production in those "dark Satanic mills" is directly linked to a switch in values towards life and well-being increasingly defined by a new quality of human interaction.[1]

More prosaic theories of development view the rise of the service economy as a potential means of pursuing growth and employment. Yet it is precisely in the pursuit of these lesser objectives that the rise of the service sector draws its heaviest and most thorough criticism.

Arguably, the scepticism of service activities emanates from their conventional economic definitions. In this framework, all forms of economic behaviour can be sorted into three broad categories. Fundamental is the primary sector. It is inextricable with the earlier stages of development, and comprises activities which can be described as "extractive", predominantly agriculture and mining. Linked to the next phase of development are those activities that are essentially "transformative" by nature. They have existed in some "marketable" form since humans made the transition from being largely nomadic, hunter-gatherers to being sedentary pastoralists. But the sector as we know it only really took shape with the Industrial Revolution. This broadening and deepening of technology began in the eighteenth century, and changed artisanal and personal manufacture into factory and mass production.[2]

As the process spread, embracing not just physical production but all forms of social behaviour, service activities emerged to facilitate the workings of the economy and changing private demand. Again, these activities existed long before services established themselves as an identifiable component of the economy. Indeed, Adam Smith — who formulated the mechanism of the market before capitalism had properly developed —

outlined one of the most basic characteristics of services: for him they were finite by definition, perishing "in the very instant of their performance".[3]

But, it was not until the 1930s that economists began to isolate services as a significant and distinct economic sector, with its own dynamics.[4] Even then, the real importance of services only emerged in the post-war world, which provided a marked economic and political stimulus to their development. As Western societies geared themselves to "mass-consumption", as the role of government expanded to administer the welfare state and Keynesian macroeconomics, and as the division of labour continued to compartmentalize business, the importance of services to employment, income, and consumption strengthened both on the supply and demand side of the economic circuit.

For much of the post-war boom the shift of resources into services passed unnoticed — and uncriticized. This was partly due to historically unparalleled growth, which tended to push long-term problems into obscurity (especially the build up of inflation during the 1960s). Yet it also followed from the fact that industry maintained and sometimes expanded its share of resources, while the retrenchment took place in agriculture and mining. During the second half of the 1960s, however, the first worries about the rise in services had emerged. In particular, they centred on the sector's low productivity growth compared to manufacturing. It stemmed from what was held to be the basic nature of services. Their "local monopoly" following from Smith's definition, their labour intensiveness, and the difficulty of investing and applying capital to their production, all placed a question-mark against their ability to generate wealth.

These concerns were concisely expressed by W. Baumol's model of unbalanced growth. His argument is based on the premise that the Western economies comprise two sectors. The first he called "technologically progressive": primarily manufacturing industry, which displays a dynamism based on innovation, capital accumulation and economies of scale. This contrasts starkly with the second "technologically unprogressive" sector. Made up predominantly of services, its activities yielded only sporadic increases in productivity at best, while many services connected with government and the welfare state manifested constant labour/output ratios. For Baumol, three major consequences followed. First, if wages grow uniformly in the economy (as unions try to maintain comparability), then the cost per unit of output must rise more quickly in services than manufacturing because of the lag in service sector productivity. Secondly, if the ratio of volume outputs for both sectors is held constant, then labour must shift from the progressive sector to the non-

14

progressive sector. Thirdly, and directly linked to this, any attempt to balance growth must lower growth for the whole economy. It also follows that if services take more and more resources, inflation will accompany the slowdown of growth.[5]

Coupled to these domestic features of economic development (which were leading to *stagflation* even before the first oil-shock) were the rising trade pressures indirectly associated with service sector growth. By the mid-1970s, Britain and the US — each with an extensive service sector — were becoming increasingly vulnerable to current account pressures. Unlike the industrial power-houses of West Germany and Japan, both suffered problems footing greater oil import bills through the expansion of manufactured exports. In Britain's case, the squeeze was acute as the country was still dependent on imports for its oil needs. As a result, the current account fell heavily into deficit and, despite a rise in invisible earnings, Britain had to undergo a large exchange rate devaluation, borrow from the IMF, and deflate to balance its payments.

To some extent, today's situation is a repetition of this trade squeeze. Then as now, there was scepticism about the ability of services to replace the wealth foregone as industry cut back. Indeed, in one of the most elaborate arguments of the time R. Bacon and W. Eltis took this reasoning one step further. For them the post-war development of non-tradeable services directly contributed to the poor performance of "tradeable" manufacturing. In particular they saw the proliferation of public sector services as the bug-bear of economic growth. By holding down productivity, pre-empting and "crowding out" resources, and discouraging private activity through high taxation, this leading component of the service sector stifled the whole "wealth-creating" process, with all the implications for domestic growth and foreign trade that followed.[6]

Despite such fears, and even the slowdown in public sector growth which has taken place within the OECD since 1975, the rise of services in all the major "industrial" economies has carried on relentlessly.[7] Does this then mean that we are doomed to slow growth unless there is a reversal of the shift into services? Is the expansion of services a bad thing which should be resisted at all costs? The answers to these questions are not as simple as present circumstances appear to make them, and hinge on how services will evolve in the future.

Seen from the widest perspective, the dynamism of services will depend on the "value" they provide to society. This, in turn, depends on changing mechanics of demand and

15

supply. In general, demand is dependent on the "utility" consumers derive or (perhaps more accurately) believe they derive from a service. By definition there is no reason why an industrial product need provide any greater "use" of "pleasure" than a service "product". They may not be the same, but there is nothing inherent in the nature of one which should make it more desirable than the other. This is especially so the more demand is determined by social and cultural factors, rather than by sheer necessity. On the supply side, the "value" of a service is also a function of the inputs involved in its "production", and hence the technique and productivity of the production process itself.

As society and the economic system continue to evolve, there is much to suggest that the expansion of services will in fact provide a contribution to growth and development — though it will remain qualified. Parallels could be drawn with the emergence of industry and the decline of agriculture (which began in Britain during the second half of the eighteenth century). An interesting comparison, for example, could be drawn with the theoretical manner in which French Physiocrat school of economics viewed manufacturing during the middle of the eighteenth century. Like Adam Smith, the Physiocrats supported the rights of the individual producers against the economic powers of an absolutist state. They attacked the concentration of economic power. Furthermore, they rejected the mercantilist and bullionist economics which Europe's emerging nation states practiced rigorously well into the century. Instead of accumulating bullion reserves through controlled trade, they argued government should encourage production and exchange. For the Physiocrats wealth lay not in hoarding idle gold and silver, but in the physical output of material things or substances. Importantly, however, they stressed that productive output could only be generated in agriculture, whereas all manufacturing was a fundamentally "sterile" activity.

History showed the Physiocrats to be grossly mistaken. With the advent of the Industrial Revolution their concept of wealth and productive enterprise became redundant. Far from being tied to agriculture, the creative process was transformed. Technology developed to harness energy to production and open up new forms of manufacturing. The division of labour and accelerated investment led not just to greater output in existing industries, but led, more significantly, to a proliferation of products and industries. Concurrently, population growth, the break-down of rural society and rapid urbanization helped shape vast new markets for industrial output.

There are signs that similar processes are at work as the Western societies move into services. During the post-war period there has been a proliferation in the types of services these societies want and produce. As a result, it is difficult, perhaps even incorrect, to speak of or to analyze the service sector as a collective entity. Instead, it could be better described as a matrix of activities and functions, often with fundamentally contrasting natures (see Table 2.1 overleaf).

It is less important to accept the total disaggregation of the tertiary sector than to recognize the diffusion of its activities. Disaggregation shows the importance of producer services as opposed to social services and personal services (the latter being the most traditional of all services). This break-down by functions and activities is also connected to what could be termed as the direction of flow of services. Thus all services can be categorized for either "intermediate" or "final" consumption. Broadly speaking, intermediate services are those whose "use" is realized at some intermediate stage in the production process. They tend to be producer services like accounting or banking, and are largely, but not entirely, consumed by firms rather than private individuals. By comparison, final services are directly consumed for what they are, usually by the individual consumer. Classic examples of such services are personal services like domestic services, and eating and drinking places. To this group must be added government services, especially those which have developed since World War II. Similarly, service activities can also classified by whether they are "marketed" or "non-marketed". Marketed services are sold to the customer in the market, at a price which covers the cost of production plus a profit margin. This definition applies to nearly all services except those which are provided by government (ie. those services provided by private suppliers). By comparison, government services tend to be non-marketed services, and are allocated to their users (be they individuals or not) free of any direct charge.

Clearly, these definitions blur and overlap. Producer services such as banking, insurance, real estate and legal activities serve the individual consumer, as well as supplying producers. Similarly, personal services (like the provision of hotel accommodation, catering, repair and laundry services) are not solely supplied to the (private) individual consumer. The distinction between marketed and non-marketed services is sharper. But, ambiguities include the provision of public services where the user partially pays for the product. Examples are postal and transport services, as well as medical services in many countries.

17

Table 2.1: AN ALLOCATION SCHEME FOR SECTORS AND INDUSTRIES

		Type of Service					
		1	2	3	4	5	6
EXTRACTIVE		*	-	*	-	*	-
1	Agriculture, Fishing & Forestry	*	-	*	-	*	-
2	Mining	*	-	*	-	*	-
TRANSFORMATIVE		*	*	*	-	*	-
3	Construction	*	*	*	*	-	*
4	Food	-	*	*	-	*	-
5	Textiles	*	*	*	-	*	-
6	Metal	*	*	*	-	*	-
7	Chemical	*	*	*	-	*	-
8	Miscellaneous Manufacturing	-	-	-	-	-	-
9	Utilities	*	*	*	-	-	*
DISTRIBUTIVE SERVICES		*	*	*	-	-	*
11	Transportation & Storage	*	*	*	-	*	*
12	Wholesale Trade	*	-	*	-	-	*
13	Retail Trade (except 32 below)	-	*	*	-	-	*
PRODUCER SERVICES		*	*	*	-	*	-
14	Communication	*	*	*	-	*	-
15	Banking, Credit, & Other Financial Services	*	*	*	-	*	-
16	Insurance	*	*	*	-	*	-
17	Real Estate	*	*	*	-	-	*
18	Engineering & Architectural Services	*	*	*	-	*	-
19	Accounting & Bookkeeping	*	-	*	-	*	-
20	Miscellaneous Business Services	-	-	-	-	*	*
21	Legal Services	*	*	*	-	*	*
SOCIAL SERVICES		-	*	-	*	-	*
22	Medical & Health Services	-	*	-	*	-	*
23	Hospitals	-	*	-	*	-	*
24	Education	-	*	-	*	-	*
25	Welfare & Religious Services	-	*	-	*	-	*
26	Nonprofit Organizations	-	*	-	*	-	*
27	Postal Services	*	*	*	-	-	*
28	Government	*	*	-	*	-	*
29	Miscellaneous Professional & Social Services	-	-	-	-	-	-
PERSONAL SERVICES		-	*	*	-	-	*
30	Domestic Service	-	*	*	-	-	*
31	Hotels & Lodging Places	*	*	*	-	-	*
32	Eating & Drinking Places	-	*	*	-	-	*
33	Repair Services	*	*	*	-	-	*
34	Laundry & Dry Cleaning Services	-	*	*	-	-	*
35	Barber & Beauty Shops	-	*	*	-	-	*
36	Entertainment & Recreational Services	-	*	*	-	-	*
37	Miscellaneous Personal Services	-	-	-	-	-	-

KEY: 1 — Intermediate
2 — Final
3 — Marketed
4 — non-Marketed
5 — Tradeable
6 — non-Tradeable

Source: H. Browning & J. Singlemann: The Transformation of the U.S. Labour Force: The Interaction of Industry & Occupation, in Politics and Society 8 Nos. 3-4, 1978.

Service types allocated by author.

Note: The classification of service types is not absolute, stating only the predominant directions of flow.

Lastly, services can be classified according to whether they are tradeable or not. Those activities which are most important to the trade in invisible exports come from the distributive and producer sectors. By definition these are marketed services and are also mainly for intermediate use. Again, the groupings are not absolute. There are some social services (for example, education and to a lesser extent health) which are marketed to foreign individuals. Alternatively, some producer (and distributive) services are exported in the form of non-marketed development aid. A big factor in the trade in services is tourism and travel. The outputs of this industry are overwhelmingly produced in the personal sector. This marks out tourism distinctly from the other tradeable services as its products are consumed by private individuals in the country of origin. They are invisible exports which are not exported.

In addition to the expansion of social services, a prime feature of the post-war diversification has been the growth of intermediate producer services. It has been a consequence of the continued division of labour. During the 1950s manufacturing activities began to farm out services, which could be provided more cheaply by independent contractors. This "externalization" had a major impact on the way output and employment statistics across sectors are accounted, although it has affected the nature of employment to a lesser degree. For example, if a manufacturing firm contracts out its cleaning or security services, its output will not change, nor is the demand for labour likely to alter appreciably. Yet, aggregate employment in the manufacturing sector will fall and its labour productivity will rise.

But, the externalization of services is more than just an accounting trick. As part of the continued division of labour it yields economic benefits through improved efficiency and even economies of scale for the specialist supplier of the service. This is especially so for the more sophisticated services, frequently linked to knowledge-based industries. These have expanded as the process of industrialization has become ever more complicated. Industrial design, management consultancy and marketing are all examples of industries that have emerged as, independent functions in the production process, where they were once carried out in-house. They reflect a deepening degree of expertise. As a direct result, their share of value added in the economy has risen continuously.

The advent of the information revolution has significantly enhanced the importance of these intermediate, marketed producer services. Information technology (IT) has allowed many services to break out of their labour and productivity constraints allowing more

19

investment in production.[8]   Be it in computer aided design and manufacturing (CAD/CAM), computerized accounting, or humbler activities like word-processing, IT has reshaped the framework of service sector development.   Complementary advances have been made in the more sophisticated producer services, as in the other main service categories.   IT has an extensive role to play in the distributive trades, where for example, more efficient stock-management (through the expanded use of "bar-coding" etc.) could improve not only wholesale and retail trading, but also storage and transportation. Likewise, IT appears to have potential for raising productivity and output in the social services.   If futuristic predictions about electronic education and medical services replacing teachers and doctors now look less likely than when they first surfaced in the late 1970s and early 1980s, IT has scope for improving such services — as well as government administration, and postal/telecommunications (PTT) services.

But, alongside such areas of growth and wealth creation, pockets of low productivity are likely to remain, and impede the development of services.   Domestic, hotel, catering, cleaning and laundry services appear more impervious to the application of technology and capital investment, as do an array of menial government and social services.   Such activities are also associated with the limited growth of value added, and hence of wages. In the US, for example, it has been estimated that productivity in food and drink outlets actually fell 0.4 percent per annum during the 1970s and early 1980s.   Such a lacklustre performance has contributed to poor earnings from these activities, which are reckoned to be nearly 40 percent below the average hourly wage in manufacturing industries.[9]

A key characteristic of services, which emerges from this description and significantly distinguishes them from manufacturing, is their heterogeneity.   There are clearly areas of high-tech activity, generating substantial value added to an economy.   At the same time, services include a large variety of labour-intensive occupations where wealth creation is limited.   This is an essential dichotomy in the nature of the service sector, and is likely to remain crucial to its future development.

Equally, if not more restrictive to the progress of services are the limitations imposed by the sector's direct interaction with extractive and transformative industries.   As the well worn phrase succinctly puts it, "services have to serve something".   Although the validity of this idea has been challenged (eg. some forms of portfolio investment management), it remains true that services rarely stand alone as economic activities.   They seldom have the capacity to reproduce or feed on themselves. Similarly, services remain linked to the use and consumption of manufactured goods.

Apposite examples of such symbiosis are provided not only by the reliance on IT products of most information services, but also by the integration of manufactured products in the provision of personal services. A strong case exists to show that the lack of dynamism of marketable personal services has been accompanied by a shift of such activities out of the market.[10] Driven, on the one hand, by the rising cost of personal services (due to high labour inputs) and the mass production/consumption of consumer durables, on the other, more personal services are being carried out in the home. Labour-saving devices (from the vacuum cleaner to the washing machine and micro-wave oven) have permitted households to internalize an array of personal services which were previously not available, or only at high cost. This migration from the market-place to the home is also noticeable in the leisure industry, widely seen as a vast area of future growth. Stereo, television and the VCR have shifted demand away from marketed, public entertainment and into the drawing room.

Patterns of consumer expenditure suggest that the emergence of a "self-service" economy has become an integrated part of the developed world. Though many of the standard modern conveniences and personal transport had become available in Western Europe by the end of the 1960s (and a good decade earlier in North America), household consumption patterns have altered little over the last 25 years. There has been no substantial shift of demand away from manufactured consumer goods into services. Despite variations in personal spending patterns across countries, there has been little change in the breakdown of expenditure within countries. The graph shows that the main cross-country trends in spending have lowered the consumption of food, while raising expenditure on rent, fuel and power. Medical expenditure in the US has taken up some of the shift away from food — given the greater role of private health care in the US than in Europe. None of the three countries has experienced any relative increase in recreational spending, or miscellaneous expenditure (made up of spending on personal care, restaurants, cafes and hotels). The only other expanding area of personal consumption, within the European countries, has been transport. But again, this is largely accounted for by the spread of the motorcar and private transport. Given that household consumption accounts for 55 to 65 percent of GDP in the developed world, and that social and political pressure is likely to maintain if not increase this share, the implications for future economic development are significant.

The emergence of a self-service economy provides an example of the potential limits to private service sector demand. It also demonstrates the interaction which is likely to continue between manufacturing industry and services. This is equally important to distributive, social and producer services and obviously plays a determining part in the propagation of information technology. Indeed, the problem of disaggregating the components of the information revolution — of splitting up the "hardware" and the "software" — combined with the revolutionary nature of IT has led some to group these activities into a "quarternary" sector.[11] Even a more limited approach has to admit the continued relevance of manufactured goods in the service economy, which the latter's evolution must take into account.

Notes and references:

1. A concise "anthology" of the ideas of post-industrialism is given in J. Gershuny's: *After Industrial Society*, Macmillan, 1978.
2. The universal breakdown used here comes from H. Browning and J. Singelmann in their article: *The Transformation of the US Labor Force: The Interaction of Industry and Occupation*, in Politics and Society, nos 3-4, 1978.
3. Adam Smith, *The Wealth of Nations*, Penguin, 1970.
4. A discussion of the early theories on services is given by P. Petit in: *Slow Growth and the Service Economy*, Frances Pinter, 1986.
5. W. Baumol, *Macroeconomics of Unbalanced Growth: The Anatomy of Urban Crisis*, in the American Economic Review, 1967.
6. R. Bacon and W. Eltis, *Britain's Economic Problem: To Few Producers*, Macmillan, 1976.
7. OECD, *The Role of the Public Sector*, 1985.
8. The concept of Information Technology (IT) used here, and its effect on services is taken from J. Gershuny and I. Miles in: *The New Service Economy*, Frances Pinter, 1983.
9. A. Kaletsky and G. de Jonquieres, *Why a service economy is no panacea*, The Financial Times, May 22, 1987.
10. The dynamics of the self-service economy described here, stems from J. Gershuny and Miles, ibid, 1983.
11. This approach is outlined by J. Gershuny, ibid, 1978.

3 International trade in services

As domestic consumption and production of services has increased in the developed economies, international trade in services has also expanded. From a theoretical point of view, trade in services can be analyzed with the same tools as trade in goods. The international services trade is driven by the same phenomenon of comparative advantage as generates trade in goods. The formulation by Ricardo at the start of the nineteenth century, has always been the basis for free trade.[1]

Ricardo's theorem states that two economies producing two types of goods will benefit if each specializes in the production of the good in which it has a comparative advantage — ie. a cost advantage in the process of production. By permitting an international division of labour, trade increases the aggregate product of both countries, making both wealthier. Although Ricardo's schematic model focused only on the production of wine and cloth in two countries, its logical principle can be extended to the trade of most products among all producing nations. This holds true for services for the physical goods of the primary and secondary sectors.[2]

Nevertheless, there are limitations on trade in services which do not apply in the same way and to the same extent as for physical products. A large part of the service sector is confined to the domestic market. Adam Smith's definition of services — that they are consumed in the instant of their performance — means that many are directly tied to a specific location. They are, by their inherent nature, non-tradeable. The clearest examples are the archetypal personal services like hairdressing. But the field is broader, accounting for a big share of GDP and employment. Thus, returning to the breakdown of service activities given in the previous chapter, most transport and distributive services are not "exportable". The same holds true for social and government services.

The classification of these services as non-tradeable is not absolute. Foreign earnings from transport services provide a source of revenue on the current account, for example. Traditionally, these have been made up largely of shipping services, but air transport has become a major factor in both freight and personal travel. Linked to these are foreign earnings accruing to domestically produced services, in the form of business travel and tourism. As previously mentioned, tourism does not involve any locational change of personal services etc., but rather entails foreign consumption in the domestic market. The same can be said of government and social services consumed by visitors to the UK, for example, which thereby generate foreign earnings.

By comparison, the main component of the trade in services today — the intermediate producer services — frequently involves substantial production in the country of the consumer.[3] Although such services are more mobile than others, their use necessitates at least some creation at the point of consumption. This arises especially because the distinction between production and distribution is often blurred. Servicing a customer under such circumstances simultaneously involves distribution and production (eg. the management consultant who tailors his product when delivering it to his client). Manufacturing firms tend to exploit overseas markets first through exports and only later through investment in foreign operations. But, international service sector companies, due to the nature of their products, are more likely to combine both approaches. Thus banks are likely to set up local branches; consulting firms (notably in accountancy) work through foreign subsidiaries; while advertising companies seek to establish local agencies; etc.

Certain activities in this branch of the service economy have a history of international practice. Banking services have been traded for centuries. But, there can be little doubt that the importance of producer services has grown as a result of the post-war boom. The "externalization" or farming out of services by industry, combined with the "internationalization" of commercial and financial activity, has catapulted these services to the forefront of invisible trade.

Table 3.1: THE SHARE OF NON-FACTOR SERVICS (NFS) AND INTEREST, DIVIDEND AND PROFITS (IDP) REVENUE IN ALL OECD FOREIGN EARNINGS

	1965	1970	1975	1980	1984
Visible Exports	71	72	72	69	68
NFS	21	20	19	18	17
IDP	8	8	9	13	16

Source: OECD, Balances of Payments of OECD Countries, 1986.

Still, a surprising picture emerges when the statistics of goods and services traded in the OECD are analyzed (this trading bloc accounting for about three quarters of the world visible trade and four fifths of the invisible trade). There has only been a marginal rise in invisible earnings relative to the total (see Table 3.1).[4] Taking figures from 1965 to 1984, the share of invisible earnings in total foreign revenues rose from 29 percent, in 1965, to 33 percent by 1984. This increase in share has been due the growth of interest,

24

dividend and profit earnings (IDPs) on foreign investments — be they physical investments in plant and equipment etc., or portfolio investments in financial assets. Accounting for 8 percent of all foreign earnings in 1965, the latter expanded to 15 percent by 1984.

Such IDP earnings do not constitute pure service sector exports — or non-factor services (NFS), as they are technically termed. Unlike the export of banking or businesses services, IDPs are not products which can be sold in foreign markets for consumption either by individuals or firms. Instead, IDP revenues are largely *rentier* earnings accruing on previously earned income or wealth which is then invested overseas. They have three main components.

The first is the foreign direct investment (FDI) of industrial and commercial enterprises (ICCs) in overseas markets. Normally, it occurs either as a form of vertical integration (when they try to gain direct access to raw materials and their processing, or set up overseas market outlets for their end products), or as a form of market penetration (when direct exporting is either impossible, because of tariffs and other barriers, or more expensive than production near the final market). Such investment is therefore connected to the production and distribution processes.

As mentioned above, this is especially the case for services. The rise in IDP earnings does, therefore, partly represent an expansion of service sector trade in its broader sense (ie. including "establishment" or "factor" trade, where the factors of production and not just the products are traded). However, the share of service sector investment in all FDI is limited. For the United Kingdom, FDI accounted for 12.5 percent of all foreign assets, and 16.5 percent of their returns in 1986. Within this slice of foreign investment, services represented little more than 30 percent, in the decade until 1984. More recently, there has been quite strong overseas investment in banking, and this will probably have pushed the share up to 35 percent. Yet, even at this level, the importance of services remains constrained. Similarly, in the other major G5 economies, the proportion of services in direct investment varies between 30 and 45 percent.[5]

Such direct investment is supplemented by investment in financial assets, and capital flows arising from international banking activities. Both practices also have long histories, in the form of bank lending — either to sovereign governments, foreign companies, or even wealthy individuals. More recently, however, such transactions have taken on new forms, as the pool of international capital and the number of financial instruments has expanded dramatically. Lending via international portfolio investments in financial assets (like securities) has supplemented more conventional banking practices to become the most dynamic component both of foreign investment and earnings. But, because of their *rentier* nature, these developments reflect more a structural shift in international ownership and debt patterns, than a rise in the real output of goods and services.

The international picture is different when such IDP earnings are deducted from the invisibles total, leaving only non-factor services (NFS). Surprisingly, NFS foreign earnings have seen their share in total OECD foreign earnings fall, from 21 percent in 1965 to 17 percent by 1984. This sluggish performance is due to a number of factors, beyond the non-tradeable nature of many areas of the service sector.

Service activities (almost by definition) tend to be more rooted in their culture of origin than manufactured products. To be sure, a German car, a Japanese television set, or an Italian garment all exhibit a certain national identity, despite the growth of global consumption and production. For services, cultural differences are stronger, and demand is more specific. This is notably so for services like management and economic consulting or advertising, and is one reason why overseas service sector markets are often exploited through local operations earning IDPs.

Cultural impediments to trade in services are frequently backed up by deliberate or non-deliberate protectionist legislation. It exists for a series of reasons, aimed at maintaining national economic and cultural independence, bolstering prestige, facilitating development, or simply curtailing current account outflows. Thus, if trade in goods is restricted by national standards, licensing arrangements, or controls on product safety and liability, the flow of international services is equally, if not more, hindered by such measures. These affect not just the product but also the producer, notably where the latter is a professional whose qualifications and services are not recognized in a foreign country. For example, there may be restrictions on imports of financial services, and consulting activities, be they connected to engineering, legal work etc.[6]

In the post-war period there has been a history of multilateral arrangements to combat such restrictions. The General Agreement on Tariffs and Trade (GATT) provides a broad international forum for the discussion of trade issues, as well as guidelines for trade practices. The GATT has concentrated on visible trade, leaving aside the problems of invisibles which, as their name implies, are more opaque and diverse. Thus, though the GATT's achievements have often been limited, the concept of free trade receives a degree of official support at a multilateral level. The same cannot be said for services sector trade, which has received little international attention to date.

This is now in the process of changing. At the GATT meeting held in Punta del Este (Uruguay) in September 1986, the developing nation members of the GATT, under pressure from the former, agreed to let services on to the agenda. In the "twin-track" compromise, the developing nations, led by Brazil and India, agreed to the inclusion of services within the GATT framework, but on condition that services would be handled separately from other issues.[7] This is clearly one step forward for de-regulation but, given the bureaucratic limitations of GATT, substantial agreements on cutting back protectionism take time to achieve.

Consequently, protectionism is likely to remain in many areas, especially those deemed to be of national importance. As in the case of strategic manufacturing industries, many countries operate protectionist or quasi-protectionist policies to preserve domestic activity in certain sectors. Most crucial, perhaps, is the control of financial services. By its nature, banking has always been a contentious international activity with the foreign control of money easily seen as a fundamental encroachment on sovereignty. This fear has become increasingly pertinent with the independence of the developing world over the last thirty years, to say nothing of the explosion of Third World lending during the 1970s. Governments in both the developed and developing world have placed limitations on foreign banking activity within national boundaries, notwithstanding the recent wave of de-regulation in the West. Similarly, insurance has been an activity many governments have sought to retain in domestic hands. The emergence of the developing nations has added to protectionism in this industry, in part to control the outflows of foreign capital. Indeed, nationalist regulation of insurance continues to characterize the developed world. Even within the EC, individual markets predominantly remain the preserve of domestic insurance companies — despite the Community's commitment to the free flow of labour, goods, services and capital. It is only with the current drive to a single market by 1992, that the EC has set about seriously opening up the service sector.

Examples of protectionism to ward off foreign intrusion and/or reduce revenue outflows are found in the other major sectors of the service economy. Earnings on tourism, for example, have repeatedly been protected by the imposition of exchange controls on nationals seeking to go abroad. Similarly, international controls on air travel — governed by the International Air Transport Association, IATA — ensure that trade (ie. air traffic) is largely regulated bi-laterally, with reciprocal landing rights. Beyond these, there exists a whole gamut of other restrictions designed more or less to impede the flow of services. To name but a few: discriminatory taxation against foreign operators; limits on royalty remittances; quotas on film or other cultural "imports"; tightly controlled labour laws to hold down the number of foreign workers (qualified or non-qualified); etc.[8]

The aim of such controls is obviously not merely to reduce developing country dependence on the industrialized world, or to improve current account statistics. Service trade restrictions must also be seen in the light of developing countries trying to foster their own nascent services. Such import substitution is seen increasingly as a vital part of the development process.[9] This appears to be especially true once a developing country has attained a certain level of industrialization, where demand for producer services accelerates as the division of labour multiplies and production becomes ever more sophisticated. Thus, for example, South Korea has already become a major exporter of civil engineering, as has Turkey, while Singapore (if it can still be described as developing) has emerged as a veritable centre for services in Asia, spanning everything from shipping to banking. Competition from the developing world has been especially tough in shipping. This has, of course, partly followed the move by companies in developed-countries re-register their fleets under flags of convenience. But, it also stems from the drive by many developing countries to expand their capacity in this area.

Consequently, in looking at a breakdown of NFS trade in the OECD, it is not surprising to find that the most dynamic component has been the residual category of "other services". This sector tends to be dominated by banking and insurance services, although it also includes a host of other major and minor activities, including engineering consultancy, management consultancy, advertising, film and television etc. Between 1965 and 1984 it expanded its share of total OECD non-factor service exports from 29 percent to 36 percent, led by the expansion of international banking services. By comparison, the least dynamic has been the transport sector, made up largely of shipping but also air transport services. It has seen its share fall over the same period from 36 percent to 31 percent of the total. Similarly, the travel sector (tourism and business travel) has also suffered a comparative retrenchment, as has the export of government services.

In comparing the UK trade position to the overall development of the OECD, the single most notable feature is that the comparative retrenchment experienced by Britain's visible trade, has been mirrored by NFS trade (see Table 3.2). In aggregate, the UK share of total NFS exports in the OECD fell from 13 percent in 1965 to 10 percent in 1984. This contraction was led by Britain's falling share of overseas transport revenues in the OECD, of which the share plummeted by 10 percent in the same period. Again, contrary to received wisdom, the performance of UK financial and other services was comparatively weak, with the market share contracting 3 percent of the total. Indeed, the only sign of buoyancy is to be found in the overall travel category. Here Britain's earnings as a percentage of the OECD total expanded from 6 percent to 9 percent.

Table 3.2:   UK SHARE OF FOREIGN EARNINGS IN OECD, FOR VISIBLE EXPORTS, IDPs, NON-FACTORS SERVICES, AND THEIR MAIN CATEGORIES

	1965	1970	1975	1980	1984
Visible Exports	11	9	8	9	8
IDP	20	14	21	25	25
NFS	13	14	11	12	10
Travel	6	7	8	9	9
Transport	19	18	15	13	9
Government	3	0	3	3	3
Other	16	17	12	13	13

Source: OECD, Balances of Payments of OECD Countries, 1986.

The record on NFS earnings contrasts strongly with the expansion of Britain's IDP earnings. If Britain's overall trade performance has been lacklustre, its revenues from overseas investments have boomed, pushing up its share of the OECD total from 20 percent in 1965 to 25 percent by 1984. As previously stated, IDP earnings are partly connected to the growth of services exports (given the necessity of establishing foreign operations). But there can be little doubt that the bulk of this increase stems from the rise in overseas portfolio investments (in financial assets). As such, the rise in IDP earnings has little to do with a surge in real activity.

To be sure, there are qualifications to such a simple aggregate analysis. By definition, any comparison will always suffer inaccuracies as separate national indicators are converted into common, comparative values. In this case, the base statistics given by the OECD are all in US dollars — with national currency values being directly converted at existing exchange rate levels.[10] Given exchange rate changes, the resulting nominal values could well distort real values or volume output. Notably, the figures for 1965 will likely exaggerate the volume share of Britain's exports, as sterling was undoubtedly overvalued until the devaluation in 1967. Similarly, those for 1984 coincide with a time of excessive dollar strength, and will therefore understate Britain's export volumes. Consequently, the nominal share contraction described above possibly exaggerates the real or volume share change.

This question of exchange rates is directly allied to the statistical problem posed by inflation. "Nominal" figures in current prices clearly do not reflect the effect of inflation on size of stocks or flows. Usually, such figures are therefore "deflated" to give "real" or volume changes. Unfortunately, however, there is no simple, single index which can be applied to *both* goods *and* services. As a result, most of the discussion about foreign earnings tends to be either comparative, or simply presented in nominal terms. This procedure is adopted in this report, although figures will occasionally be given that have been calculated using a consumer purchasing power deflator, so that some account of inflation is taken.

Table 3.3: CURRENT ACCOUNT: BREAKDOWN OF BALANCES
(in £ millions)

	1965	1970	1975	1980	1986
Visible Balance	-260	-34	-3333	1361	-8463
Invisibles:					
Services					
General Government	-270	-309	-569	-849	-1401
Sea Transport	1	-80	89	141	-909
Civil Aviation	28	46	105	395	-534
Travel	-97	50	301	223	-646
Financial & Other Services	240	709	1410	3958	9102
IDP Earnings:					
General Government	-140	-265	-225	48	-905
Private	589	860	1115	-270	5962
Transfers					
General Government	-177	-169	-337	-1782	-2216
Private	8	-13	-138	-296	59
Invisible Balance	182	829	1751	1568	8509
Of which Private and Public Corporations	761	1585	3020	4447	12972
Current Balance	-78	795	-1582	2929	46

Source: CSO, "Pink Book".

Nevertheless, despite such statistical qualifications, the overall performance NFS trade in the OECD, and of British NFS exports in particular, can scarcely be described as exceptional when compared to the trade in visibles. On both counts, a quantitative examination of the aggregate figures does seem to belie the image of an unambiguous expansion of service sector trade, in which Britain is taking a leading part. In terms of the long run development of the British economy, the rather lacklustre indicators examined above would seem to put a strong question mark against an over-reliance on service sector exports in the long term.

All this is not to say that invisible earnings are, and will continue to be, of vital importance to Britain's current account (see Table 3.3). Although NFS export revenues have fallen as a total of all credits — whereas IDP credits have strengthened their position over the last decade (in line with the above trends) — the real significance in non-factor service trade lies in the surplus it produces on the current account. Thus, if visible exports remain by far the largest generator of credits (followed by IDPs), NFS trade produces the greatest *net* revenues for Britain. Over the twenty years to 1986 these grew from £15 million to £5.0 billion. By comparison, net IDP revenues rose from £402 million to £4.7 billion, while the visible trade deficit has fluctuated greatly — falling from a record high of £3.4 billion, in 1981, to a low of -£8.7 billion in 1986.

Also, the growth in NFS revenues has been a consistent feature of foreign earnings, contrasting notably with the much more fluctuating IDPs. The success of NFS trade has been overwhelmingly led by the growth of net earnings accruing to the *residual* "financial and other service" sector. Over the two decades to 1986, it succeeded in boosting its net foreign receipts from £350 million to £8.4 billion. This contrasts with a contraction of earnings by for sea transport (from £5 million in 1975 to -£940 million) and the mediocre or fluctuating results for Civil aviation and travel.[11]

Notes and references:

1. David Ricardo, *Principles of Political Economy and Taxation*, Everyman, 1978.
2. B. Hindley and A. Smith, *Comparative Advantage and Trade in Services*, in The World Economy Vol. 7, Dec 1984.
3. M. Kakabadse, *International Trade in Services: Prospects for Liberalization in the 1990s*, Atlantic Institute Paper N 64, 1987.
4. Customarily, export earnings are used as the proxy for calculating change and growth of trade patterns.
5. D. de Laubier, *La percée des services dans les investissements internationaux*, Economie Prospective Internationale, Centre d'Etudes Prospectives et d'Information Internationales (CEPII), to be printed in 3rd quarter 1988.
6. A. Sapir and E. Lutz, *Trade in Non-Factor Services: Past Trends and Current Issues*, World Bank Staff Working Paper No. 410, 1980.
7. M. Kakabadse, ibid, and Banque Paribas, *L'éveil des échanges internationaux de services*, in Problèmes économiques N 2002, 1986.
8. A. Sapir and E. Lutz, ibid.
9. A. Sapir and E. Lutz, *Trade in Services: Economic Determinants and Development-Related Issues*, World Bank Staff Working Paper No. 480, 1981.
10. All aggregate statistics used here for the OECD, as well as Britain's relative position within the the OECD, are taken or calculated from *Balance of Payments of OECD Countries*, OECD, 1986.
11. CSO, *United Kingdom Balance of Payments, The "Pink Book"*, HMSO, 1987 edition.

PART 2

4 The transport industries

Introduction:

Until the early 1970s transport consistantly provided one third of Britain's invisible earnings. Since then, there has been a quite dramatic decline in the relative importance of the industry: less than 10 percent of current invisible earnings are derived from transport. To a great extent this is the logical result of the relative increase in the financial sector, as seen in the preceding chapter. But within transport, there has been an undeniable revolution in global trends, a revolution that has been to the detriment of the UK industry.

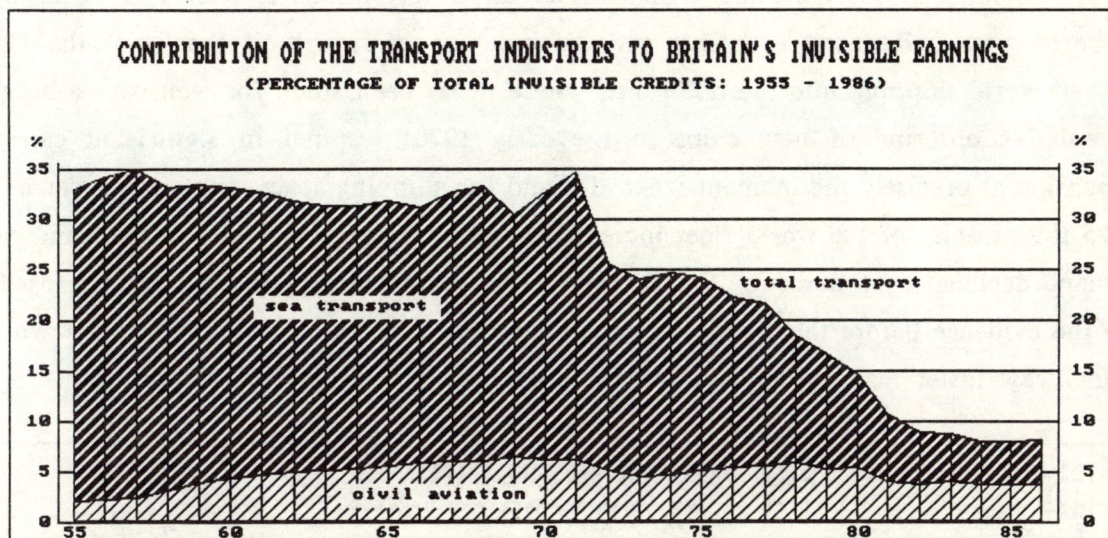

CONTRIBUTION OF THE TRANSPORT INDUSTRIES TO BRITAIN'S INVISIBLE EARNINGS
(PERCENTAGE OF TOTAL INVISIBLE CREDITS: 1955 - 1986)

Two major trends stand out. First, over the past fifteen years there has been a relentless diminution to the role and contribution of shipping. Not only has the British fleet dwindled almost to the point of extinction, but also changing trading patterns (both geographic and as regards composition of the goods) have reduced the nation's requirement for shipping space to carry her exports. The UK now trades considerably more with her European partners than it did twenty years ago, as such, average sea voyages have been reduced. Furthermore, the higher unit values of manufactured goods, which provide most of Britain's exports, are not reflected in tonnages shipped. The second trend follows from this, which is the rising importance of air transport.

The following discussion begins with an international overview of the major transport industries (shipping and aviation — Britain has only one land frontier, with the Republic of Ireland, in consequence the contribution of road haulage to the balance of payments is negligible). A closer look at the position of Britains ship and aircraft operators indicates a worrisome situation. The merchant navy fleet has shrunk considerably, while Britain's airlines are not yet well positioned relative to foreign carriers. In conclusion, the components of transport's contribution to the balance of payments are examined, with a view to deriving the probable net position of the sector in the coming years.

Shipping

The fortunes of the maritime industries are inexorably linked to trends in world-wide seaborne trade. Reduced economic activity brought on by the oil shocks of the 1970s pushed world shipping into the doldrums, where it has been stuck for well over a decade. Speculative ordering of new ships in the early 1970s resulted in significant capacity expansion at precisely the moment when demand for shipping space went into reverse. In 1975 the capacity of the world fleet increased by some 12 percent while in that same year demand declined by 6 percent. For the next eight years shipowners apparently refused to see the evidence before them. Fleet capacity continued to rise as new ships slid down the launchways faster than old tonnage was scrapped.

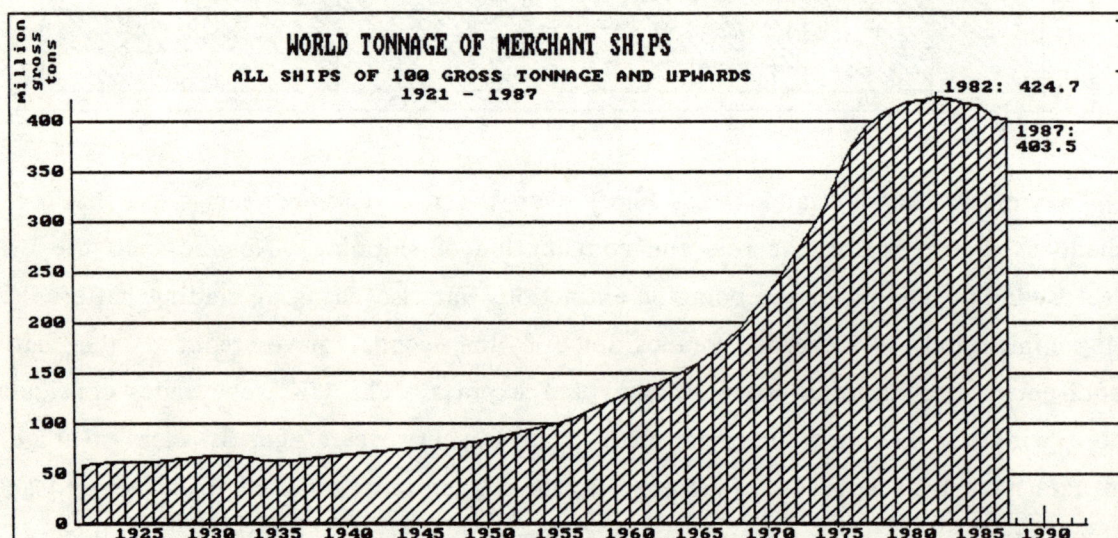

By 1983 more than one in four of all merchant ships in the world was surplus to requirement. This overcapacity forced freight rates to loss-making levels, in many instances, and brought a sharp fall in the value of second-hand vessels. Low freight rates seriously affected the ability of ship operators to service the formidable loans they had contracted to increase their fleets, while the lower asset value of the ships resulted in poor collateral for those who had advanced the finance. The inevitable happened. A number of famous shipping companies were forced into bankruptcy (Burmah Oil, Sanko, and US Lines to mention a few) while ship arrests by creditors and complex debt renegotiations became almost commonplace.

Nearly every comment about shipping's dilemma concludes that the industry can return to better times only by a reduction in the mismatch between supply and demand. But how can this be done? If world seaborne trade were to increase by some 25 percent, then the present fleet could be fully employed at its currently low operating performance rates. The most optimistic forecasts for total world trade volume growth in the next few years allow for around 4 percent per annum. With the trends towards adding value to primary materials at source and relocating production units closer to the end-user markets, this moderate increase could even be translated into a relative decline in shipping requirements.

Another way of achieving full ship capacity utilization would be to slash the size of the world fleet by a quarter. Yet this could only happen if there was some sort of "community spirit" within the shipping fraternity. Owners of modern fleets will be unwilling to send good ships for scrap while fleets of rusty ageing hulks continue to ply for charter. Large numbers of ships consigned to scrap would put pressure on scrap prices. Owners might sell surplus vessels at knockdown prices to operators in the developing countries, eager to increase their fleets at bargain prices, but this offers no solution to the problem of global overcapacity. Furthermore, at current scrapping rates it would take over a decade to achieve a balance. Yet scrapping rates can only increase if there is a significant growth in scrapping facilities world wide (even at today's low turnover there are queues at most breaker's yards). This is unlikely as scrap prices would be bound to fall with a glut of unwanted ships, and as the longer-term need for such facilities is doubtful.

A third way of reducing the disequilibrium would involve lower operating efficiencies. This is not a viable option either, because even present levels are sustainable only at a high economic cost. Fleet efficiency, as measured by miles steamed fully laden, was cut almost in half in the decade from 1973. If all ships operating today increased their efficiency to rates equivalent to those of the early 1970s they could carry more than twice the cargo presently on offer. Current overheads are barely covered by income from available trade.

Even lower efficiency would lead to a major shakeout in the industry, to the detriment of traditional maritime nations. Lower freight rates would make life increasingly difficult for those operators who borrowed heavily in the 1970s. If they were forced into liquidation (as would be likely), their more modern tonnage would be sold by their creditors to the highest bidder. As newer second-hand ships lost value, older vessels also would slide down in price to a level little above scrap value. At this point, without the burden of heavy financial charges, the operators of older tonnage would be able to cover their costs at far lower freight rates, forcing the spiral one twist further down. The hardest hit would be the owners of the more modern and more expensive fleets to operate (with higher financial charges, manning costs, etc).

TRENDS IN WORLD SHIPPING: 1970 - 1986

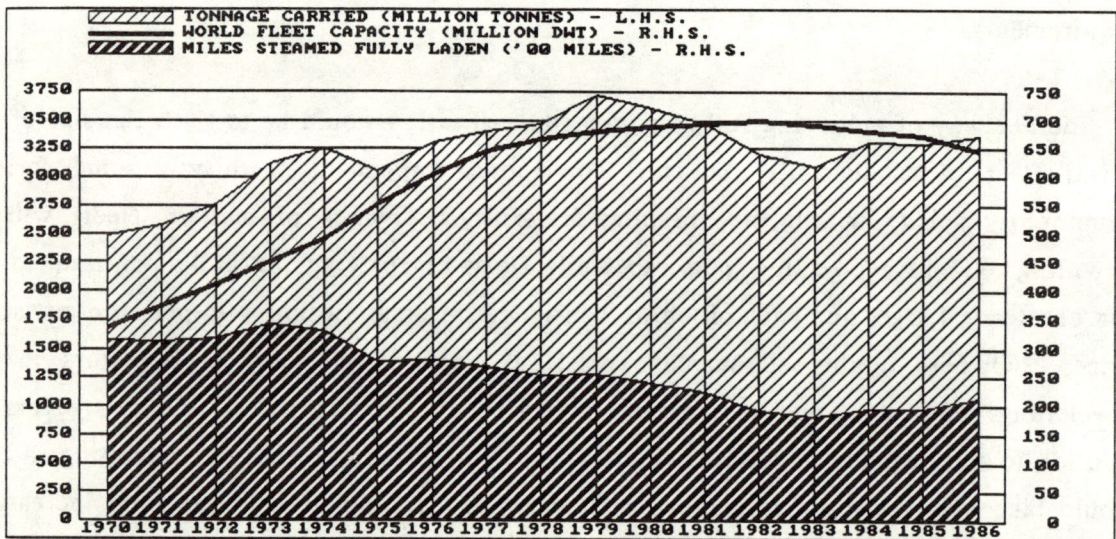

These arguments would seem to indicate that, in the industrialized countries at least, the future for shipping will be bleak for the next decade or so. Yet there is increasing evidence that, at last, the worst of the crisis may be over. The above diagram charts the evolution of shipping supply and demand, as well as showing the trend in capacity utilization (as measured by the distance steamed fully-laden per tonne of cargo space), the surrogate for fleet efficiency. Two years ago only a brave man would have predicted an upturn in shipping demand. The results for 1985 were ambiguous: fleet capacity had declined, but by a small amount relative to the total overshoot, although seaborne trade shrank by almost the same amount. However, figures for 1986 appear to confirm a general improvement on all three indicators. Of course it may be overly optimistic to deduce a watershed in the crisis from one single year of reasonable performance, but other factors serve to reinforce this hope.

First, the reduced real price of oil could stimulate economic growth and hence global trade, while also increasing demand for tanker space (which comprises roughly 40 percent of all ship capacity). But there are negative aspects to this. Lower fuel prices make older ships more economic relative to the fuel-efficient vessels built in an era of high oil prices. In addition, that part of the world fleet involved in the oil trade has been most responsive to changing conditions. Tanker scrapping rates have been far higher than for other ship types (8 percent of tanker space disappeared in 1986). As a result, prices for second-hand tankers have risen by over 50 percent since Autumn 1985 (the nadir in recent history) and this section of the market, while still straining under overcapacity, is much healthier than it appeared a year or so ago.

Second, there has been a rapid evolution in the "flag" profile of the world fleet. In 1970, 65 percent of all ships sailed under flags of the OECD nations. In 1986 such ships accounted for only 39.3 percent of the fleet. Shipping operations based in these countries are, by and large, more heavily regulated than in the open registry countries (Liberia, Panama, Cyprus, etc), whose fleets have risen from 18 percent of global tonnage in 1970 to 27.5 percent in 1986. It has been increasingly tempting for OECD-based owners to transfer their bases of operations to less regulated flags, thus reducing their operating costs. (Shell and BP have both recently deserted the British flag, while two-thirds of the ships owned by US companies fly the flags of other countries.) This trend has meant a significant loss on the sea transport account for the more advanced nations, some of which are introducing measures designed to stop this hæmorrhage. Thus ship operators can expect some improvement in their fiscal status, failing which they will continue to take advantage of the benefits to be gained from flagging out to tax havens like the Bahamas, Bermuda, the Caymen Islands, Gibraltar, Malta, and other small countries with disproportionate merchant fleets.

Somewhat surprisingly, while the size of the OECD fleet continues to dwindle (from 216 million grt in 1980 to 159 million grt in 1986), the traditional open registry fleets (Liberia, Panama, Cyprus, etc.) have not been the principal beneficiaries: indeed, with 111 million grt in 1986, their fleet is 3 percent smaller than in 1980. In the last six years the fleet of the developing countries has grown considerably, together with that of dependencies of the OECD countries (Gibraltar, the Isle of Man, Kerguelen, etc). This proliferation of quasi-open registries has resulted from the adoption of the UN Convention on Conditions for the Registration of Ships, which says that there does not need to be an economic link between flag and vessel, provided that the administrative and judicial responsibility is accepted by the country of registration. Many countries have made registration by non-nationals very much easier (hence the boom in ships registered in Malta, Honduras, St. Vincent, Gibraltar and the Cayman Islands). At the same time, many OECD countries have established "offshore" registers. In mid-1986 France established the Kerguelen register (French Antartica), which allows non-oil bulk carriers to use the French flag but employ up to 75 percent non-French seamen. In the United Kingdom there has been an extensive transfer of shipping to the Isle of Man, which had some 5 million dwt on its register by mid-1987. Norway has set up a new "international" register designed to attract back national owners from the flags of convenience. Other countries are considering similar expedients: land-locked Luxembourg intends to establish a register, as does Spain in the Canary Islands, while Sweden, Finland, the Netherlands, Belgium and Japan are pressing their governments to do the same.

Table 4.1:   THE DEVELOPMENT OF THE FLAG PROFILE OF THE WORLD FLEET
(PERCENTAGE SHARES OF THE MAJOR NATIONAL GROUPS)

	1970	1975	1980	1981	1982	1983	1984	1985	1986	1987
OECD countries[1]	64.7	58.1	51.4	50.7	49.6	47.0	45.1	42.8	39.3	35.5
Open Registry Countries[2]	18.0	24.3	27.3	24.9	25.0	25.3	26.2	26.8	27.5	29.8
USSR/Eastern Europe[3]	8.2	8.0	7.6	7.7	7.7	8.0	8.0	8.2	8.6	8.8
Developing Countries	7.7	8.5	11.0	14.1	15.0	16.6	17.5	18.5	20.4	21.1
Rest of the World[4]	1.4	3.1	2.7	2.6	2.7	3.1	3.2	3.7	4.3	4.8

(1) Including the Great Lakes Fleets of the USA and Canada (3 million grt in 1987).

(2) Bahamas, Cyprus, Lebanon, Liberia, Oman, Panama and Vanuatu.

(3) Albania, Bulgaria, Czechoslovakia, East Germany, Hungary, Poland, Romania and the USSR.

(4) Bermuda, Cuba, China (PR), Faroe Islands, Falkland Islands, Gibraltar, Israel, North Korea, Monaco, South Africa, Vietnam.

Source: OECD. Maritime Transport (various issues)

Third, and more important, the very seriousness of the situation suggests that bitter medicine will soon be swallowed voluntarily, or forcibly administered. Clearly, from the foregoing analysis, any initiative to bring shipping supply into balance with demand will have to come from operators of more modern ships, or their backers. If present conditions are allowed to persist the insolvency rate among such owners will increase relentlessly, causing significant losses to their financiers. Ship finance institutions have had to accept losses of at least $15 billion over the past three years and forecasts of loan write-offs over the next three years vary from $10 to $30 billion per annum. As the present value of the oldest quarter of the world fleet is variously estimated at between $3 and $6 billion, it would appear sensible (and likely) for some "mopping up" operation to be launched, taking older tonnage out of circulation to allow more modern tonnage to cover costs — either by the bankers who risk losing their collateral, or by other interested parties such as trade associations or governments (subsidies paid to shipbuilders in order to make the price of new vessels competitive in the world market represent $5 billion annually, according to the OECD).

Linked to this, there is heightened awareness by international organizations that something drastic needs to be done. In November 1986 the United Nations Conference on Trade and Development (UNCTAD) urged a combined assault by governments, shipowners, shipbuilders, and bankers on the disequilibria in the maritime industries. This initiative was quickly followed by one from the EEC, which launched an "urgent study" into further proposals to ease the plight of Europe's dwindling merchant shipping fleet. But perhaps more practical has been the changing attitude by ship financiers to lending money against doubtful collateral. The spate of bankruptcies has forced bankers to take a far more active interest in their ship finance portfolios. The introduction of hedging programmes in the freight futures market (through the Baltic International Freight Futures Exchange — BIFFEX — and other similar institutions) offers financiers a tool for securing guarantees on shipping loans, or monitoring the positions of their loan portfolios, while also introducing a measure of stability in the notoriously volatile market for freight rates.

In sum, therefore, although the situation is still critical, particularly in the traditional maritime nations where many operators are unlikely to weather the next couple of years, the prospects for world shipping seem less bleak today than they did a short while ago. Shipping is an "inertial" business: the decision to build or to scrap a ship is not taken lightly and cannot be easily or quickly reversed. Thus once a course is set, the industry will follow it naturally — regardless of short-term fluctuations. Nevertheless, even with a significant improvement in demand for shipping volume, freight rates will remain depressed, while prudent owners will continue to seek reduced costs wherever they can, fostering further reduction in merchant fleets flying the flags of the traditional maritime nations.

THE BRITISH MERCHANT NAVY FLEET
GROSS TONNAGE OF SHIPPING REGISTERED UNDER THE BRITISH FLAG: 1921-1987

'000
gross
tons

1975: 33157.4

1987
8504.6

1940-47
NO DATA

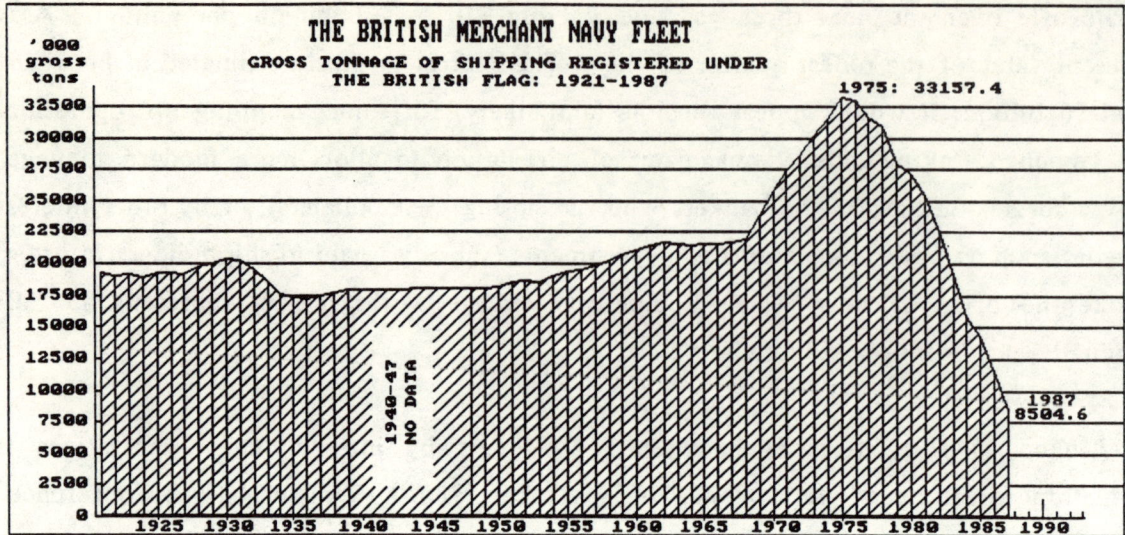

The rapid decline in Britain's merchant navy fleet over the past twelve years has prompted a wave of concern. Since 1975 the gross tonnage of shipping registered under the British Flag has been falling at a vertiginous rate — in that time the fleet has been halved twice. This rapid absolute decline in tonnage since the mid-1970s is by and large due to the global influences set out above. As the figure above shows, the size of the British fleet varied very little from the early 1920s until the late 1960s. The sharp increase from 1968 to 1975, when the fleet expanded by 50 percent, was almost entirely due to investment in large bulk oil-carrying vessels.

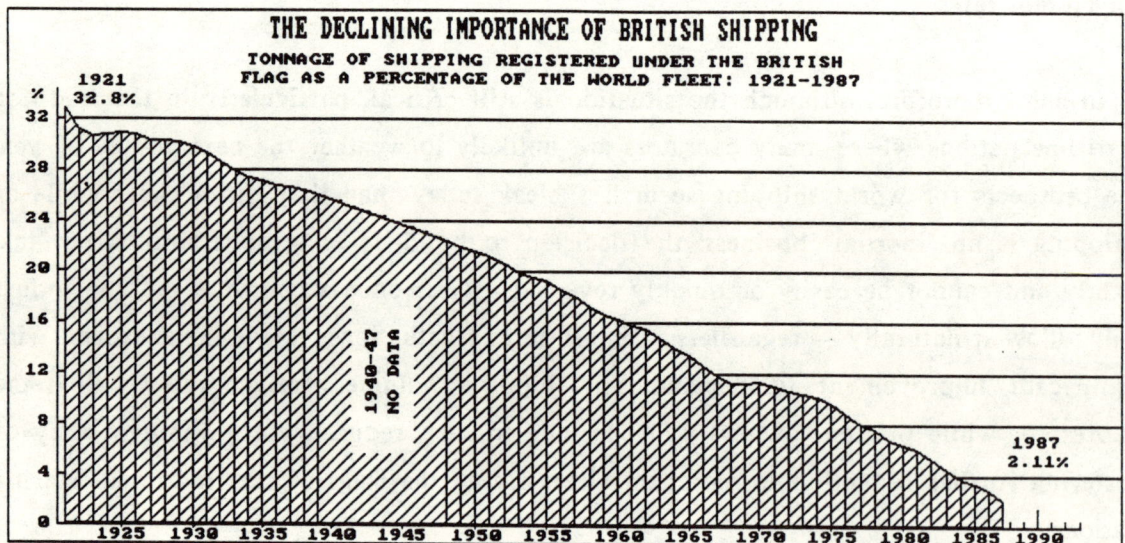

THE DECLINING IMPORTANCE OF BRITISH SHIPPING
TONNAGE OF SHIPPING REGISTERED UNDER THE BRITISH FLAG AS A PERCENTAGE OF THE WORLD FLEET: 1921-1987

%

1921
32.8%

1940-47
NO DATA

1987
2.11%

42

Yet this pattern which appears so significant when looking at the British fleet in isolation, is barely perceptible when put into the context of Britain's position in the world fleet. In 1921 Britannia ruled the waves: one third of all tonnage sailing around the world was flying the Union Jack. By 1987 barely 2 percent of the world fleet flew the British flag. This long-term decline has continued unabated, and at a steady rate. Even the dramatic surge in the fleet to 1975 was insufficient to arrest the relative decline. Indeed, the 50 percent increase in tonnage between 1968 and 1975 was entirely due to a 70 percent increase in average ship size: the number of ships of over 100 registered tonnes in the fleet actually declined (from 4000 in 1968 to 3600 in 1975).

While the total number of UK owned and registered ships has fallen to 2150 since 1975 (and tonnage has been slashed by 75 percent), the decline in the various types of ship has not been uniform. The breakdown of the tonnage of the UK fleet in 1975 and in 1986 was as follows:

Table 4.2:   COMPOSITION OF THE UK FLEET
(Ships of 100 grt and over)

Ship Type	% in 1975	% in 1986
Oil Tankers	49	38
Ore & Bulk Carriers	24	19
General Cargo	19	22
Miscellaneous*	8	21

* Including fishing vessels, fish factory and carrier ships, chemical and other non-oil tankers, liquefied gas carriers, barge & vehical transporters, passenger ships & ferries, research ships and other civil non-trading vessels.

Source: Lloyd's Register of Shipping quoted in OECD, Maritime Transport.

Apart from the expected decline in the importance of the bulk oil transporters, this table shows a considerable increase in specialized ship types. Shipping is now considered as far more than a necessary stage between the manufacture and marketing of products; it has become a vital component of the whole manufacturing/delivery process. As such, competition in the transport industry for this more sophisticated business has forced the pace of evolution of different modes of carriage.

One of the immediate consequences of the decline in British-owned tonnage has been the falling share of Britain's trade handled by the national fleet. In 1986, only 22.2 percent of the 150 million tonnes of goods exported were carried in British ships (although these goods accounted for 36 percent of the value of all exports). This is a considerable decline on previous years, and represents a decline that is greater only in the smaller fleets of Denmark and Spain.

Table 4.3: SHARES OF VARIOUS NATIONAL FLAGS IN NATIONAL SEABORNE TRADE

Flag of Register	Share of National Export Trade								Annual Rate of Change 1980-85
	1978	1979	1980	1981	1982	1983	1984	1985	
United Kingdom	36.5	33.1	36.9	30.0	27.1	23.5	24.0	22.9	-10.0
Belgium	8.3	6.1	5.0	5.2	4.7	6.2	5.6	5.2	0.8
Denmark	25.3	23.5	25.0	21.5	17.4	17.1	17.4	11.7	-16.4
France	25.7	18.1	19.4	18.5	21.2	20.7	21.7	....	2.8
Finland	45.4	42.0	37.1	46.9	48.1	46.5	46.7	41.9	2.4
Germany	22.6	24.7	24.4	21.8	20.0	21.2	20.1	20.4	- 3.6
Greece	45.0	44.6	45.0	43.9	46.5	43.3	41.4	....	- 1.7
Italy	17.6	16.7	17.7	17.3	15.6	18.5	....	....	1.5
Netherlands	9.1	8.5	8.1	8.9	8.7	8.2	8.5	8.7	1.4
Norway	40.5	44.3	48.5	51.9	57.4	64.3	64.1	65.5	6.2
Spain	20.1	18.1	15.5	13.5	15.4	14.4	14.4	8.9	-11.7
Sweden	28.3	26.2	28.7	29.6	29.1	28.5	28.5	27.7	- 0.7
Japan	24.6	23.8	24.6	23.5	23.6	22.6	22.7	20.8	- 3.4
United States	4.6	4.0	3.9	4.1	3.5	3.8	3.7	4.3	1.9

Source: OECD, Maritime Transport

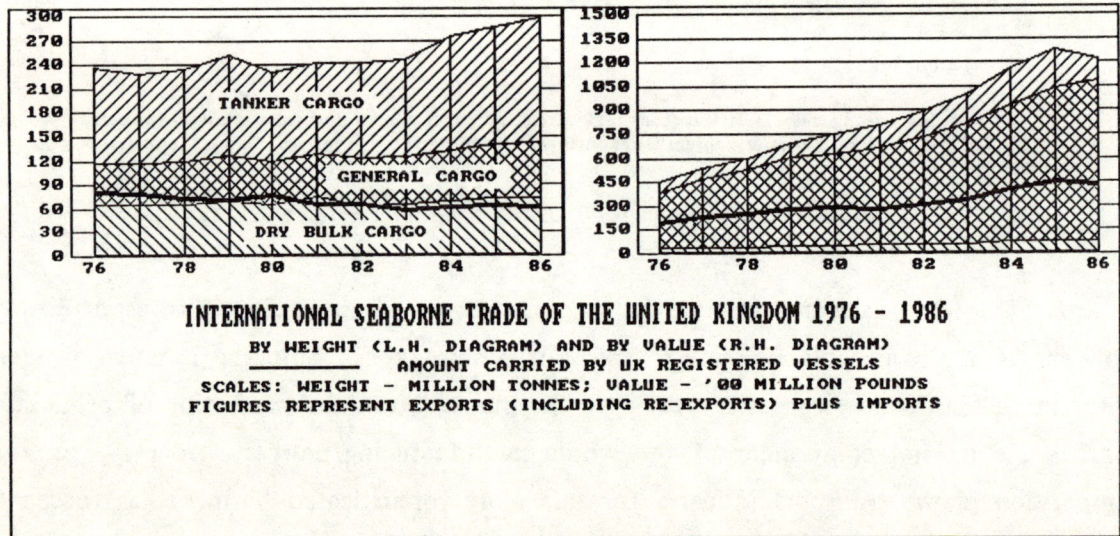

INTERNATIONAL SEABORNE TRADE OF THE UNITED KINGDOM 1976 - 1986
BY WEIGHT (L.H. DIAGRAM) AND BY VALUE (R.H. DIAGRAM)
AMOUNT CARRIED BY UK REGISTERED VESSELS
SCALES: WEIGHT - MILLION TONNES; VALUE - '00 MILLION POUNDS
FIGURES REPRESENT EXPORTS (INCLUDING RE-EXPORTS) PLUS IMPORTS

Another trend which has been damaging for the prospects of the merchant fleet is a shift in the pattern of British trade. In 1975, 53 percent of the tonnage carried by UK-operated ships was intercontinental (deep sea trading): ten years later only 28 percent of shipments were over such distances. Thus while the volume of trade grew over the decade, the demand for shipping space (a function of tonnage and distance measured in

44

tonne-miles) actually declined. This trend is unlikely to reverse, particularly with increased trading with Europe and the tendency to make smaller shipments to one major port (Rotterdam, for instance) where goods are transferred to other vessels for farther-flung destinations.

Civil aviation

Civil aviation has come a long way in its short history. In half a century it has grown from a swashbuckling entrepreneurial activity, undertaken only by the intrepid and the adventurous, to an integral part of modern life. In the United States, for example, where flying is now the normal choice even for short-distance travel, 450 billion passenger-kilometers were logged on internal flights in 1986 (for a population of around 250 million). Two out of three citizens of the US are customers of the airlines.

In Western Europe, where air travel is still regarded by many as somewhat extravagant, there is tremendous scope for expansion. Only two in thirty Europeans flew last year. Nevertheless, growth rates in passenger traffic have been impressive over the past ten years or so, averaging between 5 and 7 percent per annum.

Table 4.4: SELECTED OUTPUTS OF AIRLINES 1975 - 1985.
(average annual growth rate on scheduled services)

	Aircraft km	Passenger km	International Passenger km	Freight tonne-km
United Kingdom	2.5	6.2	6.7	7.2
Germany	1.1	5.5	6.2	10.3
France	-2.2	5.7	5.1	11.2
Italy	0.7	5.0	4.2	7.2
Netherlands	2.3	6.6	6.6	8.8
Spain	2.1	5.0	4.2	7.2
EEC (12)	0.9	5.7	5.9	8.9
Switzerland	2.5	5.5	5.7	7.2
Japan	4.0	7.9	10.0	13.2
USA	3.5	7.4	9.5	3.1

Source: Transport Statistics Great Britain 1976-1986, HMSO, 1987.

Growth in passenger traffic is the major determinant of trends in civil aviation. In the United Kingdom, for example, revenue from freight amounts to less than 10 percent of overall income. (Indeed, with an average loading of 95 tonnes for a Boeing 747 freight transporter, air freight rates are such that only valuable and urgent deliveries are considered for this mode.) The least optimistic estimates for passenger growth through to the end of the century allow for 3-4 percent per annum — estimates that may easily be exceeded should air traffic deregulation in Europe follow the US example.

In 1978, President Jimmy Carter introduced the Airline De-Regulation Act in an attempt to open the US domestic market to free competition. Under the threat of anti-trust legislation, US airlines were forced to abandon IATA (the International Air Transport Association, the cartel which controls routes, capacities, frequencies and tariffs throughout the world), or force it to relax its rules.

The results of this freedom in air services have been ambiguous. Initially there was a flood of new entrants into the US market, hitherto 90 percent dominated by the ten major carriers. Cut-throat pricing wars enabled passengers to travel, on average, for 30 to 50 percent less than in the days of regulation, and to have a wider choice in the number of destinations. Competition forced airlines to serve the needs of the consumer better — flying where he wanted, when he wanted — rather than imposing its schedules on the travelling public.

But the bigger airlines were able to undercut the lowest prices on routes where the new low-cost operators tried to establish a foothold by cross-subsidizing cheap fares with higher fares on less competitive routes (and also by retaining the full-fare business traveller which permitted a number of bargain-price seats to be offered on most flights). Few of the new market entrants were able to stand the pace for long. The geographic spread of the major carriers provided the competitive muscle such that, today, the ten largest airlines in the US again resemble an oligopoly, commanding 94 percent of domestic traffic.

The majors have re-established their dominant positions by buying out the smaller companies, or forcing them to work closely in harmony with their own services. This has come about as much from the deregulatory shake-out as from the new geography of air travel in America. Large airlines have adopted certain major regional airports ("hub" airports), as their home bases. From these hubs they fly small feeder services to lesser "spoke" airports in the region, as well as make connections to other "hub" airports across the country. At St. Louis International airport, for example, 82 percent of the passengers landing or taking off in 1986 did so in TWA aircraft; at Pittsburgh, 80 percent flew with USAir. Indeed, at 15 of the top airports in America, 50 percent of traffic is controlled by one airline or two share 70 percent or more.

Each airport only has so much space available on the ground. Once an airline becomes established at an airport it is in a strong position to keep its rivals out by physically occupying the space. By leasing most of the gates at these airports from the local authorities, the big companies control which others can handle passengers. For airport expansion has not kept pace with passenger traffic growth. Once an airline achieves a dominant position, it can exert pressure on the airport authority for expansion plans suiting itself.

Deregulation not only opened the American domestic market to free competition; it also affected routes originating in the US. North Atlantic air travel accounts for 30 percent of the international market. Over the last decade, the number of carriers serving the route has doubled. The scramble for passengers has brought fares tumbling down in a succession of price wars. But even here, the competitive edge has been gained by the larger companies (using similar tactics to those outlined above). Brave attempts to establish new services (Laker and People Express are prime examples) foundered against the might of the majors.

Comparisons between the experiences in the United States and the likely deregulation of European airlines should be made with caution. For while route-fixing and fare agreements are an undoubted constraint to free trade wherever they occur, Europe still represents a group of different nation states separated by frontiers. The prospect of 1992 and the free circulation of goods, labour, and services throughout the European Community has led some to think that the single European market will resemble that of the US. For many reasons (cultural, linguistic, infrastructural, not to mention monetary and political), it cannot, and will not — at least for the next decade or so. According to Umberto Nordio, chairman of Alitalia: "The stark, Darwinian process through which the US mega-carriers emerged as survivors in the deregulated US environment would, since its inception, meet with several obstacles in the European environment of today. In Europe, extinction or mutilation of a national airline would elicit strong protests from all the vested interests that in time have grown around it. A suggestion might then follow again to rely on the old panacea of subsidizing the ailing airline so as to satisfy both vested interests and customers' expectations. The Darwinian process would thus be thwarted."[1] Few European countries will willingly accept their national flag-carrier being dominated by the airline of another country (which would be the case if the US model applied). This is the heart of the fractious arguments that have been going on in Brussels for the past couple of years.

Fewer Europeans than Americans travel by air. The distances between destinations within each country rarely warrant air travel for non-business purposes (in France the high-speed train service can move passengers from the centre of Paris to that of Lyon quicker than any airline, allowing for time to reach the airport and for checking in). And unless prices are cut, families travelling on holiday will rarely consider air travel before road or rail. Though the numbers are small relative to those flying in America, the infrastructure available in Europe is hard-pressed to cope with current demand.

We are all familiar with the annual crop of complaints about airport delays due to congestion on the most popular tourist routes in summer. Flights from Britain to Spain and Greece, in particular, are frequently hostage to the limitations (physical and human) of the airport services in the countries of destination. Indeed, the constraints to airport size that have marred the deregulation process in the United States are, if anything, even greater in Europe. Already, in France, Britain, the Netherlands and Germany, the national carrier is firmly established at the major port of entry (Paris CDG, London Heathrow, Amsterdam Schiphol, and Frankfurt). The same is true for the smaller members of the European Community; each takes pride in its national airline and gives it preferential landing rights. Some of these airports have already almost reached their physical capacity to receive flights (either due to lack of space on the ground, runway constraints, or air traffic control limits). At present there are no major plans to overcome these difficulties. It is not easy to see how any process of deregulation could succeed if it increased the number of flights.

Deregulation, almost by definition, is bound to increase air traffic regardless of the numbers of passengers flying. In the US, the practice before 1978 was for airlines to operate just two or three flights each day to major destinations, using large bodied aircraft. Consumer demand transformed this operating pattern, encouraging airlines to offer more frequent flights, but with fewer places on each aircraft. Thus, while the number of passengers increased, the number of air traffic movements increased even more. In Europe, this trend has emerged already on the most popular routes (London to Paris, London to Brussels, for example), while any move towards the hub and spoke network typical of the US would increase the frequency of shorter journeys (on smaller aircraft) as well as longer-haul flights.

If the demand for European air traffic increases in line with forecasts, there will, very soon, be a pressing need for additional airports and flight-control facilities. This poses a

48

major problem for planners and legislators alike. Only airline passengers like airports to be close to big cities; environmentalists and residents fight any proposals for extending runways or operating times. In addition, air traffic control systems throughout Europe are already close to saturation at peak hours. Greater numbers of aircraft movements would inevitably lead to delays, or threaten the viability of the current system. Neither airport terminals nor air traffic controllers can be created overnight. The long lead times for construction and training will cause difficulties over the coming years.

If deregulation does come to Europe in the near future (as the European Commission seems determined it should), those countries which react the quickest will be best placed to establish themselves as major hubs of air travel in Europe. Those less swift to react may be relegated to spokes on the continental network. In a hub and spoke air transit system, those countries with the largest facilities available will emerge as leaders in civil aviation in the 1990s. Britain, with its huge facilities at Heathrow and Gatwick — the two largest airport terminals in the world measured by international passenger movements — will be in a very strong position, as will the Netherlands, France, Italy and Germany, with their facilities at Schiphol, Paris, Rome and Frankfurt.

Civil aviation in Britain

The recent takeover of British Caledonian by British Airways has created the only airline company in Europe that can be compared with the mega-carriers in North America. True, BA has held the blue riband for international passenger-kilometers flown for some time (hence its advertising slogan: "The World's Favourite Airline"). But this accolade is due in part to Britain's relatively small land area. Of the 645 million kilometers flown by UK airlines in 1986 more than 88 percent were international: in terms of passenger kilometers flown, the percentage is even higher (95 percent of 87 billion passenger-kilometers).

Thus British Airways will primarily be operating in the future, as in the past, in an international competitive environment. The company's success or failure will be determined by its ability to attract business in the international market, as much as from its capacity to retain the custom of British travellers. BA is in a strong position at present, having weathered some very uncertain years in the late 1970s and early 1980s.

49

PERCENTAGE DISTRIBUTION OF PASSENGER AND AIRCRAFT MOVEMENTS AT BAA AIRPORTS

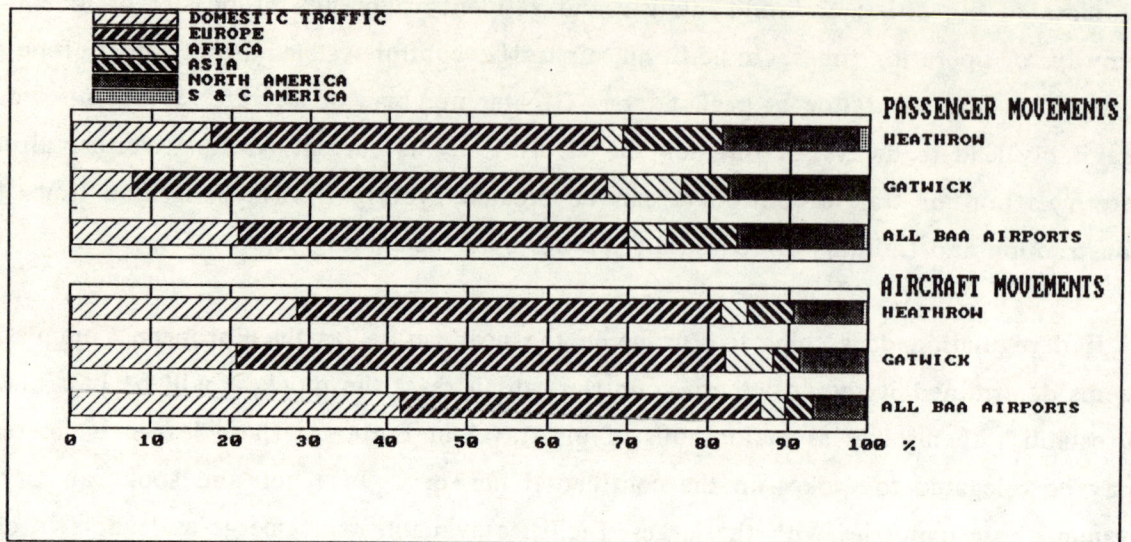

But as seen in the previous section, the future of civil aviation in Britain, and its contribution to the balance of payments, is related to more than the relative health of the national flag carrier. Also important is the competitivity of Britain's airports: their capacity to handle the expected increase in demand both on the ground and in the air. In a "hub and spoke" aviation network there can be room only for a certain number of "hubs". While there is little doubt that London will remain one of the primary European air transit centres in a deregulated Europe, and the hub for Britain, passengers departing from other national locations could be enticed to take a shuttle flight to or from Paris, Frankfurt, or Schiphol, for example, if the price was right and transit delays were kept to a minimum. This may not be so easy to do with passengers whose starting point or final destination were London or the home counties of Britain (who account for 70 percent of passengers through Heathrow and Gatwick at present). But for a traveller from Manchester or Edinburgh, for example, the promise of a less stressful flight via Amsterdam could attract business away from the ever more crowded terminals of Heathrow and Gatwick (where passengers on scheduled flights already try to avoid the summer package-tour rush hours).

Britain's major airports are managed by BAA (formerly the British Airports Authority), which has made considerable efforts to upgrade the terminals at Heathrow and Gatwick, and has plans to boost the passenger capacity of Stansted from 1 million to 7 or 8 million per year. But there are limits to the extent to which extra passenger handling facilities can increase the capacity of an airport.

At Gatwick, the terms of the BAA agreement with the local authority, the physical size of the airport, and public opposition to expansion together preclude the possibility of building a second runway, for the time being. The current capacity of Gatwick is estimated at 25 million passengers per annum, a figure that will be reached in the mid-1990s. Heathrow also faces a theoretical physical limit of 50 million passengers (again, a figure that could easily be reached within the next decade). Furthermore, a ban on night flights restricts the absolute number of movements that can be handled in any given day at both London's major airports. In these circumstances, the only possible expansion of the South-Eastern airports would have to come at Stansted, or by building a completely new airport.

If the number of flights across the South-East of England were to be boosted in some way, there would be a heightened need for increased air traffic control facilities. Already the number of near-misses that are reported in the London region airspace has raised considerable concern. If passenger traffic is to expand at anything like the rate projected, a careful overall strategy will have to be developed that ensures safety and environmental considerations, while allowing the continued commercial development of aviation.

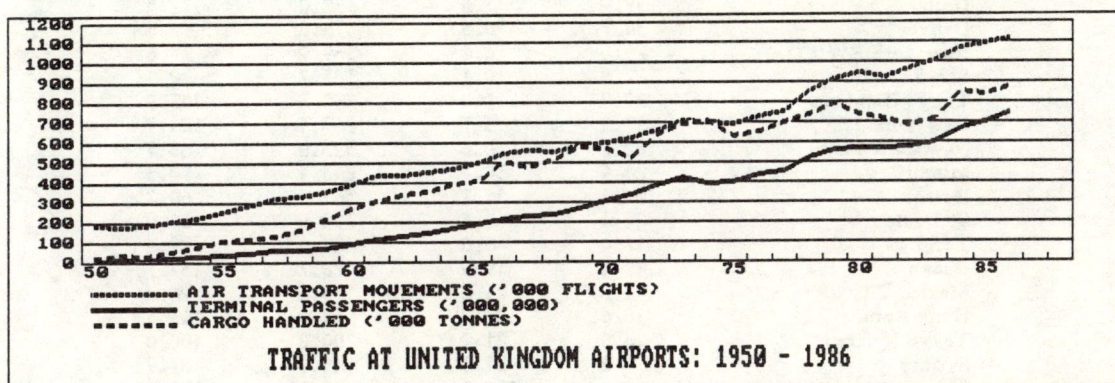

TRAFFIC AT UNITED KINGDOM AIRPORTS: 1950 - 1986

AIR TRANSPORT MOVEMENTS ('000 FLIGHTS)
TERMINAL PASSENGERS ('000,000)
CARGO HANDLED ('000 TONNES)

Table 4.5: MAJOR EUROPEAN AND INTERNATIONAL AIRPORTS – TRAFFIC, 1986

(passengers, air transport movements, and average aircraft loading)

Airport	Passengers (million)	% Internat'l	Air Transport Movements ('000)	Loading* Pass/aircraft
London Heathrow	31.3	82.1	289.3	108.5
Frankfurt	19.8	73.8	235.0	84.3
London Gatwick	16.3	93.3	154.7	105.4
Paris Orly	18.5	38.9	164.2	112.9
Paris CDG	14.4	89.4	144.9	99.6
Rome	12.6	49.4	143.3	87.8
Amsterdam	11.7	99.3	158.6	73.7
Madrid	10.8	45.7	113.4	95.6
Stockholm	10.6	41.3	188.2	56.3
Copenhagen	10.0	78.4	157.4	63.3
Palma	9.9	78.5	74.8	132.6
Athens	9.6	55.8	110.2	114.8
Zurich	9.3	94.8	131.8	70.2
Dusseldorf	8.5	59.8	97.1	87.5
Milan	8.3	59.2	102.3	81.4
Munich	8.0	48.6	122.6	65.1
Manchester	7.5	73.0	85.5	88.1
Brussels	7.5	99.7	89.9	63.8
Oslo	6.3	51.4	94.3	66.7
Geneva	4.6	82.8	76.6	59.9
Helsinki	4.4	64.2	57.6	76.5
Lisbon	3.3	73.9	38.1	86.9
Dublin	2.9	94.5	54.6	53.1
Chicago O'Hare	54.8	6.8	642.1	85.3
Atlanta	45.2	3.1	569.6	79.3
Los Angeles	41.4	15.5	507.5	81.6
Dallas	39.9	1.3	552.0	72.4
Denver	34.7	0.6	373.6	92.8
New York EWR	29.4	4.4	369.9	79.6
San Fransisco	27.8	10.1	385.7	72.1
Tokyo Handea	27.2	1.8	262.3	103.9
New York JFK	27.2	56.5	267.1	101.9
New York LGA	22.2	0.6	323.2	68.7
Miami	21.9	34.9	243.1	90.3
Boston	21.8	11.2	361.8	60.2
St Louis	20.4	0.5	398.9	51.0
Toronto	17.4	46.0	220.4	78.8
Osaka	17.4	19.9	126.7	137.7
Mexico City	10.8	25.6	113.6	94.7
Hong Kong	10.6	100.0	64.9	163.5
Tokyo Narita	10.0	81.9	100.2	100.0
Sydney	9.2	31.3	104.9	87.9
Singapore	8.9	100.0	68.3	130.5
Montreal	8.1	47.0	128.0	62.9
Jeddah	7.2	49.4	70.1	102.7
Bangkok	7.2	81.5	63.1	113.6
Rio de Janeiro	6.7	38.4	96.3	69.6
Riyadh	6.1	28.9	57.9	105.8
Delhi	5.0	37.1	45.3	109.9
Taipei	4.6	100.0	37.4	121.6

* Average number of passengers per flight movement.

Source: British Airports Authority

Until quite recently Britain's earnings from the provision of transport were generally in balance with the amount paid to foreign operators for such services. In the twenty years to 1975 the net balance only twice exceeded plus or minus 5 percent of total transport credits. The first oil shock disturbed this rough equilibrium. In the following six years transport earnings comfortably exceeded outgoings by more than 5 percent (largely due to the surplus earned by maritime oil transporters). Since 1980, however, the tide has been running against the UK industry. In 1987 Britain spent £1.57 billion more on transport than it earned — a 22 percent shortfall of credits over debits.

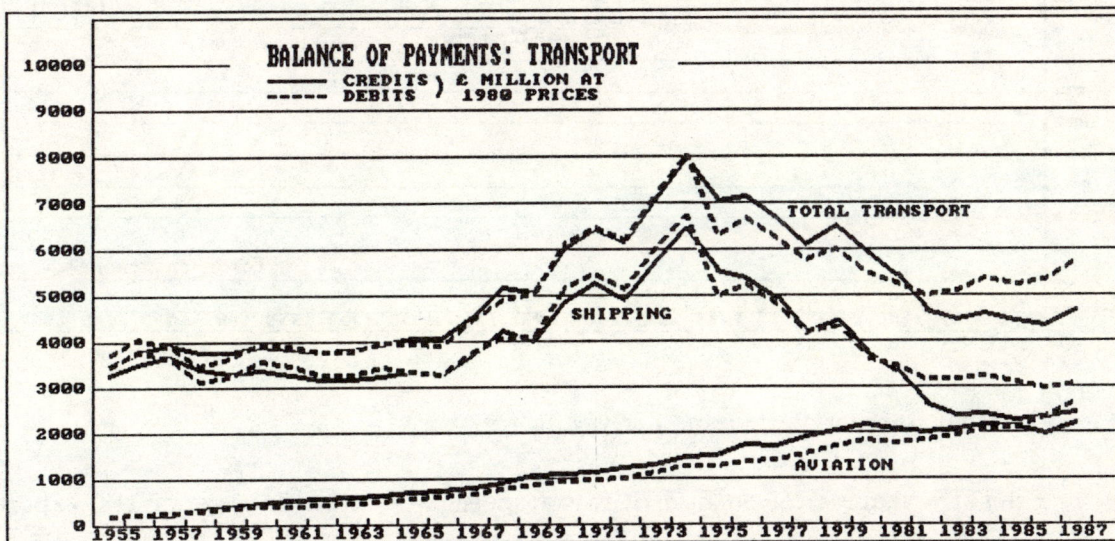

BALANCE OF PAYMENTS: TRANSPORT
—— CREDITS) £ MILLION AT
---- DEBITS) 1980 PRICES

The balance of payments on the transport account shows three clear phases since the mid-1950s. Until the mid-1960s there was little variation in real income derived from transport[2], which was primarily supplied by shipping services. In the decade to 1974, income from both shipping and aviation almost doubled, with the boom in global trade, while spending kept pace so that the net position remained in balance. Since 1974 shipping credits have collapsed: but in the period to 1981, at least, aviation credits continued to grow at a steady rate, outstripping debits, so that the overall net position remained reasonably healthy. In 1980 the trends diverged, since when the account has moved strongly into deficit. Shipping credits have fallen significantly below debits, and earnings from aviation have stagnated such that the net contribution of aviation to the overall balance has narrowed, sliding into deficit in 1986.

The reasons for this quite spectacular slide into the red on the transport account are as many as the items on the balance sheet. By and large, however, the bulk of the discrepancy can be accounted for by the change in Britain's shipping fortunes since 1980. Until then, the Sea Transport account had been approximately in balance, but in the ensuing five years the gap between income and expenditure widened considerably so that by 1985 expenditure was 25 percent greater than income.

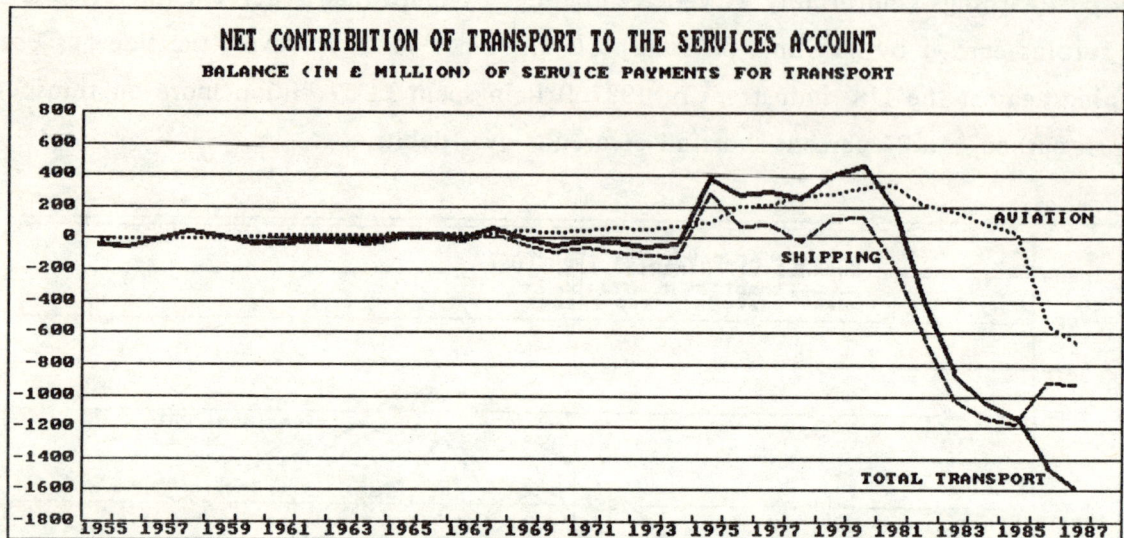

NET CONTRIBUTION OF TRANSPORT TO THE SERVICES ACCOUNT
BALANCE (IN £ MILLION) OF SERVICE PAYMENTS FOR TRANSPORT

Income from transport services is derived in five ways:

1.   Freight revenue received by British transporters from the carriage of UK exports to overseas markets.

2.   Freight revenue received by British transporters from the carriage of goods between two overseas locations (cross trading).

3.   Charter receipts by British owners from the hiring out of transport equipment to overseas transporters.

4.   Passenger revenue received by British transporters from the carriage of overseas residents.

5.   Disbursements made in the UK by overseas transporters (the purchase of fuel, stores, and other running costs, etc.).

On the debit side, expenditure on transport services arises in similar ways:

1.   Freight payments made to overseas operators for the carriage of UK imports.

2.   Charter payments overseas for the hiring in of transport equipment.

3.   Passenger revenue earned by overseas transporters carrying UK residents.

4.   Disbursements made overseas by British transporters.

Thus the transport accounts can be disaggregated first, according to the mode of transport and, second, into four principal components: freight charges, charter payments, disbursements by operators, and passenger revenues. In the following tables all statistics are derived from CSO statistics.

Shipping

Freight earnings by UK ship operators can be broken down two ways, by the nature of the cargo (liquids or dry goods) and by the nature of the trade — into revenue from the carriage of UK exports, and income from cross-trades. Total freight credits have fluctuated widely since 1976. While income from cross trading in dry goods grew by some 40 percent over the period (largely thanks to the fleet of British container ships), the slump in the oil trade wiped out all the gains. Significantly, while the value of British exports more than tripled over the same period, freight earned on UK exports has fluctuated around the £400 million level, in current terms, representing a real contraction. This implies a considerable loss of business to overseas carriers, and is confirmed by the steady rise in dry cargo freight payments to foreign operators. Freight debits are only incurred on imports to the United Kingdom.

Table 4.6:   SEA TRANSPORT – FREIGHT ACCOUNT
£ million, current revenue/expenditure

Freight Credits	1976	1977	1978	1979	1980	1981	1982	1983	1984	1985	1986
Dry Cargo											
UK Exports	445	528	459	461	462	372	428	369	417	494	391
Cross Trades	507	558	520	516	616	637	650	539	624	608	710
Wet Cargo											
UK Exports	32	37	48	63	84	73	65	79	125	75	136
Cross Trades	1020	1036	907	1296	1160	1117	653	666	685	517	665
Total Credits	2004	2159	1934	2336	2322	2199	1796	1653	1851	1694	1902
Freight Debits											
Dry Cargo	765	860	1020	1268	1380	1550	1583	1654	1907	2094	1929
Wet Cargo	200	170	140	168	97	123	147	168	229	238	258
Total Debits	965	1030	1160	1436	1477	1673	1730	1822	2136	2332	2187
Freight Balance	1039	1129	774	900	845	526	66	-169	-285	-638	-285

The second largest item on the shipping account was, until 1980, revenue from time charters. Throughout the last ten years, overcapacity in the world fleet led ship operators to reduce chartering activity wherever possible. In the five years to 1986, however, such credits have been cut by two thirds. Charter payments overseas also fell in most of the period, although there was a strong rebound in 1986.

These two items, freight and charter income, provide a clear reflection of the shrinkage of Britain's merchant fleet. Between them, they account for roughly two-thirds of the shortfall on the transport sector balance of payments.

Table 4.7: SEA TRANSPORT - CHARTER ACCOUNT
£ million, current revenue/expenditure

Charter Credits	1976	1977	1978	1979	1980	1981	1982	1983	1984	1985	1986
Dry Cargo	384	395	294	300	268	240	172	97	118	131	111
Wet Cargo	267	217	219	349	317	382	243	224	118	128	108
Total Credits	651	612	513	649	585	622	415	321	236	259	219
Charter Debits											
Dry Cargo	85	110	101	77	88	105	159	110	109	127	172
Wet Cargo	717	727	615	650	546	518	473	493	550	436	566
Total Debits	802	837	716	727	634	623	632	603	659	563	738
Charter Balance	-151	-225	-203	- 78	- 49	- 1	-217	-282	-423	-304	-519

Despite the decline in the British fleet, disbursements made by UK operators overseas have failed to follow suit. This is not as surprising as might be indicated by a first glance. As seen above, many British operators and owners have changed the national flag of their ships, for the purposes of seeking less restrictive environments. Others have chosen to remain under the Union Jack, but have sought to cut their operating costs by hiring foreign crews (at lower wages) to man their ships. Thus, despite a 75 percent reduction to the UK fleet since 1975, disbursements overseas have remained roughly constant.

There is another discrepency, between the trends for dry goods and liquids. Disbursements linked primarily to the oil trade have been cut by 70 percent whereas those in the dry cargo trade have increased by 30 percent. This is a reflection of the disastrous decline of business in the oil trade (which has borne the brunt of the merchant fleet collapse and where manning levels are relatively low), and the increase in cross trading in dry goods (see freight credits above). The doubling of credits earned when foreign ship operators take on supplies in the UK is directly related to the relative shift in the flag composition of the world fleet.

Table 4.8: SEA TRANSPORT - DISBURSEMENT AND PASSENGER ACCOUNTS

£ million, current revenue/expenditure

	1976	1977	1978	1979	1980	1981	1982	1983	1984	1985	1986
Disbursements											
Credits	437	500	532	617	672	721	740	726	774	819	681
Debits											
Wet Cargo	600	583	480	664	604	710	477	432	369	221	180
Dry Cargo	738	849	759	782	878	852	961	1117	1110	1190	1042
Disbursement Balance	-901	-932	-707	-829	-810	-841	-698	-823	-705	-2230	-1903
Passenger Revenue											
Credits	141	162	170	202	237	242	316	354	393	499	537
Debits	50	46	47	68	82	86	90	93	112	130	130
Passenger Balance	91	116	123	134	155	156	226	261	281	369	407

The fourth pillar of sea transport earnings is provided by passenger revenues. Indeed, since 1983 income from this source has surpassed receipts from chartering out British ships. Of all the items on the transport account (both for shipping and for aviation), it is the only one that has remained consistently in credit, and has expanded in real as well as nominal terms. The bulk of the revenue from passengers is earned by Britain's cross-channel ferry companies, who have a dominant position in their market. These receipts, which provide a welcome respite on the transport account, will doubtless be affected by the opening of the Channel Tunnel (due in May 1993) but may be expected to remain in surplus for the forseeable future.

Table 4.9: SEA TRANSPORT - CONSOLIDATED ACCOUNT

£ million, current revenue/expenditure

	1976	1977	1978	1979	1980	1981	1982	1983	1984	1985	1986
Freight											
Total Credits	2004	2159	1934	2336	2322	2199	1796	1653	1851	1694	1902
Total Debits	965	1030	1160	1436	1477	1673	1730	1822	2136	2332	2187
Freight Balance	1039	1129	774	900	845	526	66	-169	-285	-638	-285
Charter											
Total Credits	651	612	513	649	585	622	415	321	236	259	219
Total Debits	802	837	716	727	634	623	632	603	659	563	738
Charter Balance	-151	-225	-203	-78	-49	-1	-217	-282	-423	-304	-519
Disbursements											
Credits	437	500	532	617	672	721	740	726	774	819	681
Debits	1338	1432	1239	1446	1482	1562	1438	1549	1479	1422	1222
Disbursement Balance	-901	-932	-707	-829	-810	-841	-698	-823	-705	-2230	-1903
Passenger Revenue											
Credits	141	162	170	202	237	242	316	354	393	499	537
Debits	50	46	47	68	82	86	90	93	112	130	130
Passenger Balance	91	116	123	134	155	156	226	261	281	369	407
Totals											
Total Credits	3233	3433	3149	3804	3816	3784	3267	3054	3254	3270	3339
Total Debits	3155	3345	3162	3677	3675	3944	3890	4067	4386	4436	4276
Overall Balance	78	88	-13	127	141	-180	-623	-1013	-1132	-1166	-937
Partial Balances:											
Ships Owned by UK Residents	1014	1024	975	1144	1150	1123	821	615	691	739	979
Ships Chartered by UK Res.	-358	-360	-313	-130	-122	-245	-364	-439	-349	-261	-281
Ships Operated by For. Res.	-578	-576	-675	-887	-887	-1038	-1080	-1189	-1474	-1643	-1636

Credits and debits on the civil aviation account can be broken down in much the same way as for sea transport, into passenger revenues, freight payments, disbursements (including charter payments), and other items.

Until 1986 the trends in the components of the aviation account were moving in very different ways. The passenger balance declined from 1978 until 1982, and then picked up strongly until the collapse of 1986. In the same period the freight balance moved from a healthy 45 percent surplus to a 70 percent deficit. The disbursement balance, having been almost 60 percent in deficit in 1976, moved into credit in 1980, peaked in 1981, and has since slid back to a 43 percent deficit. The reason for this is due more to a failure to earn credits from foreign airline's disbursements (in decline since 1980 in real terms), rather than to any significant increase in UK spending overseas.

Table 4.10: CIVIL AVIATION - BALANCE OF PAYMENTS

£ million, current revenue/expenditure

	1976	1977	1978	1979	1980	1981	1982	1983	1984	1985	1986
Passenger Revenue											
Credits	615	690	847	901	1004	1026	1119	1304	1560	1749	1653
Debits	327	393	459	582	791	903	1016	1126	1240	1296	1651
Passenger Balance	288	297	388	319	213	123	103	178	320	453	2
Freight Payments											
Credits	105	134	149	129	154	134	129	146	175	180	209
Debits	60	71	89	107	183	168	233	281	333	335	355
Freight Balance	45	63	60	22	-29	-34	-104	-135	-158	-155	-146
Disbursements											
Credits	285	351	394	641	955	1101	1110	1083	1078	1030	947
Debits	448	515	623	773	905	935	1003	1074	1249	1399	1354
Disbursement Balance	-163	-164	-229	-132	50	166	107	9	-171	-369	-407
Other Items											
Credits	44	28	65	84	97	98	113	132	118	119	113
Debits	5	5	5	5	7	6	5	7	7	8	11
Balance of Other Items	39	23	60	79	90	92	108	125	111	111	102
UK Airlines Balance	316	337	438	341	350	323	358	508	604	649	621
Overseas Airlines Balance	107	118	159	53	26	-24	144	331	502	609	1070
Overall Balance	209	219	279	288	324	347	214	177	102	40	-449

The radical change in the passenger balance raises some difficult questions. How could the account slide so far (with a revenue decline of 6 percent) when the total number of passengers carried, seat occupancy and passenger-mile performance all registered gains? The answer, most probably, comes from the relative importance of American passengers on transatlantic flights to Britain. As seen in the section on tourism, receipts from that source fell remarkably in 1986 due to the falling dollar and terrorism: 27 percent fewer

Americans visited Britain in 1986 than in 1985. The jump in spending on foreign airlines by British passengers may also be explained by trends in tourism, particularly the reliance of package tour operators on foreign airlines for a large share of the charter business. Thus, with more normal transatlantic traffic in 1987 and the following years, passenger credits should resume their growth pattern while debits, also, will grow at the same, or a faster rate.

Income from freight is still relatively minor compared to passenger receipts on the aviation account. Nevertheless, British airlines appear to be losing out to foreign competition. While the tonnage carried by UK airlines grew by 40 percent in the decade to 1986, cargo carried by foreign airlines increased by 56 percent. And in revenue terms, the difference has been even more stark. Credits have barely doubled over the period, while debits have multiplied six-fold.

Outlook

The importance of transport can be assessed by considering what would be Britain's position in the extreme case where the country had no transport industry. What would be the balance of payments impact of a total dependence on foreign shipping and aviation services? In such a case, Britain's balance of payments would be debited for freight charges on all goods imported into the country, and also for all foreign travel of UK residents.

In 1986 the UK imported 150 million tonnes of goods by sea, 80 percent of which were carried by non-British shipping lines. The cost to the country for this freight amounted to £2.5 billion. If all goods had been carried by non-British shippers, the cost would have been of the order of £3.1 billion. Balancing this would have been expenditure by these foreign shipping lines in the UK, probably amounting to some £850 million. Thus the net loss to the country would have been some £2.3 billion. In addition, UK shipping lines earned some £875 million from carrying passengers in 1986, £335 million of which came from UK residents. Passenger revenue earned by foreign shippers from UK residents in the same year amounted to £130 million. Thus, without a British fleet, a further £465 million would have been be added to the freight deficit. In this hypothesis, the country would have had a deficit of almost £2.8 billion on its balance of payments due to the absence of a merchant navy. A similar calculation can be made for civil aviation where, in the absence of a native industry, the loss would have been some £1.4 billion.

The development of such hypotheses is not totally academic. The present government appears unconcerned about the parlous state of British shipping. Britain's merchant navy has shrunk by 75 percent in the last ten years and, according to Lord Brabazon, the Minister for Shipping: "Some sectors of the fleet may contract further and in some there may be further transfers to other registries."[3] Such an attitude, while honouring Britain's firm adherence to the principles of free competition, may bring about undesired economic effects if pursued to the bitter conclusion, which in turn could encourage a re-examination of the situation. Civil aviation growth, in the near future, will be constrained unless a more far-sighted infrastructure development programme is developed.

As seen above, there is a strong correlation between the size of the fleet flying the British flag and the net sea transport balance of payments. There are measures which could be taken to forestall the decline of the industry, if not improve the overall situation. The creation of an "offshore" registry (as has been done by Norway, France, and other countries) providing fiscal and legislative benefits to national operators could attract shipping to the British flag.

For the time being Britain does have a domestic transport industry, one which earned a net £1.3 billion in 1986, and saved a further £1.5 billion by handling UK imports and transporting UK residents. This is a not inconsiderable contribution when the overall balance of payments position (£1 billion deficit in 1986) is considered.

Notes and references

1) International Herald Tribune, June 15, 1987.
2) Real income obtained by deflating current income by the consumer price index.
3) Written parliamentary reply given in February 1988 to opposition MP Alexander Eadie, who had asked the government to support the NUMAST proposal for urgent action to stem the decline of the British merchant fleet by providing tax incentives for owners and seafarers, the appointment of a special minister, the abolition of cabotage within the EEC, and the carriage of government-sponsored cargoes in UK ships.

Other references include:

Transport Statistics Great Britain (annual publication). Department of Transport, published by the Government Statistical Service, HMSO.
Statistical Trends in Transport 1965-1983, OECD, Paris.
UK Balance of Payments & Monthly Bulletins, Central Statistical Office, London.
Statistics Bulletin (various), Department of Transport, London.
Maritime Transport (annual publication). OECD, Paris.
Lloyd's Register Annual Report (annual publication). Lloyd's Register of Shipping, London.
Statistical Bulletin (various), Civil Aviation Authority, London.
"Transport", in *International Management*, July 1985.
Le Commerce International, Cahiers Français No. 229, La Documentation Française, Paris.
"Shipping", A Special Report in *South*, June 1988.
Measures of Assistance to Shipbuilding, OECD Paris, 1987.
Problemes Economiques No. 2008, La Documentation Française, Paris.
Problemes Economiques No. 2057, La Documentation Française, Paris.
"Increased Scrapping to Boost Recovery", in *The Naval Architect*, London, March 1984.
"Not Just a Bunch of Grumblers", in *The Naval Architect*, London, June 1985.
"Aviation Brief", in *The Economist*, February 27, 1988.
"Aviation", A Special Report, in *The International Herald Tribune*, May 1985.
"Why Predators are on the Prowl", in *The Financial Times*, September 1985.
"The Giants in Command Again", in *The Financial Times*, September 18, 1986.
"Aviation: Changing the Rules", in *The International Herald Tribune* Special Report, June, 1987.
"BA: A Bumpy Take-Off - and a Bumpy Ride?" in *Financial Weekly*, Decemeber 18, 1986.
British Airways: The Path to Profitability, Alison Corke, Pan Business Profiles, London.
NCEIS Aircraft Forum: An Industry in Transition, 1986, NCEIS, Georgetown, USA.
Air traffic distribution in the London Area (CAP 522), Civil Aviation Authority, London.
"Regional Airports", *Financial Times Survey*, March 1985.
"A Special Report on Airports", in *The Times*, September 1986.
"London's Airports", *Financial Times Survey*, March 1988.

5 Tourism

Introduction:

Unlike such traditional and élite services as banking, insurance and shipping, "tourism" (or "travel") is above all a modern industry — the product of technology and mass consumption.[1] Its prehistory dates back no further than the age of steam, when in 1841 Thomas Cook harnessed the iron-horse to the temperance movement, providing the working man with an upright way to spend what little leisure time and money he had. The Grand Tour was already as a splendid undertaking for the upper classes. For the first time international travel emerged in pursuit of pleasure and culture, rather than commerce and empire.

Today's package tours of "sun, sea and sex" may seem far removed from Cook's Victorian propriety, just as the hordes of "back-packers" who loaf about bellow the arches of Florence's Uffizi bear little resemblance to the dilettantes of old. But the economic, social technical forces which gave birth to the travel industry are still driving it on at the end of the 20th century. They have propelled this economic activity to the top of the world league. Taken at its broadest, the global travel turnover reached $2 trillion in 1986, or 12 percent of the world's GNP.[2]

To be sure, the bulk of this awesome figure stems from domestic travel, while it is international travel, and especially Britain's share of that market which concerns this report. Nevertheless, both forms of travel are linked, with the historical factors responsible for this spectacular growth affecting them simultaneously. These can be placed into four major categories: 1) the development of transport, 2) the expansion of leisure time, 3) the rise of wealth and especially surplus personal income, and 4) the geographical expansion and integration of all business activities. They have undergone a revolutionary advance since 1945.

In the field of transport, two great changes have occurred. The first was the proliferation of the car as the prime form of personal mobility, spurring domestic and overseas travel. Although this development was already well underway before the war, most notably in the United States, it was not until the post-war era that the car became widely accessible to the average consumer in the "First World". The second has been the growth of the air travel. With the introduction of the jet engine into civilian aviation during the early 1950s, and emergence of the wide-bodied jet two decades later, air transport has become a cheap, fast form of domestic and especially international travel. It too is available to most consumers in the industrialized countries.

The development of transport, of course, occurred as part of an unprecedented phase of industrial and economic growth. Now called the long boom, this expansion had an equally remarkable impact on the private, disposable income of the mass populations of the industrialized countries. For the first time in history, and in stark contrast to the privations of 1930s and 1940s, the bulk of society began to earn an income which permitted a high degree of discretionary spending. Goods and services above and beyond the immediate necessities of life became available to the average consumer within a short time. The demand for travel as a generic product rose accordingly.

The expansion of leisure time, a further manifestation of the rise of wealth, has also precipitated and sustained the growth of tourism. This is especially true with regard to paid holidays, which now run for 4 to 5 weeks in most European countries (though still only 2 weeks in the USA and Japan). By combining leisure time with pay, they provide the two preconditions needed for consumer desire to turn itself into economic demand for tourism.

The most recent distinctive feature within the travel industry has been the rise of business travel. Again, it is not new. But its identity as a separate part of the industry only really goes back to the early 1970s. Furthermore, although this sector accounts for between 20 and 30 percent of international passenger and revenue flows (together with other forms of non-discretionary travel), it remains difficult to define and quantify precisely. This stems from the frequently overlapping nature of private tourism and business travel. Nevertheless, it is a sector which shows distinctive factors.

A service export for final consumption:

Moving from the wider history of travel, the most distinctive characteristic of travel as an export service industry is that it is largely, though not exclusively, geared to final consumption. Unlike producer services which are consumed at an intermediate stage in the production process, tourism is an end product consumed largely by private individuals, although the rise of business travel has introduced an element of ambiguity. The

64

consequences are vital to the way tourism functions, setting it apart from all other export services.

Being largely a consumer product, tourism corresponds closely to the classical definition of a service. To return to the words of Adam Smith, tourism is amongst those services that are consumed "in the very instant of performance".[3] As a result, consumption also takes place at the point of production. Unlike with the consumption of goods, or indeed many producer services, it is the customer who physically moves to the point of production/consumption, rather than having the product transported to the point of consumption. This feature of tourism is significant because it enables services which are overwhelmingly non-tradable to generate foreign revenue. Thus, for example, personal services like hotel accommodation, catering, and entertainment do contribute to the external economy, although they are not usually seen to.

Directly linked to this is the fact that tourism does not really comprise one service, but rather a large bundle of services. The basic requirements of a traveller are quite broad, the discretionary motives and needs exceedingly varied. The typical, traditional classification separates the desire for personal travel into two principal parts. The first is "wanderlust". It is above all the search for novelty — not necessarily in the form of high adventure, but more generally in the quest for that which distinguishes a foreign culture from one's own. As such "wanderlust" is more likely linked to international travel. The second is "sunlust". It includes not just the quest for sun, but the search for all leisure amenities. Consequently, it does not have to be linked with international travel, when the sought-after amenities are available in the tourists home country. In reality, travel is of course motivated by a huge number of physical (ie. health), cultural, interpersonal (eg.family) and prestige factors, all of which can act singly, but tend to act together in an infinite variety of combinations. To these private motivations for travel, it is increasingly necessary to add business and other non-discretionary motives like study, conference travel, competition in sports events, government service and so on.[4]

As the result of such diversity, the demand for services generated by travel spreads over a wide range of sectors. Returning to the Browning and Singlemann classification of given above (see Chapter II), it immediately becomes clear that tourism specifically involves the supply and demand of the following particular services:

Distributive services:
1.   Transportation.
2.   Retail trade.

Personal services:
3.   Hotels and lodging places
4.   Eating and drinking places
5.   Barber and beauty shops
6.   Entertainment and recreational services.

In addition, tourism also involves the significant consumption of physical goods, like souvenirs, luxury purchases etc.

The role of government:

A further trait setting tourism apart from other export services can be found in the impact of government on the sector. This takes the form either of direct involvement at a micro-level, affecting the immediate workings of the industry and its constituent parts, or by indirect action on the overall social and economic framework in which tourism functions.

Taking the latter influence first, it is clear that government regulation concerning the provision of paid leisure time (ie. statutory stipulations on annual holidays as well as other national holidays) clearly has an important effect on tourism. Similarly, the way governments arrange holidays, and especially the timing of school holidays will affect the industry. The more concentrated these are — especially to summer holidays — the greater the seasonal oscillation of the travel industry, and hence the greater the inefficiencies arising from fluctuating capacity utilization.

Another social constraint is government legislation on the retirement age. It is increasingly a key variable affecting tourism. The demographic aging of the industrialized world, together with rising wealth and savings patterns, as well as the specific attempts in many countries (especially in Europe) to cut unemployment by lowering the retirement age, are all factors enhancing demand from the older members of society.

More specific intervention by government arises in the form of exit and entry requirements at borders, as well as currency movement restrictions. Policies in these areas may not be reacting immediately to economic developments in a country's tourism trade, but there can be little doubt that they have a direct impact on the industry. Tight entry controls in the forms of visas etc. (especially where these are of limited duration), to say nothing of exit controls on nationals obviously have a direct effect on the flow of tourists. Similarly, exchange regulations, which are often implemented as part of overall measures aimed at supporting a country's current account, will restrain expenditure flows.

At the industrial level, government intervention in tourism arises when the market cannot or will not undertake certain functions. A significant example can be found in the form of official overseas promotion of the host nation. It occurs for a number of reasons. In the first place, worldwide diplomatic representation provides a good infrastructural base for any promotion, especially when such marketing involves the cooperation of foreign governments (eg. a drive to expand bi-lateral tourism as part of a strategy for strengthening cultural ties). Secondly, general government action is often the most efficient, and even sometimes the only way to secure promotion overseas. This stems from the fact that most travel services are supplied by small enterprises, who by themselves would not be able to mount promotion, except perhaps through umbrella organizations. The latter, however, tend to be discouraged from such activity because the benefits do not fall exclusively to their members — given that tourism represents demand for a bundle of goods. Promotion, especially where it occurs abroad, tends therefore to become the responsibility of government.

From the point of view of production, government is also often an important catalyst, if not actual agent, in generating tourist products and attractions. Again, such intervention arises out of the nature of the costs and benefits involved. Thus, legitimate intervention occurs in areas like environmental protection (eg. maintenance of national parks and the restoration of historic monuments) or the development of leisure facilities (eg. sports complexes and cultural centres). By their nature, such projects provide general value to the community at large. They are diffuse. Costs, however, are concentrated, and this asymmetry tends to dissuade pure market-driven activity. Also, from the point of view of the wider social costs and benefits, governments often aim to encourage projects in tourist activities with the aim of generating employment. Though impact of such action on foreign revenues is only secondary, it must nevertheless not be discounted as an important factor in the expansion of the industry.

Altogether, therefore, the effect of government action, be it at a general and national level, or a specific and municipal level weighs heavily on the development of tourism both in the domestic and the international context. It distinguishes tourism from most, though not all, other export services which are predominantly market driven in their nature.

The growth and present state of the international market:

In trying to asses the international market for tourism, two indicators are most commonly used. The first measures the flow of people. More specifically, it based on the number of "arrivals" at nation's frontiers, who stay for more than 24 hours.[5] The major shortfall of this statistic is that it says nothing about the length of visit. Consequently, statistics stating the number of nights spent are also frequently used.

The second major indicator relates to the international flow of revenues. Typically these are measured by the foreign receipts accruing to a country from all spending by overseas (ie. non-resident) visitors. For the sake of international comparisons, individual country figures are usually converted into US dollars. The problem of using dollars as such a gauge, stems from the distortion that nominal figures (ie. figures in current prices) suffer due to inflation, and currency fluctuations. For example, total OECD receipts rose from $74.4 billion in 1985 to $92.2 billion in 1986, representing a nominal increase of 24 percent. However, much of this nominal rise can be attributed to a substantial fall in the dollar over the same period, so that the real growth only amounted to 5 percent.[6]

Table 5.1:   WORLD TOURISM : ARRIVALS AND RECEIPTS

	Arrivals (millions)	Receipts (US$ billions)
1950	25.3	2.1
1960	69.3	6.9
1970	159.7	17.9
1980	284.8	102.4
1981	288.8	104.3
1982	287.0	98.6
1983	293.9	98.3
1984	315.4	102.5
1985	333.0	109.6
1986	340.0*	129.0*
1987	355.0*	150.0*

* Estimates.

Source: World Tourism Organization.

68

Looking at the aggregate figures for international travel over the last three and half decades, it is immediately apparent that the industry has undergone considerable expansion. Since 1950 the number of worldwide "arrivals" (as measured by the World Tourism Organization — WTO) has risen from 25 million to 340 million in 1986. This rise has resulted from average annual growth of 8.6 percent over the whole period. By comparison, international revenues have expanded from $2.1 billion in 1950 to $129 billion in 1986, translating into an average annual real rate of growth of 7.5 percent (see Table 5.1).[7]

Breaking down these figures gives a different picture to the one of smooth long term growth, and a number of important factors stand out. Most significantly, there appears to have been a secular decline in the number of arrivals throughout the whole period. With each successive decade, the growth rate has fallen. By comparison, real growth in receipts has fluctuated considerably.[8] Notably, receipts from international tourism grew more quickly during the 1970s than the 1960s. This is perhaps particularly surprising given the stagnation of the world economy which followed the first oil-shock.

Indeed, the resilience of earnings in the face of such economic turbulence, led to the general impression that the world travel industry was much more capable of weathering recession than other activities. The experience of the 1980s, however, turned this wisdom upside down. For the first time, aggregate arrivals actually fell in 1982, by just under 2 million. Although growth in arrivals did resume in 1983 (even exceeding the record of 1981), this was not reflected in earnings. Thus, in 1983 total receipts fell for their second year running, not only in real terms, but actually in nominal terms. Looking at the 1980s so far, therefore, average annual growth in arrivals has been a mere 3 percent, while real earnings have remained flat. This is despite two years of record expansion in 1985 and 1986.

The cause of this sad performance lies with the world recession that followed the second oil-shock. The reason why the impact on tourism was so much greater than after the first oil-shock stems probably from the length of this recession. In contrast to their previous response, most governments throughout the world reacted to the oil-price explosion by depressing activity — as part of a general anti-inflation policy in the industrialized world, and anti-debt policy in the developed world. As a result, the recession lasted much longer, and precipitated much greater unemployment, both of which will have directly contributed to the contraction of travel.

A more detailed lesson of the 1980s is found in the geographic volatility. As with most consumer industries, tourism is obviously subject to swings in fashion, which can quickly shift demand from one area to another. The development of tourism in 1986 showed how strong the effect of non-economic factors on the flows of tourism can be. This was the year European industry will remember as the one during which the Americans stayed away. US traffic into Europe had already been under pressure when the dollar began to depreciate in February 1985. But, the real turning point came during the first months of 1986. In the wake of the terrorist attacks at Rome and Vienna airports, a further attack in Berlin, the US air-raid on Libya, to say nothing of Chernobyl's radioactive outpourings across the Continent, US tourist arrivals and expenditure plummeted. If the absence of "Rambo" star, Sylvestor Stallone, at the Cannes film festival personified this sudden lurch, the naked statistics were equally dramatic. In Italy, Greece and France arrivals from the US were down by over 45 percent on the year before, in Germany by nearly 30 percent, and in Britain (the loyal ally whose government supported the Libyan raid) arrivals fell by over a quarter.[9]

These events highlight the potential for fluctuations in international earnings both globally and across regions. It is a point worth underlining, because travel is frequently represented as an industry of unlimited and unproblematic growth. The global experience since 1981 shows that this is simply not the case.

The rise of business travel:

The volatility of private tourism during the last few years has been less evident in business travel. The sector also includes travel movements undertaken by diplomats, government officials (including members of the armed forces), competitors at sports and other events, delegates to congresses and conferences etc., but continues to be dominated by people involved in business. Although as old as commerce itself, this sub-sector of travel has only properly existed with a distinct identity since the early 1970s.

The business traveller began to be recognized for his (and increasingly her) specific needs in the international airline market. The development of special services for this customer occurred because of the substantial volume growth which took place in the air-passenger market during the 1970s. In an effort to counter the impact of exploding fuel costs, airlines across the world set about raising capacity utilization, under the motto that any passenger, paying no matter how small a price for a seat, is better than no passenger at all. Through the introduction of cheap discounts, this had the effect of bringing substantial numbers of low-budget travellers into the market. As happens so often, however, the pursuit of a particular policy in one area had adverse consequences in others. In this case, the influx of low-budget travellers became a considerable irritant to the business traveller, with the result that airlines eventually responded by developing "business class" travel, sandwiched between "economy class" and full-blown "first class".

Although the airline market is the most striking example of a new service evolving to cater specifically for the business traveller, parallels can be found in many other industries. Thus, for example, the international hotel industry has begun to introduce segregated "executive" areas or floors into its accommodation, car rental agencies offer discounts to corporate clients, and travel agents provide whole packages of services to their business customers.[10]

The motivation behind such efforts is not hard to understand. Total non-discretionary travel accounts for about 30 percent of the international market — with strict business travel alone taking 20 percent. What makes it interesting to the producers, however, is its consistency. The fact that the business traveller frequently has no choice but to travel even when times are bad (unlike the private tourist), underpins the market. Also spending in this sector tends to be more concentrated, with the vast bulk of expenditure going into transport and hotel services. Thus, it has been estimated, for example, that about 50 percent of all airline revenues, about 70 percent of car rental income and over 75 percent of hotel earnings are derived from business travel (both domestic and international).[11] Furthermore, the higher frequency with which individuals travel for business, compared to personal motives, creates greater potential for nurturing customer loyalty. Add to this the internationalization of commerce (and especially finance) and it is not hard to understand why suppliers in the market assiduously court their customers.

The main international players:

Like most economic activity, and certainly most export service activity, the international trade in tourism is dominated by the OECD bloc. Thus, in 1986 aggregate receipts of these countries at $92.2 billion accounted for 71 percent of the world total.

71

When offset by overall expenditure, the net balance for the whole of the OECD consisted of a small deficit of $3.9 billion — contrasting with a small surplus in 1985 of $0.9 billion. Indeed, viewed over the long term, the OECD tends to be in broad balance on its travel account — a phenomenon which is largely though not entirely explained by the fact that the member countries are their own most important suppliers and customers.

Within this group, and as also within the world travel economy, the European market stands out as the single largest trading zone. Europe's share of OECD travel receipts amounted to 75 percent in 1986, giving the region just under 60 percent of the world market.[12] The reasons for this dominance are. Given the overall population of the Continent, its comparative wealth, and the concentration of a large number of relatively small countries, intra-European travel is substantial, and this weighs heavily in collective international figures. Furthermore, in terms of receipts (though not arrivals) the relative position of Europe in world trade has actually expanded during the 1980s, by about 3 percent.

By comparison, aggregate receipts in North America have been falling. This is the world's second most important region, but its share has fallen nearly 4 percent between 1981 and 1986, to 24.2 percent of the global total. East Asia and the Pacific, on the other hand, the third largest earner, has seen its proportion of world receipts grow to nearly 11 percent — a rise of just under 2.5 percent in the period 1981 to 1985. All the other regions of the world in the WTO classification — Africa, the Middle East and South Asia — have witnessed small contractions in their limited shares.

Table 5.2: WORLD'S TOP TOURISM EARNERS AND SPENDERS - 1986

| | Receipts | | Arrivals | | Expenditure |
	US$-billions	% of total	millions	% of total	US$-billions
United States	12.9	10.1	22.0	6.5	17.8
Spain	12.1	9.4	29.9	8.9	1.5
Italy	9.9	7.7	24.7	7.3	2.8
France	9.7	7.6	36.1	10.7	6.5
United Kingdom	7.9	6.2	13.8	4.1	8.7
Germany	7.8	6.1	12.2	3.6	20.7
Austria	6.1	4.8	15.1	4.5	3.3
Switzerland	4.2	3.3	11.4	3.4	3.4
Canada	3.9	8.0	15.7	4.6	4.3
Mexico	3.0	2.3	4.6	1.4	2.1

Source: World Tourism Organization

Looking at revenues by countries rather than regions, it is immediately apparent that there is a concentration of earnings. Thus, the five largest earners travel account for just over 40 percent of the world's revenues, and the top ten for over 60 percent. Heading the league in 1986 was the United States. With receipts totaling $17.8 billion — or 10.1 percent of the world total. The next seven places were taken by European countries, led by Spain and Italy. Then came France, followed by the United Kingdom with just over 6 percent of the world market. The only other non-European countries in the top ten were Canada and Mexico, both of whom are strongly tied to the US market, and benefited in 1986 especially from Americans switching their travel destinations away from Europe (see Table 5.2).

The relative weight of international travel in the OECD economy:

In assessing the importance of travel in the international economy, three main indicators are normally used. The first centres on the share of GDP which foreign earnings generate, either in an individual country, a group, or the world as a whole. In the case of the OECD, these revenue flows accounted for just under 1 percent of total GDP. This, hardly spectacular figure again indicates that by far the largest share of turnover is domestic. Even in Europe the proportion of international travel in GDP only just reached 2 percent in 1985, while in the US it represented a mere 0.3 percent.

The importance of spending on international travel as a share in total private consumption is also modest, if not marginal. For the whole of the OECD, overseas travel accounted for only 1.4 percent of final private consumption. Again, at 2.6 percent the European share was higher than the average, and has been rising over the last ten years.

The third most widely used indicator of the overall importance in travel earnings stems from their relative size in aggregate current account earnings. Here such revenues, which generate just over 4 percent of all foreign earnings in the OECD, do make a significant impact. Furthermore, this average figure hides the immense importance tourism has for particular countries, most notably those in the Mediterranean. For Spain and Greece tourism in 1985 brought in more than 20 percent of all foreign currency, while its shares for Austria and Portugal fell on either side of 15 percent. From the perspective of the current account there is little doubt that tourism plays a vital role in many countries.

The UK market:

The travel industry of the United Kingdom fits in well with the general pattern of growth in the developed world. It is an industry that has grown to prominence since World War II, driven largely by rising wages and the expansion of paid holidays. In the late 1930s less than a third of Britain's population took an annual holiday. Even in 1951 only 3 percent of all full-time manual workers with holiday entitlements had more than two weeks paid holiday a year. By 1974, 98 percent of these workers were receiving more than 3 weeks per annum. In turn, this turn led to roughly 60 percent of the total population taking an annual holiday. The subsequent extension by 1984 to 96 percent (of manual workers) having more than 4 weeks paid holiday, has not however led to a further rise in the proportion of adults actually taking annual holidays.[13] This places Britain squarely amongst the northern (and richer) countries of the EC.[14]

Given its population size, per capita income and geographical location, the UK is both one of the world's largest producers and consumers of travel services. With an overseas income in 1986 of £5.4 billion (or $7.9 billion) Britain was in fifth position in the world. At the same time, spending of £6.1 billion (or $8.9 billion) made the UK the world's third largest importer of travel services. The scale of these flows and their relative balance places the UK in the same bracket as the two other major north European economies, France and Germany. Whereas the former tends to be characterized more as a net earner and the latter as a net buyer of travel services, both exhibit significant flows in either direction, as does the UK. This contrasts, for example, with the two largest European earners, Spain and Italy, which are very small spenders.

In the long term development of British tourism, the single most important feature is that the share of all international earnings has risen slightly over the last two decades. In 1965 the UK accounted for 4.2 percent of the total world receipts. By the late 1970s it had expanded to around 6.7 percent, before falling back by 0.5 percent during the 1980s.

As with global earnings, Britain's real growth in travel revenue has suffered a slow down over the last twenty years. Indeed, the average rate of growth recorded during the 1970s was only as half that of the 1960s. Growth underwent a further contraction by over two fifths during the 1980s. Despite, this discouraging long term trend, however, it is significant that real earnings did actually rise between 1980 and 1986 at an annual average rate of 3.8 percent, contrasting strongly with no growth in aggregate world figures (see Table 5.3).

Table 5.3: VISITORS TO AND FROM THE UK AND THEIR EXPENDITURE

| | Arrivals in the UK | | UK residents visits abroad | | |
	No ('000,000)	Receipts (£bn)	No ('000,000)	Expenditure (£bn)	Balance (£bn)
1970	6.69	0.43	8.48	0.38	0.05
1975	9.49	1.22	11.99	0.92	0.30
1980	12.42	2.96	17.51	2.74	0.22
1985	14.45	5.44	21.61	4.87	0.57
1986	13.77	5.41	24.53	5.93	-0.52

Sources: Employment Gazette, August 1987, Department of Employment.
Business Monitor: Overseas Travel and Tourism, 1985, HMSO.

The most important feature has been the gradual rise of business related earnings. Over a three-year average, these contributed to 22 percent of the total in 1970. By 1985, the three-year average had risen to 25 percent of the total. The net impact of this part of the market on the UK current account has tended to be positive. Whereas the balance on the leisure account has shown considerable fluctuations over the last two decades — with a record surplus of £971 million in 1977, and a record deficit in 1986 of £1010 million, the balance on business travel has always been in the black. Given the size of the leisure account compared to the business account, the overall balance has also fluctuated violently. After having been in surplus between 1968 and 1980, net earnings on travel went into deficit in 1981, where they have remained in every year except 1985.[15]

The main traits of travel in the UK:

The essential characteristic of international travel to the UK is the dominance of London. Over 60 percent of all visitors to Britain spend some time in the capital. The importance of London diminishes somewhat in total earnings. Because 60 percent of nights are spent outside London, the city receives a smaller share of receipts.[16] By way of contrast, the emphasis placed on London in domestic tourism is very weak, with the capital representing only 7 percent of visits and 4 percent of spending (BTA press release, January 1988).

Linked to the location of London, travel in the rest of Britain is concentrated in the south of England. This region accounts for more than 40 percent of nights spent by all foreign *and* British tourists in the UK, and 50 percent of their spending. Other parts of England represent less than 40 percent of nights and only 30 percent of receipts of both domestic and international travel. Similarly, other countries of the UK attract less than 20 percent of nights and expenditure from all tourism.[17]

This geographical distribution, and the divergence between foreign and domestic travel, highlights many of the major factors which determine the nature of Britain's net travel balance. Beginning with the earnings side of the account, the role of London underlines the importance of Britain's man-made attractions to the tourism, which satisfy many of the "wanderlust" and "sunlust" demands of the foreign visitor to Britain. London is Britain's main cultural centre. In historical monuments, museums, theatre, music and other entertainment, it provides a concentration of facilities that no other city or region of the UK can rival.

London is not just Britain's main outlet for its own multinational business but also a global centre for commerce, most notably in banking and other financial services. Together with the transport links it offers as the world's largest crossroads for international air travel, its accommodation and general business facilities, London has therefore become the major market for business travel in the UK, and a key player internationally. It ranks, for example, as the world's second largest conference centre behind Paris. As a result, it was estimated that London earned the UK £900 million from overseas visitors in 1983.[18]

Table 5.4: OVERSEAS ARRIVALS IN THE UK AND EXPENDITURE BY
COUNTRY/REGION OF ORIGIN IN 1985

	Arrivals (000')	% of total	Expenditure (£mn)	% of total
United States	3167	21.9	1478	27.1
Canada	631	4.4	231	4.2
EC:	6557	45.3	1392	25.5
France	1620	11.2	250	4.6
Germany	1484	10.3	241	4.4
Ireland	968	6.7	255	4.7
Netherlands	762	5.3	115	2.1
Other European	1313	9.1	440	8.1
Middle East	588	4.1	649	11.9
Africa	633	4.4	432	7.9
Australasia	556	3.8	304	5.6
Japan	211	1.5	94	1.7
Other	794	5.5	432	7.9
TOTAL	14449		5451	

Source: Employment Gazette, August 1987, Department of Employment.

Linked to the dominance of London in British tourism are the private and business arrivals from the United States. Behind Canada and Mexico, Britain was the third main destination for Americans in 1985, taking 9 percent of all foreign tourists. In turn, these visitors accounted for 22 percent of all arrivals in the UK, and 27 percent of all earnings. By comparison visitors from the EC represented 45 percent of all arrivals, but only 26 percent of spending (see Table 5.4).[19]

The attraction of Britain to travellers from the United States (both for pleasure and business) is further tied to less tangible, cultural factors such as the English language and Britain's colonial history. There is a danger in overstating their significance, but they may represent a comparative advantage of British tourism within the European market.

In contrast to this man-made or cultural dimension of Britain's tourism is the natural environment. It cannot be said to exert a strong pull on foreign visitors, and acts as a force pushing out British tourists. "Green and pleasant" though England's lands may be, neither they, nor even Scotland's rugged Highlands, are of unrivaled attraction in Europe. When it comes to Britain's infamous weather, however, a more emphatic observation can be made. Though the reputation may not be entirely warranted (eg: it rains almost as much in Paris as in London), weather and especially its unpredictable nature do have a negative impact on tourism in Britain. This shows itself most dramatically in the foreign visits abroad made by UK residents. The spectacular growth of the package tour industry led 10 million British tourists to head for the Mediterranean in 1986. As the most important destination for British tourists inside Britain is the seaside (accounting for 35 percent of all trips and 48 percent of spending) a large part of the British tourist industry is in direct competition with the Costa del Sol etc., and so clearly suffers a definite disadvantage.[20]

The economic impact of tourism:

The direct benefits of tourism are felt in two main ways. First is the macroeconomic impact on the current account, already dealt with above. Stemming from this a more detailed, sectoral breakdown of the income inflows can be carried out.

It reveals, not surprisingly, that the largest share of receipts is accounted for by spending on accommodation, food and drink. Yet, in aggregate these services only take just over 40 percent of all foreign earnings. The relatively modest size of this share can be explained by the very substantial proportion in spending which the retail trade takes. Spending in shops, on all manner of souvenirs, mementos, typical British luxury goods and even necessities, accounts for upwards of 35 percent of all expenditure by overseas tourists in the UK. Two further areas of spending are on inland transport and entertainment, recreation and miscellaneous services. Each attract about 10 percent of foreign spending.[21]

The other major economic impact of tourism stems from its role as a generator of employment. The absolute size of the tourist workforce is difficult to gauge precisely. Given the general nature of tourism, and especially its seasonal fluctuation, the sector occupies a large number of of part-time workers, either as employees, or as self-employed participants. It is difficult when calculating such figures, based on employment in the various individual industries which serve tourism, to know precisely what share is attributable to tourism and what is not. The Department of Employment gives an average figure of 1.26 million full-time workers and another 524,000 part-time female workers in all tourism related industries. However, given that these include the services of restaurants, public houses, night clubs, libraries, sports centres etc. not all this employment is due to tourism. At the same time, these figures do not include jobs created in other areas by tourism (eg. retailing, banking etc.). Weighing up such problems, the CBI report on tourism published in 1985, estimated that between 900,000 and 950,000 jobs were directly attributable to tourism.[22]

The role of government in British tourism:

Though the employment aspect of tourism is not relevant to this study, it is indirectly significant because of its effect on government policy. Given the labour intensity of many tourism related services, there is considerable scope for boosting work in this sector, especially in those regions of the country where unemployment is above average. The priority attached to this component of tourism was underpinned when the government shifted overall responsibility for tourism in the UK away from the Department of Trade and Industry and to the Department of Employment, in September 1985.

The more traditional agents of government policy in this domain have been the national Tourist Boards. Set up under the Development of Tourism Act 1969, the Boards

78

of England, Scotland and Wales have acted as catalyzing agents over the last years for developing the industry. By offering part-finance for individual projects, they aim to attract private sector money into tourism investment. Thus, for example, the English Tourist Board spent £11.5 million in grants during 1985/6 on 542 projects whose aggregate capital cost amounted to £98.4 million. As a result, a total of 1960 jobs were created.[23] Recently the government has also turned to the Manpower Services Commission and its Youth Training Schemes (YTS) to boost tourism employment through the expansion of vocational training schemes.

Alongside the national boards is the British Tourist Authority. Its function is to promote tourism overseas, and so generate invisible earnings. The main points of its international marketing strategy can be defined as follows:[24]

1. Enhance Britain's position in established markets and develop new ones.
2. Exploit the UK's historic and cultural attractions, while fostering product evolution as market tastes alter.
3. Expand the proportion of business travel, notably in the conference market.
4. Reduce seasonal fluctuations.
5. Promote the regions of England, Scotland and Wales.
6. Boost London's role as an international crossroads and tourist centre.

In pursuing this strategy, the BTA lays weight on co-operative programmes with private enterprise. This supplements its government grant, which amounted to £20.6 million in 1986/7 and £22 million the following year. These programmes range from large exhibitions like the World Travel Market (which was held at Olympia in 1986, and attracted 35,800 trade visitors) to advertising campaigns conducted overseas in conjunction with British or local sponsors. Thus in 1986, the BTA carried out over 100 campaigns in 26 markets with 36 separate commercial partners. Their total spending amounted to £3.8 million, of which the BTA contributed just under 60 percent. In addition, the BTA ran a further 209 joint marketing schemes which continue to be the main vehicle for co-operation between the Authority and its private partners. Altogether these schemes involved 169 commercial sponsors (including 73 foreign participants), whose support amounted to nearly 70 percent of the £7.22 million record expenditure.[25]

Shaping the future:

The variables likely to affect the further development of tourism are numerous. The most significant are the expansion of world income, or more specifically, the growth of personal disposable income, and the evolution of leisure time. But these do not act in isolation, being directly and indirectly connected with an array of other factors. The following list provides a general outline of the main forces at work in shaping the future course of tourism.[26]

1.   The progress of the world economy, including current account, exchange rate fluctuations, and relative cost of energy.
2.   Demographic developments, especially in the main consuming nations.
3.   The future growth of disposable leisure time.
4.   Changes in international relations.
5.   Progress in transport, lodging and marketing.
6.   Competition from other forms of leisure.

Taking the non-economic factors first, it becomes apparent that each of these variables comprises a constellation of factors. Thus, looking at the main demographic forces which affect tourism, it is necessary to account not only for overall population growth, but also how it is broken down across age groups, social categories and so on.

Nevertheless, for the western world the single most important demographic factor likely to affect tourism in the long term is the decline in birth rates. Over the longer term (ie. from the mid-1990s onwards) this will lead to an accelerating population shrinkage, especially in Western Europe and Japan. In the more immediate future, the main impact will be to shift demand towards middle and older age groups. Baby-boomers and pensioners, with relatively high disposable income, will provide an increasingly important source of demand. However, there is a significant qualification to the growth of travel amongst the aged. It arises from the necessity of catering to their specific needs. Suppliers of tourism services will have to shape their products around the specific requirements of this market, paying particular heed to features centered on comfort, security and health.

Other social and demographic factors likely to spur the growth of tourism in the intermediate future include the rising marriage age in most industrialized countries, the increasing tendency for people to live alone and the continued induction of women into the labour market, increasing disposable household income.

Allied to these demographic factors is the continuing expansion of leisure time. It appears likely that retirement ages in the developed world will continue to fall, albeit it at a slow pace. Similarly, it is certain that annual paid holidays will continue to rise over the long term (and indeed are likely to spread in the increasingly affluent developing countries, notably the Newly Industrialized Countries of South East Asia).

There is, however, a vital qualification to this, especially in Europe. As shown above, the percentage of adults in the UK taking annual holidays has remained unchanged since the early 1970s at about 60 percent, despite the continued expansion of entitlements. A similar ceiling of between 60 and 65 percent exist in the rest of the EC.[27] This would imply the potential for growth is limited.

But there are countervailing factors. To begin with, tourism will be encouraged if the expansion of leisure is packaged so that it permits the continued growth of shorter, more frequent trips, like travel over long weekends. These have become a growing phenomenon not just in domestic tourism, but also intra-European tourism. This trend also has the advantage of reducing the seasonal fluctuations in activity.

More important, is the continuing expansion of international tourism relative to domestic tourism. At present, for example, only a quarter of all British tourists go abroad. For West Germany the share is two thirds, which clearly suggests that the scope for expanding international travel is considerable. This would appear to be especially true of so for tourism from southern Europe as these countries get richer, and for tourism from the US and Japan, where the levels of international travel are still small. Although such a realignment amounts to little more than a redirection of demand, it could act to the benefit of certain countries, like Britain.

Crucial to such developments are changes in tastes and consumer preferences. Although much of the theory of the post-industrial society has been debunked, and there has not been a massive switch in consumer spending away from durables to services (see Chapter II), it cannot be denied that the post-war world has seen a growing internationalization of cultures. Education and communications have exposed different races and nations to each other, even if they have not brought them together. The continuation of such developments is likely to strengthen further the desire not just for international, but also inter-continental travel.

To what degree such desire is translated into economic demand, will in the final analysis depend on the growth of personal income, relative to the costs involved in travel. On the supply, or cost, side the major advances are likely in transport. The proliferation of high-speed trains (like France's TGV) across Europe, the construction of the Eurotunnel, and the deregulation of European air-fares are all likely to reduce transport costs the European traveller. Also, technical developments in the airline industry, like the development of short-haul jets, to say nothing of the introduction of the prop-fan engine (calculated to save up to 30 to 40 percent of aeroplane fuel costs) will also cut transport costs to carriers and so to travellers.

From the point of view of demand, the single most important factor is world economic growth. Before the early 1980s it had been thought that the demand for travel was fairly inelastic compared to short-term growth fluctuations. It was a conclusion derived largely from the resilience of the sector in the face of the first oil-shock and world recession. Since the early 1980s, however, the appraisal of tourism has altered fundamentally. The contraction of volume in arrivals and receipts showed the potential for volatility stemming from a slowdown or slump in growth.

When the crunch came, it was also reflected in long-term estimates of the performance of tourism. Thus, for example, one WTO estimate before the slump predicted 5 percent growth in arrivals throughout the 1980s, translating into a total of 460 to 480 million by 1990. The optimism was subsequently revised. In 1983, S. Medlik calculated annual growth for the decade would only average 4 percent, yielding approximately 400 million arrivals by the end of the decade. Subsequently, as growth and tourism picked, the European Travel Commission again predicted 5 percent growth between 1985 and 1990, leading to 415 million arrivals.[28]

Since the slump, the annual percentage change in arrivals has fluctuated quite substantially. 1984 witnessed a strong rebound, with arrivals surging by 7.4 percent. The following year also turned in a healthy performance at 5.6 percent. Then in 1986 growth slowed again to 2.4 percent, but has been provisionally measured at 4.4 percent in 1987. Given the secular tendency for growth in arrivals to fall over the last three decades, it seems most likely that growth over the next years will probably not average much more than 4 percent. This would take the total to 400 million by 1990, and up to nearly 490 million by 1995. Alternatively, growth of only 3 percent would reduce these figures to

390 and 440 million, while faster growth at 5 percent would lift them to 410 and 520 million.

Pinning down growth in receipts becomes a more precarious process. The figures given above for real growth since the 1950s are based on deflating growth in current US dollars by the American consumer price index. Such a calculation is better than nothing. However, it does not account for the currency fluctuations which have affected the value of the dollar since 1971. As these gyrations have become more volatile during the 1980s, estimating real world growth by deflating dollar values in current terms has become increasingly inaccurate.

Figures for the real growth in earnings by the OECD (as a proxy for world growth) over the last few years tend to parallel the fluctuations in arrivals, though running at a slightly lower level. Thus in 1983 volume growth expanded by a mere 2 percent. 1984 witnessed a substantial jump to 7 percent. This was again followed by a respectable 5 percent rise in 1985, whereas 1986 saw no change in real earnings. This trend would suggest that if arrivals grow at about 4 percent, receipts will probably rise less, say at between 2 and 3 percent. Growth at these rates would produce total receipts in 1990 of $140.7 billion and $150.7 billion — calculated in dollar and exchange rate values prevailing in 1986. By 1995, the aggregates would be $155.4 billion and $174.7 billion. Given that the WTO has already estimated world receipts in 1987 at $155 billion, shows how difficult such statistical prediction can be.

Notes and References:

1.   The terms "travel" and "tourism" are generally used synonymously in the literature covering the industry — ie. most "tourism" data and qualitative analysis also covers the increasingly important business travel sector.

2.   S.R. Waters, *Travel Industry Yearbook: The Big Picture — 1987*, Child & Waters Inc., 1987.

3.   see Chapter II.

4.   Concise, general descriptions of the main motivations for travel are given by S. Popadopoulos in *The Tourism phenomenon: an examination of important theories and concepts*, The Tourist Review, N 1/1987, and by Dr. K. Socher in *Tourism in the theory of international trade payments*, The Tourist Review, N 3/1986.

5.   This is the definition most widely accepted, given by the World Tourism Organization amongst others. It distinguishes the tourist from the "excursionist" who spends less than 24 hours away from home or his/her point of work.

6.   OECD, *Tourism Policy and International Tourism: in OECD member countries*, 1987.

7.   This rise in revenues is based on deflating the nominal dollar value of annual international revenues by the US consumer price index.

8.   It is important to note that the "real" figures given here are the nominal earnings deflated by the US consumer price index — reference year 1967. Consequently they do not account for currency movements against the dollar. As the currency has tended to fall since the collapse of Bretton Woods, the figures for the 1970s and 1980s probably overstate overall real growth in volume terms.

9.   ibid OECD.

10.   Financial Times surveys, *Business Travel*, 19 April 1985, 12 March 1986, 21 May 1987.

11.   R. Cleverdon, *International Business Travel: A New Management*, Economist Intelligence Unit, London, 1985.

12.   ibid OECD and Waters.

13.   Professor S. Medlik, *Paying Guests*, a report of the CBI, July 1985 and ibid S. Popadopoulos.

14.   Commission des Communautés Européenes, Service du Tourisme, *Les Européens et les vacances*.

15.   CSO, *The "Pink Book", UK Balance of Payments*, 1987 Edition, HMSO.

16.   ibid S. Medlik.

17.   ibid S. Medlik.

18.   ibid R. Cleverdon.

19.   Employment Gazette, *Travel and tourism — latest statistics*, August 1987.

20.   British Tourist Authority, *Britain's Tourism*, January 1988.

21.   ibid Medlik.

22.   ibid Medlik.

23.   ibid OECD.

24.   based on the OECD, *Tourism Policy and International Tourism: in OECD member countries*, 1986.

25.   British Tourist Authority, *Annual Report*, 1987.

26.   This list is based on a series of variables proposed by the WTO at a Seminar on the development of international tourism in Europe until the year 2000. 2nd/4th June 1987.

27.   ibid the European Commission.

28.   The predictions given here have been taken from a report by O. Protard and P. le Galès, under the direction of H. de Jouvenel, *L'avenir du tourisme: analyse et perspectives*, Association Internationale Futuribles, 1986.

PART 3

6 The background to the City

Perhaps of all Britain's economic activities, and certainly its services, the business of the City and its institutions arouses the most controversy.[1] If politicians of every persuasion are *for* British manufacturing industry — as they are for peace and justice — the same cannot be said about financial services. The criticism most frequently levelled at the City, is that it is (and has been) primarily concerned with its own affairs and profits, oblivious to the interests of Britain's domestic economy and industrial performance. Far from being the financial motor of British growth and development, the City, and banking in particular, is often accused of being preoccupied with investments and business overseas. Some would even go further. They see passive negligence as actually a definite conflict of interests, especially during phases in Britain's economic history when industry has suffered badly, as was the case during the first half of the 1980s.

The origins of the conflict go back a long way and are well entrenched in Britain's economic development. Even before the industrial revolution, London had established itself as a leading financial centre. With the rising domination of British shipping and overseas trade during the eighteenth century, British finance, insurance began their ascendancy in Europe and the world. As British fleets replaced those of the United Provinces, so too London pushed aside Amsterdam as the world's major centre for financial and other trade-related services. Thus, by the end of the century much of the atmosphere and even the structure of the City had already been established. The creation of an industrial society did little to alter this development. Despite the vast need for capital investment generated by industrialization, London's financial markets appear to have played a limited role in this economic transformation. Retrospectively, this phenomenon may appear premeditated. But, a conspiracy theory of finance deliberately eschewing industry does not bear closer scrutiny.

Arguably, overseas investment was and remains a more exciting field of activity for the enterprising financier. Supplying funds to open up the Americas would certainly have been more glamorous than supporting the development of the domestic steel industry or the emerging technological industries of the second industrial revolution during the 1870s. But, it does not seem unreasonable to assume that investments then, as now, were predominantly determined by rates of return. Where profit was to be made at home, enough domestic finance existed, as was shown by the rapid, speculative proliferation of railways during 1830s and 1840s.[2] Also, being the first to industrialize British industry had greater control over the speed and direction of its development. With its monopoly position in world (and subsequently protected Empire) markets this gave industry sufficient room for manoeuvre to finance its own expansion. In short, it cannot satisfactorily be argued that British industry was starved of cash during the nineteenth century, due to deliberate action by the City.

That said, there was a failure to foster industrial progress in the last quarter of the nineteenth century, and before the First World War. With hindsight, there is little doubt that Britain's industrial capacity to compete had been greatly eroded by 1914. In particular, American and German industry had not only outpaced Britain in traditional sectors like iron and steel, but had also taken a strong lead in the increasingly important science-based industries. This failure to develop, encouraged by the closed imperial market, ultimately brought British industry into direct conflict with finance after *la belle époque* had been destroyed by war. Aside from the social misery it caused, the determination with which the Government, aided and abetted by the Bank of England, set about restoring the gold standard appears ludicrous today. By 1925, Winston Churchill and Montagu Norman had achieved their noble goal: the pound had returned to its pre-war parity with gold. Sterling's importance as the world's reserve currency had prevailed, and London's position in international finance was upheld. But the cost to industry was enormous. After a brief post-war boom, domestic demand was continuously deflated. A stringent regime of balanced budgets and tight monetary policy were applied to squeeze out the effects of wartime inflation and its attendant devaluation. The impact on industry was catastrophic. In particular, the staples, like shipbuilding, textiles, iron and steel and coal, suffered a substantial contraction.

Far from trying to re-establish anything like the pre-war regime after World War II, Britain followed the US into the ordered international monetary system of Bretton Woods. Thus, following an initial effort to value the pound at $4.03, the Labour Government pegged sterling at $2.80 in 1949. Yet, by the late 1950s even this major devaluation was proving insufficient, as the inter-war conflict between finance and industry began to resurface, albeit in a moderated form. Despite broad commitment to the *laissez-faire* of *Pax Americana*, Britain's balance of payments and the value of sterling were propped up by import and currency controls: specifically, a partial continuation of pre-war quotas on manufacturing imports, and a restriction on the convertibility of sterling by foreign residents. Both measures were removed in the late 1950s, with unfortunate consequences.

Far from being a technical formality of marginal impact — as the Bank of England argued on behalf of the City — free convertibility soon put sterling under pressure as Britain's trade balance deteriorated. When Labour came to power in 1964, the battle to preserve the pound became all the more acute as the socialists struggled to maintain confidence in the City. But, the impact on the trade balance of the Labour's policies for faster growth eventually forced Harold Wilson to cave in. Sterling was dramatically devalued to $2.40 in 1967.[3]

It can well be asked why the battle for sterling was fought so intensely. Retrospective analysis strongly questions the economic rationale for dogmatically pegging the pound to $2.80. Yet such a debate tends to ignore not only the psychological pressures of Britain's international status, but also the importance attached to the strength of sterling, notably by the City. But, there can be little doubt that the increasing over-valuation of the pound eroded the competitiveness of British industry, and so will have contributed to the deterioration of the trade position.

Tensions between industry and finance have re-emerged under the Thatcher government, though in a different form. Following the imposition of high-interest rates — to bolster the credibility of monetary policy in the markets — and the coincident rise of earnings from North Sea oil, sterling appreciated dramatically until well into 1981. The resulting squeeze on industrial competitiveness did much to enforce the contraction of British industry during this period. At the same time, while speculative foreign capital flowed into Britain pursing high nominal interest rates, domestic capital began to pour out. Following the removal of exchange controls by the Conservative Government in 1979, Britain exported so much capital that by the end of 1985 it became the world's second largest net creditor nation. Given the plight of British industry (and especially unemployment), the outflow of such vast quantities of investment capital has been controversial. Once again it appeared as though the Conservatives had helped their friends in the City, at the expense of Britain's domestic economy.

It is not the function of this report to adjudicate in the debate. There can be little doubt that, by international standards, British industry (once again) suffered from under-investment during and after the second oil shock. Nor can there be much doubt that removal of exchange controls — as part of a broader non-interventionist strategy by the Thatcher government — has helped consolidate the success of the City. But it does not automatically follow, that a more *dirigiste* governmental policy would necessarily have produced better results — especially given the historical separation between Britain's finance and industry. Nevertheless, what is important to the future of financial service exports is the possibility of a future change in policy which may seek to limit or direct the present activities of the City. A change in government could well alter the financial environment. The introduction of measures to reduce overseas investments; the implementation of tighter, statutory, outside regulation, backed up by tougher measures against criminal offenders; higher taxes on the conspicuous super incomes now earned etc. could all act to restrict the City's free-wheeling growth. Such a change in government policies would have a direct effect on invisible earnings.

Notes and references:

1.   The use of the term "the City" here follows that of the CSO *Pink Book* on the UK Balance of Payments. Consequently, it is defined as a group of institutions and not the geographical place, although clearly there is a large overlap between the two.
2.   see E.J. Hobsbawm, *Industry and Empire*, Penguin, 1968.
3.   see D. Jay, *Sterling*, Oxford Paperbacks, 1986.

7 Banking

The role of London and the Euromarkets:

For all the brouhaha made about preserving the remnants of sterling's international status, developments in the rest of the British economy were relentlessly undermining its strength and importance. Despite their historic separation, there can be no doubt that British finance during the nineteenth century had come to dominate the world riding on the back of industry. Britain's huge *rentier* economy, and the complementary creation of the sterling area, were ultimately the result of a sustained trade surplus by British industry. By 1914 foreign investments totalled £4 billion, yielding an annual revenue of £180 million.[1] The World Wars, combined with the Depression, laid waste this vast accumulation of assets. Worse still, although Britain experienced unparalleled growth during the twenty years after 1945, there was no denying the comparative decline of British exports in world trade. Not only was the US consolidating its position as the world's strongest industrial power, but Britain was losing ground to its European competitors. In short, the economic foundation for London's role no longer existed.

The key to explaining the continuation of the City as a major centre for international finance is, on the face of it, equally straightforward. It has become an entrepôt for foreign business. By providing a funnel through which foreign savings can be channelled into foreign investments, London has created for itself a new function in the international world of post-war finance. It cannot be said that this development was the result of either government or the Bank of England policy. To be sure, the City did strive to maintain its international position, and its internationalist traditions always made it a potential centre for foreign business. But, the real impetus came from developments in the world economy over which Britain had little or no influence, and to which the value of sterling was peripheral at best. In fact, London owes its present role to the burgeoning role of the dollar in the post-war world economy.

The origins of this process lie in the emergence of the "eurodollar" during the 1950s. This currency was created as dollars flowed out of the US after the war, financing aid, trade, and overseas investments. The prefix "euro" arose because these dollars originally found their way to Europe, but the term actually covers all currency (dollars or any other currency) held outside its country of origin. No precise date or event marks the exact moment when the eurodollar emerged as part of the world banking system. But, its first major use occurred when the Soviet Union shifted its dollar assets out of the US into Paris during the Cold War. Although this transaction was tiny, compared to the subsequent growth of the "euromarkets", the transfer underlined one of the salient features of the euromarkets, namely their independence from national government action. The political autonomy of European (and especially City) banking remains an important factor in luring business away from the US, such as the re-routing of Arab investments.

Another crucial comparative advantage the City had in attracting the eurodollar market was its relative freedom from government regulation. When there has been political intervention, it has occurred primarily to restrict the export of sterling through the use of exchange controls. The actual practice of banking has been relatively unregulated in Great Britain. The shift to free-convertibility in 1958, followed by the limitation of interest rates under the Kennedy administration (Regulation Q), as well as other controls on investments in the US, lured foreign capital to Britain when the Euromarkets first emerged. More recently, in Britain, the freedom of banks to carry out personal or commercial banking along with investment banking and security trading has been a major factor in encouraging foreign banks to move to London. By comparison, the City's two rival markets — New York and more recently Tokyo — are still subject to the statutory separation of these activities, under America's Glass/Steagall Act and Japan's Article 65.

This specific deregulatory lead is being steadily eroded, however. For some time, the Glass/Steagall Act has been under attack in the courts. More recently, it came under under legislative assault, when the Senate Banking Committee approved a bill in March 1988 that would repeal major portions of the the Act. Crucially, the Financial Modernisation Bill, presented by Senators William Proxmire and Jake Garn, would allow commercial banks to underwrite securities — expect corporate equities. It seems most likely that the bill will pass the full Senate, after which Congress must decide on the issue by 1st April 1991. In the latter house, it will likely face stiffer opposition from more populist Congressmen. Nevertheless, a provision forbidding mergers between banks with more than $30 billion in assets and securities houses of over $15 billion, combined with the persuasive argument that maintaining Glass/Steagall is simply driving business abroad, could help it through. Were this to happen it could well spark a similar repeal of Article 65 in Japan, already under heavy pressure from the commercial banking industry.

Global securitization of the money markets:

The importance of being free to conduct both types of banking within one company stems from the developments in banking since the turn of the decade. The traditional (Anglo-Saxon) division of labour in banking is based on two main types of activity. The first, most public, function of banking is the collection, administration, and investment of personal assets, as well as the handling of daily and short term transactions made by businesses. Known as retail banking, or commercial banking in the US, it is carried out by banks with large branch networks. These collect funds from the individual customer, in the form of current and deposit accounts. The accumulated capital is then lent out. Generally it is passed back to individuals (through the form of over-drafts, and personal loans) or to companies both large and small. Sometimes, retail banks have also participated in making larger international loans, most notably during the 1970s. But, from the historical perspective, the bulk of their activity has been domestically oriented.

In Britain, commercial banking has traditionally been carried out by the so-called five major clearing banks: Barclays, Lloyds, Midland, National Westminster, and (in Scotland) the Royal Bank of Scotland, which have recently be joined by the TSB. They are called clearers because they have the power to clear personal cheques, rather than simply act as deposit takers. Over the last decade, the old monopoly these banks held on commercial banking has been greatly eroded following domestic deregulation. Most notably, this has led to the building societies carrying out many of the basic banking services geared to the private customer.

In contrast to the huge, bureaucratic organization of the retail banks are the much smaller investment banks — or merchant banks as they are usually called in the UK. Where the retail banks collect and invest money on a small scale, the investment banks have handled larger transactions. As agents in a market between wholesale lenders and borrowers. Without the asset base of the retailers, the merchant banks typically did not act on their own account in the past. Their main source of money has been individual or corporate wealth, which has been lent to other commercial enterprises and even governments. As the global economy has progressed, the affairs of the investment banks have been dominated by transactions involving ever larger "institutional" entities. Significantly, the global inter-bank market has emerged as a key area of activity for investment banks.

In addition to these functions the investment banks carry out two other tasks, both of which have expanded since the war. First, they are responsible for organizing the issue of equity by companies. The banks' role in this process is to find buyers for stock that is to be floated. If they do not succeed, they are obliged, as "underwriters" of the equity issue, to buy up any remaining stock at the issue price. By doing so, they guarantee the share price and hence the issuer's capital. Secondly, the investment banks are responsible for selling off government debt in the form of bonds (called "gilts" in the UK due to the gold colour of the paper they are printed on). These bonds are redeemable after a certain period of time, during which they pay interest (usually at a fixed rate, though sometimes linked to changing, market rates). Again the investment banks have the responsibility for finding buyers of the debt.

Given the nature of their business, investment banks have tended to have a more glamorous image than the retail banks. Where the retail banks are large, bureaucratic, hierarchical and more domestic (if not provincial) in their outlook, the merchant banks tend to be smaller, less formal, more loosely organized and more international. Furthermore, unlike the retailers, which by their nature are geographically diffuse, the investment banks concentrate in the main national and international financial centres.

Yet, for all the jealousies and proclaimed clashes of culture, the last decade has seen a cumulative breakdown of the division of labour in US, British, and Japanese banking (in contrast to the "universal" Continental banks which have traditionally carried out both tasks). Under the impact of information technology, financial de-regulation and internationalization, the lines of demarcation have become blurred. Already during the 1970s, the big clearing banks moved into large-scale international finance. The two oil shocks suddenly switched massive wealth away from the developed world to OPEC. The international banking system became the tool for channeling these funds back to the oil consumers — notably the non-oil producing developing countries. This "re-cycling" as it became called, provided the commercial banks with opportunities for moving into international banking. A huge business was built as commercial and investment banks clubbed together to form "syndicates", providing huge loans to the developing world.

But, when Mexico started to have servicing difficulties in August 1982, this vast multinational undertaking lurched to a halt. Almost overnight new lending to the developing world stopped, as bankers across the globe woke up to their excessive exposure. Instead of continuing the flow of wholesale finance, the private banking system

94

turned to the IMF and World Bank to organize some form of damage control. "Rescheduling" and payments deferral became the order of the day. This rapid change in the international banking equation had a number of major consequences, as the international banking community turned its attention back to the developed world as an outlet of investment. There it found two sources of financial demand. The first came from the recently elected Republican Administration in the White House, which was piling up a unique, peace-time federal debt. With a tight monetary policy being pursued by the independent Federal Reserve, this deficit was overwhelmingly financed through the issue of US government bonds. The second major source of demand came from the private sector, both individuals and corporations. As US growth pulled out of recession in 1983, personal consumption in the US rocketed, while the corporate sector emerged as a significant consumer of finance to fund investment and the vast merger-wave that has swept corporate America.

The ensuing bout of corporate borrowing occurred through the issue of company bonds or "securities" rather than through an expansion of conventional bank loans. The advantage of raising money in this fashion stems from the greater freedom it gives to the borrower, while at the same time creating a "debt market" for the lender (ie. bond holder), who can chose to retain or sell the debt he holds. Unlike a bank loan which takes place between two contracting parties, a bond or security can be more widely distributed and circulated throughout its life. This not only reduces the long term risk for the lender when the issue is made, but also increases the liquidity of the capital markets.

Once it got underway, this process of "securitization" began to feed on itself. Not only has it spread to include a large share of European corporate finance, but the development of new financial instruments has generated a vast number of new markets. The most common have included: floating rate notes (FRNs) which link the interest payments on bonds to LIBOR (the London Inter-Bank Offered Rate); swaps on interest payments and currencies that permit the repackaging of interest payments on debts (across currencies if need be); and more recently the development of bonds with "warrants" which permit the bond holder to convert his bonds into equity. These instruments have expanded the ways in loans can be put together and marketed, further raising overall market liquidity. As a result, it has been possible to accommodate the rise of personal and corporate assets available for investment.

The "Big Bang" and London's bid for the world markets:

These international developments have been the most important forces behind the drive to reform Britain's domestic equity and government bond markets — colloquially termed the Big Bang. Technically, it was triggered by the investigation of the Office of Fair Trading (OFT) into the restrictive practices of the London Stock Exchange (LSE), begun under the last Labour Government. Seeing the need for British financial services to keep up with international trends, the Conservatives let the OFT procedures go ahead. It was a decision inspired not just by the competitive ideology of Mrs Thatcher. Instead, it also met the aims of the Bank of England, which had specifically noted that the bulk of Britain's capital outflows since exchange controls were abolished in 1979 had been handled by foreign banks.[2]

To pre-empt a legal decision, and maintain its influence over reform, the Chairman of the Exchange, Sir Nicholas Goodison, came to a compromise agreement with the then Secretary for Trade and Industry, Cecil Parkinson. In return for a suspension of the OFT investigations, and the maintenance of self-regulation by the Exchange of its affairs, the government secured two major concessions. First, the fixed commissions of broking charges were to be abolished; and second, membership of the Exchange was to be opened to outsiders, including foreigners. The market for gilts, which are traded through the Exchange, was to be similarly opened.

Though there were some in the City who believed that the agreement had gone too far, most observers felt that the Stock Exchange had got off lightly. Once again the Conservatives appeared to be pampering financial interests. But, as it has turned out, international financial developments pushed what seemed to be modest changes into a revolution. Far from allowing the *ancien régime* to continue, the Goodison/Parkinson agreement has subjected the Exchange to the full blast of international competition. It has pulled down the barriers between Britain's domestic banking and the international capital markets which have grown up in London.

The rise of this international activity based in London can be traced to the growth of the global markets. Once the eurodollar had emerged as a source of finance outside the control of any government, it was largely a matter of time before a complementary method for tapping this source emerged. At first, the bulk of eurodollar (or indeed any other expatriate currency) lending was largely carried out through traditional banking channels. This process culminated in the re-cycling of Arab oil revenues after the two oil shocks of the 1970s. With the sudden flow of huge amounts of capital from the oil importing nations, the OPEC countries were faced with the task of investing their wealth. Given the constrained growth in the OECD, much of the money was funnelled to the developing world. This was a process in which London played a significant role. More recently, the position of London as one of the world's main centres of the eurocurrency markets has been underpinned by the surge of global securitization, and its role as the home of the the eurobond.

The founding father of the eurobond in 1962 was Siegmund Warburg, an aggressive newcomer to London who, in 1946, set up his own merchant bank, Warburg's (today part of Mercury Securities). This bond functions much like any other. Its astounding success stems from the fact that it exists outside the control of any country or government, making it the perfect logical counterpart to the eurodollar, and all other expatriate currencies. It is a truly international form of debt. Also, being a "bearer only" bond, the eurobond underpins its freedom from government control by guaranteeing the complete anonymity of its holder. In the early days this made the eurobond an ideal form of investment for the private individual seeking to avoid national controls and tax on his or her private capital. The "Belgian dentist" was the archetypal investor who funnelled his money through Switzerland into eurobonds, where it would be untraceable, and earn a higher rate of interest than in a bank account. Today, the private individual still plays a role in the eurobond market, but the bulk of activity has shifted towards the larger financial institutions. In the process, and greatly boosted by securitization, total volumes of eurobond issues and trading have soared. Thus, by 1985 market turnover was estimated at $2.2 trillion per annum with new issues running at $130 billion. In 1986 these figures expanded respectively to about $3.2 trillion and $180 billion.[3]

By handling three-quarters of the eurobond market, and being an important host to inter-bank lending, London has partially succeeded in holding on to its share of international lending. Thus in 1985, London still accounted for nearly 24 percent of all international lending, although its share has been falling over the last decade.[4] Its importance is also reflected by the presence of the international banking community. During the same period, the number of foreign banks registered in London rose by over 50 percent to nearly 500, making London the most international of all the world's banking centres — see Table 7.1.[5]

Table 7.1: GEOGRAPHICAL BREAKDOWN AND STATUS OF FOREIGN BANKS IN LONDON - END 1985

Region of Ownership	Representative Offices	Branch Operations	Consortium Banks	Subsidiary Operations	Total
Western Europe	60	83	4	24	171
Eastern Europe	10	2	2	2	16
Japan	15	24	2	2	43
North America	181	49	2	23	92
Caribbean	7	1	-	1	9
Latin America	16	9	4	-	29
Middle East	15	20	6	2	43
Others	14	64	-	9	87
Total	155	252	20	63	490

Source: Bank of England Quarterly Bulletin, September 1986.

Table 7.2: FOREIGN EARNINGS BY BRITISH AND RESIDENT BANKS
(in £ million)

	1976	1978	1980	1982	1984	1986
Financial Services:						
Credits	257	257	466	669	913	1223
Debits	24	36	31	85	99	59
Balance	233	321	435	584	814	1164
Direct Investment Income:						
From Subsidiaries	131	190	350	142	-76	212
Due to Overseas Affiliates	233	236	317	675	762	646
Balance	-102	-46	33	-533	686	-434
Portfolio Investment:						
Income	10	40	80	350	1423	2621
Interest and Discount on :						
Export Credit	168	233	390	558	816	910
Foreign Currency:						
Credits	4423	6179	15261	33924	35449	28677
Debits	4487	6183	15324	33207	35121	29421
Balance	-64	-4	-63	717	328	-750
In Sterling:						
Credits	214	198	474	1158	1717	2398
Debits	341	343	1203	1899	2316	3620
Balance	-127	-145	-729	-741	-599	-1222
Net Earnings	118	399	146	935	1944	2295

Source: CSO, "Pink Book", 1987.

Table 7.3: ESTIMATES OF BANK'S OVERSEAS EARNINGS FROM FINANCIAL SERVICES

£ million	1983	1986
Foreign Exchange	252	438
New Issue Fees	49	101
Portfolio Management Fees	712	129
Miscellaneous Earnings	353	540
Total	726	1208

The two sets of figures given here are based on two successive inquiries by the Bank of England on the overseas earnings of some 500 banks.

Source: Bank of England, Quarterly Bulletin, August 1987.

98

In the process of this rise in international activity, the invisible earnings of banking have grown substantially. Non-factor earnings by British and foreign banks registered in Britain have gone up from £243 million in 1976, to £1.2 billion by 1986. Although much of this six-fold increase stems from inflation, real earnings have still grown nearly two and a half times or by an annual average of 8.5 percent — see Table 7.2.[6] According to the Bank of England, the major component of these earnings arises from London's foreign exchange business. With an average daily turnover in early 1986 of about $90 billion, London has about a third of the world's currency exchange business, and this alone contributes to over a third of bank service earnings. The other two major individual service earnings are fees for issuing new securities, and managing client portfolios. Combined, these two functions account for a further fifth of NFS revenues, with the remaining income arising from miscellaneous services — see Table 7.3.[7]

Of the same order in 1986 were the IDP earnings by the banks — see Table 7.2. As has been explained in the introductory chapter on invisible trade, such revenues are generally of a different nature to NFS earnings — being predominantly interest earned on previously accumulated capital. Accordingly they are dealt with in a subsequent section which analyses the breakdown of overseas investments and their returns. Nevertheless, given the nature of banking, such IDP earnings are intimately linked with the non-factor services provided by the banks. Put at its simplest, the transaction charges arising on a loan are accounted as NFS income, while the interest earned on the same loan are accounted as IDP revenue.

Stemming from London's role in the euromarkets, it is not surprising to see that the largest volume of IDP flows arises from borrowing and lending in foreign currencies. Over the last few years, interest debits and credits on foreign currency transactions have been in the order of £30 billion per annum. Given that borrowing has tended to exceed lending — so that the stock of liabilities is greater than assets — the net balance is usually in deficit. The same is true for transactions in sterling. The reason why both the net asset and net earnings position are negative lies largely with the presentation of capital account statistics. Notably, these transactions are separated from portfolio business. This is a logical differentiation for examining the overseas investments of the economy as a whole. For example, it provides a better picture of the investment behaviour of other financial institutions, like pension funds or insurance companies. But, it is somewhat artificial for banking, where portfolio investment simply constitutes another form of financial activity, often inseparable from other activities. Still, a crude calculation of the

99

interest rate differential on such borrowing and lending with non-residents shows an average spread of about 1/2 percent during the last decade, while an aggregate calculation which includes the portfolio balance tends to yield a surplus.

The flows on direct investment also indicate the way in which NFS and IDP earnings are interlinked. For British-based banks, such IDPs arise from the build up of foreign operations, needed to sell banking non-factor services overseas. The same is true for the repatriation of profits from foreign subsidiaries set-up in Britain to their parent operations abroad. (For a more detailed examination of such revenue flow see the chapter on IDPs.)

The growth of the eurobond market, however, also highlights the main problems facing British banking, and which have intensified since the the Big Bang. Although the eurobond was developed by a British merchant bank, and Warburg's remains a key player in the market, trade in these bonds has been dominated by foreign investment banks. For years, the US-Swiss conglomerate Crédit Suisse-First Boston had been top of the trading list, followed by all the big names in US securities and some of the larger continental universal banks like Deutsche Bank. More recently, however, the eurobond market has been under strong attack from the Japanese. As a result, Nomura Securities has shot to the top of the table since the end of 1985, closely followed by the other main Japanese securities houses.

TABLE 7.4:   PERCENTAGE SHARES OF INTERNATIONAL BUSINESS IN LONDON
BY NATIONALITY GROUPS

	US	GB	Japan	Others	(EC)	Consortium
1975	38	21	13	23	(6)	6
1980	25	23	20	27	(10)	5
1985	16	19	31	31	(12)	3

Source: Bank of England, Quarterly Bulletin, September 1986.

Given that this market was born and has grown up in London, the absence of a substantial presence by the British merchant banks is significant. Clearly London has maintained its position as an international centre, but its role has increasingly become that of an entrepôt for foreign activity, with domestic banking playing a diminishing part — see Table 7.4.[8] What has to be asked, therefore, is whether the same forces that led to foreign domination of the international eurobond market will now also lead to foreign domination gilts, UK equity and international stocks on the Exchange.

By lifting fixed commissions and allowing outsiders to trade on the Exchange, the Big Bang has subjected a comfortable marketplace for domestic participants to the full vigours of international competition. This becomes clear when the technical aspects to trading on the Exchange are examined. Under the old system of "single capacity" trading, dealing was carried out through brokers and jobbers. Each had a very specific and separate function, with brokers acting as agents for clients seeking to buy or sell stock, while the jobbers actually owned and dealt in stock. Given his capacity as an agent, the broker's earnings came from his agent's fee or (fixed) commission. By comparison, the stock jobber made his profit on the difference between the prices at which he bought and sold stock (the jobber's "spread"). With the legal enforcement of single capacity trading abolished by the Big Bang, many of the main participants in the market are now "dual capacity" market-makers, who carry out the function of both broker and jobber.

This makes equity trading on the Exchange much more like trading in bonds — as was formally reflected by the merger of the Stock Exchange with the International Self-Regulatory Organization (ISRO), which supervises London's trading in international securities. But, the new, homogenized structure clearly puts British, domestic market-makers into direct competition with their overseas rivals. As these firms have already come to dominate the London eurobond market, there can be little doubting their long term threat to the British equity and gilts markets. The bigger American and Japanese houses have larger asset bases and wider international networks with which to carry out their dealings. This gives then a number of advantages in trading. In particular, it leaves them better placed to underwrite larger share or bond issues. It also allows them to spread their risks and their losses across markets and instruments. Given that the abolition of fixed commissions has increased the importance to banks of dealing on their own account, the benefits of a larger asset base are substantial.

To try to meet this challenge and capitalize on the world securities boom, British stock broking, jobbing and banking has undergone a fundamental a re-structuring. Brokers and jobbers sought to expand their underlying asset bases, while the banks aimed at developing their securities business. During the merger wave which hit the City in the wake of the Goodison/Parkinson agreement, three main tactics were employed in the frantic, even haphazard, struggle for survival. The first has been the trend to create integrated market-makers, aimed at meeting the international challenge head-on. Arguably the most ambitious and celebrated of these new creations is Barclays de Zoete Wedd (BZW), the investment bank of Britain's second largest clearer. A composite "super-firm" of Barclays Merchant Bank, the stockbroker de Zoete & Bevan, and the jobber Wedd Durlacher Mordaunt, BZW approached the Big Bang with a staff of 1400 people, and a capital base of £240 million.[9]

More traditional was the response from those brokers who aimed to maintain their position as agents. Given that only 35 Exchange members registered themselves as market-makers in equities, this group of 244 made up the overwhelming majority of members at the time of the Big Bank. Their prime goal was to exploit customer desire for anonymity and impartial service, not logically guaranteed by the single-capacity market-makers. Furthermore, agency brokers were aiming to compete through maintaining an advantage in non-price competition. Blue chip brokers like James Capel and Cazenove clearly set out to take advantage of their reputations in quality service and research. This approach overlaps with the third defence strategy developed: namely that of the specialist, seeking to offer more sophisticated and better informed "niche" services in a limited number of areas and activities. It is a strategy not just been applied just by stockbrokers, but also by some of the banks, perhaps most noticeably Lazard Brothers. Under the stewardship of former Cabinet Minister Sir John Nott, Lazards opted to retain its image as a more personal merchant bank, concentrating on client relationships and private banking. Its strategy has been to remain relatively small, with the aim of pursuing profits by keeping down costs. In view of the overheads to which the more ambitious players of the new market have exposed themselves, this would seem to be an intelligent, if somewhat lacklustre, tactic.

The battle in the domestic markets and the rise of international equity trading:

It is still too early to tell which will ultimately prove to be the most successful approach, if indeed a homogeneous ideal exists. Original predictions — made during the run up to the Big Bang, and held until the world stock market crash in October 1987 — suggested that only those firms which installed large trading capacity, capable of offering all investment banking services, would thrive. All other competitors would either be driven out of the market, or become highly specialized. Such views reflected the conventional wisdom of the world banking industry, which maintained that business would inevitably come to be dominated by a small number of international "super banks". More recently, it is becoming apparent that the market offers scope for a much greater variety of structures.

Looking at New York's experience with de-regulation, it is clear that the transition in London could continue for quite a while yet. Though fixed commissions were abolished on "May Day" 1975, commission charges were still falling five years later, by which time their share in earnings for the securities had fallen from 50 to 20 percent.[10] Nevertheless, events since Big Bang have first proceeded quickly, while the dramatic crash of the world stock markets in October 1987 creates a much greater exogenous pressure upsetting the market. The impact of the latter will undoubtedly continue to act as a catalyst of change, unless a bull market reestablishes itself. Six months after the crash, there was however no sign of this happening.

The immediate aftermath of the Big Bang saw a substantial fall in commissions, especially on larger transactions. According to the Bank of England, rates on deal ranging from £100,000 to £1 million commissions from about 0.4 percent to 0.2 percent. In trades of over £2-3 million, commissions even fell to as low as 0.125. By comparison, rates on small transactions (of £1000) remained broadly at their pre-Big Bang level of 1.65 percent.[11]

As a result of these falls, earnings were significantly squeezed. To some extent, these were partly offset by the continued bull market in shares which ran until late summer of 1987. It enabled market-makers, especially, to profit trading on their own account, while at the same time bolstering commissions through the much greater volume of trading which followed Big Bang and was encouraged by stock performance at the beginning of the year. Though this rise in turnover did lead to severe "back-office" problems in the settlement of transactions. Nevertheless, even before the spectacular October reversal, it was clear that numerous areas of the London market were suffering from considerable over-capacity, making a significant shake-out likely sooner or later.

This is most true for the market in British government bonds, or gilts. Where previously the gilts market had been dominated by only two jobbers, there were 27 registered market-makers, or primary dealers after the Big Bang (capitalized at £700 million). They are chasing a market which had a turnover of £350 billion in 1986. Although daily turnover grew four-fold during the first half of 1987, it was still very small when compared to the *daily* turnover of $100 billion of US government bonds, which is handled by 38 primary dealers.[12]

Given these constraints, the long term determination of foreign dealers to gain market share will be critical in shaping its ultimate structure. Nearly half the new primary dealers are foreign owned, or have overseas links. Included among them are many of the big battalions in international bond dealing, such as Goldman Sachs, Salomon Brothers, Merrill Lynch, and the Union Bank of Switzerland (which has linked up with British stockbrokers Phillips & Drew). With their substantial experience in US Treasury and eurobonds, as well as huge asset bases, these competitors are pushing Britain's domestic houses very hard. By early 1988, fierce competition had already cut down the number of market-makers to 23, with the most prominent departure being Lloyds Bank, which withdrew from the market by June 1987. Should Noruma and Daiwa Securities be granted their licences to become primary traders, competition will surely worsen further, if their aggressiveness in the eurobond market is anything to go by. (Their applications were blocked at the last minute in May 1988, allegedly as a reciprocal response to the problems of access experienced by British firms in the Tokyo market).

To try to spread the competition, and also offset the limited size of the UK domestic market, the Stock Exchange is actively developing itself as a marketplace for the trade in international equity. It was a primary factor in bringing about its merger with ISRO, and was further underlined when the LSE officially re-Christened itself as the International Stock Exchange of the United Kingdom and the Republic of Ireland Ltd.

In many ways, the emergence of international stock trading is the apotheosis of the move to global securities trading. Its rise has been driven by a complex set of factors on the one hand, backed up by marked changes in regulation and progress in technology on the other. International share ownership is the logical counterpart to multinational production in the real economy. It allows companies to spread their capital raising activities into countries where they are directly investing and/or targeting as markets. At the same time, it permits investors to widen the national composition of their portfolio holdings. In theory, such behaviour should lead to a more efficient global allocation of capital. In practice, the expansion of international equity has helped the re-cycling of capital as a result to international trade disequilibria, primarily between the United States and Japan.

Yet the growth of international share ownership also creates considerable difficulties. At the most general level it touches on the issue of political sovereignty. In the first place, an absence of capital controls is absolutely essential to the expansion of the market.

For the moment, government legislation across the industrialized world is moving to every greater freedom of capital movement, even though this is causing problems to national monetary authorities in the control of the domestic money supply. More problematic are the political repercussions resulting from the changes of ownership sparked off by international share trading. The raucous surrounding Carlo de Benedetti's attempted takeover of Belgium's Société Générale, or the disquiet voiced about Nestlé's takeover of Rowntree are only the most immediate manifestations of the difficulties likely to arise as international share ownership broadens.

At the market level, the trade in international equities also faces considerable hurdles. Compared to global market for bonds, the equity market remains relatively small and illiquid. Before the Crash, monthly turnover in international equities in London (both on and off the Stock Exchange) was unofficially estimated between £25 billion and £30 billion, clearly a figure which is dwarfed by the size of the world bond markets.[13] Furthermore, the nature of equity trading is considerably more complex than for bonds. Legal constraints on foreign ownership of domestic industry, cultural differences, the degree of company and market specific information required to deal in equities etc., all combine to create a heterogeneity in equities not found in bonds. Such characteristics will continue to impede the the internationalization of the market.

The crash of '87:

The rush to Big Bang occurred during a period of great optimism. When the US government loosened its monetary policy in the third quarter of 1982, it triggered a long term fall in nominal interest rates which did so much to spark-off and then underpin the bull market. By the spring of 1987 the tide began to turn. Despite the substantial devaluation of the dollar, American trade figures, to say nothing of the Federal deficit, were showing little sign of improving. Indeed, the US was heading for another record annual deficit on its current account.

In response to the continued currency weakness, threatening a future rise in inflation, market pressure on prices began to push up yields in the bond market. Specifically, the Japanese were beginning to cut down their acquisitions of US Treasury bonds (T-bonds) due to mounting currency losses against the yen. Given their paramount role in financing Federal debt, this growing reluctance to buy T-bonds put downward pressure on prices, and upward pressure on interest rates. Market anxiety was also nudged by trade friction between the US and Japan spilled over into legislative action when the US imposed import controls on semiconductors, again leading to further pressure on interest rates. Lastly, the Federal Reserve Board, weary of rising inflation began tightening monetary policy through the use of interest rates.

In the early autumn the Fed, under its new Chairman Alan Greenspan, pushed up rates a further notch. Subsequently, a definite rift between movements in the bond and stock markets emerged, as the latter continued to rise. When, however, James Baker, the US Treasury Secretary, threatened further dollar devaluation to redress the intransigent trade deficit, Wall Street went into its tailspin. On Monday, 19 October, the Dow Jones index crashed 508 points.

The size of the crash, which was mirrored across all stock markets (except Tokyo) imposed heavy losses on many securities houses, especially where these were caught with stock as market-makers. Since the crash, both stock and bond markets across the globe have remained fragile, again with the very notable exception of Tokyo which has recovered to pre-Crash levels. As a result, the earnings squeeze continues. Market-makers are finding it very difficult to profit by trading on their own account. Furthermore, the contraction of private investor activity, caution by the financial institutions, and a switch by companies away from stock flotation to raise capital have led to a near halving of turnover volume on the main exchanges, with the attendant squeeze on agency commission.

For London, the Crash has depressed activity not just in domestic equities, but also international stocks and the eurobond market. Since Black Monday, international equity has been especially badly hit due to the inherent difficulties in trading in such assets, enhancing the overall problem of liquidity. Notably, new Japanese investment in foreign equities has slumped worldwide since the Crash, and this is affecting business in London.[14]

Equally worrying for London has been the reversal of the eurobond market experienced during 1987. The writing for a market downturn was on the wall long before the Crash. Towards the end of 1986 a liquidity crisis hit the market for FRN "perpetuals", subsequently battering the whole FRN trade which had been one of the most vibrant eurobond sectors during the early to mid-1980s. At the same time, the full-scale assault by the Japanese houses to gain market share was also wiping out profitability.

A further key problem for the market has arisen from the progressive weakness of the dollar. Although other currencies have been introduced into the eurobond market, it was the dollar on which it had been built up, and which continued to remain its major currency. With the on-going devaluation of the US currency, investor demand for dollar-denominated bonds steadily weakened. To some degree, this has been offset by the growth of euroyen and euroDeutschmark bonds. Nevertheless, other such eurocurrencies have not been able to plug the gap. Given all these factors, it was therefore not surprising to find that the market suffered a substantial reversal during 1987, as new issues fell by 22 percent to $143 billion.[15]

Into the future: the American and Japanese challenge:

In assessing the course of Britain's invisible earnings on banking services three major issues stand out. First, British domestic (and international) banking is experiencing increased competition. This need not affect London as a location for international activity *per se*. It has been estimated that foreign banks contribute about half of banking NFS earnings.[16] But, if foreign banks succeed in gaining a significant share of the British domestic market, it too will be increasingly subject to strategic planning outside the UK, as has always been the case for London's international activity. Given the spread of communications technology this would mean that business presently carried out in London could move elsewhere. It has already, for example, been suggested by some Japanese houses that primary dealing in yen-denominated eurobonds should move to Tokyo. It does not seem unreasonable to suggest that trading in British equities, if not gilts, could be similarly relocated.

There seems little doubt that the relative share British banks' activity within the London market will decline, as the foreign houses move into certain areas of the market: notably international equities, and to some extent gilts and domestic stock. The retreat by Lloyds bank from gilts and Midland's withdrawal from equities demonstrate clearly the strength of competitive pressures and their consequences for market-makers, especially where these are newcomers to the business. Heavy losses in 1987 have also led to a contraction of securities activity by County NatWest. This leaves Barclays de Zoete &

Wedd as the only major market-maker set up by a British clearing banks. Indeed, along with Warburg's it remains the only British investment bank capable of offering a sufficiently wide range of services, on a large enough scale, to tackle foreign competition at all levels.

The cream of the agency brokers like Cazenove and James Capel have also been successful since the Big Bang. Contrary to original expectation, they have not been simply muscled out of the market on pure price competition. However, their deliberate concentration on broking effectively limits their role. Consequently, though the solidity of their business may inspire envy, their strategy — along with that of the more specialized "niche" operators — by definition leaves other areas of the market open to foreign penetration.

If the relative position of British banks declines, the real challenge to the City becomes a geographic one. At its broadest level it can be be divided into the global battle between London, New York and Tokyo, and the regional struggle taking place within Europe.

The threat posed by New York and Tokyo is great. Both centres, and their national banking industries have advantages over London which makes direct competition very tough. To be sure, London is most likely to remain the third pole of the inter-continental triangle. Nevertheless, it is highly feasible that a significant amount of the business could be transferred to one or both these markets.

Above all, there can be no doubting that both American and Japanese finance have a scale advantage over the British. This stems largely from the size and strength of their respective domestic economies. In addition, their finance industries have been markedly boosted by bond and stock activity over the last few years. The doubling of the US government debt to over $2 trillion since the turn of the decade has created a vast new pool of bond business for the main American houses. Given that this Federal Government debt has been accompanied by a huge influx of international capital, its "benefits" have spilled over to the Japanese capital markets.

Mirroring the growth in America's trade deficit has been Japan's trade surplus. Rising to over $90 billion in 1986, the surplus has provided the Japanese economy with an unprecedented amount of capital to invest overseas. Part of it has gone into direct foreign investment by Japanese industry, especially in Asian economies like Korea. But, a greater

108

share has been invested in financial assets, notably in US government bonds. It has been estimated that such investment amounted to between $35 to $40 billion annually during the mid-1980s. Thus, although the US federal and trade deficits may have helped undermine domestic industry, they clearly have done wonders for American and Japanese finance. Coinciding with this huge expansion of the bond market, was the stock market boom experienced by both the US and Japan. Though faster rises may have been registered in some of the European markets, the size of the US and Japanese exchanges made their growth much more important.

For the securities houses involved in both the US and Japan the last years have therefore been a period of substantial growth. As a result, their asset and capital bases have expanded dramatically, giving them a significant edge over even the largest British houses. Where, for example the NatWest Investment Bank was capitalized at £310 million at the time of the Big Bang, the four largest American houses have a capital base in excess of $9 billion, while the Japanese "big four" are touching $13 billion.[17]

Backing up their capital strength, the American houses must also be counted as among the leaders in financial expertise. If, perhaps, the British benefit from the innate gambling spirit for the generalist and amateur, the Americans prosper on being the scientific technocrats *par excellence*. Leaving aside the broader cultural questions like a stronger commercial and competitive ethos, US finance has traditionally been noted for its flexibility and power to innovate. Many of the major advances made in all areas of banking over the last twenty years (from travellers cheques and credit cards to financial futures and currency swaps) have been pioneered by the Americans. This gives US finance two advantages. First, by developing new instruments US banking enhances the services it offers its customers. Secondly, being the first to move into new areas of activity tends to raise the profit rate for those involved, by generating temporary "monopoly" or "super" profits.[18]

Added to this creative ability is the manner in which US banking has harnessed technology. Computerization has affected all banking, but the Americans have remained at the forefront of new technology, and in particular banking software. Although floor trading may still be dominated by the hustling generalist, the back-room is increasingly controlled by high-tech boffins presiding over awesome computer power. These "rocket-scientists" are not trained in the art of banking or even trading. Instead, their ability stems from the sciences: pure mathematics, physics, statistics, and electronics. With these skills, they are developing sophisticated forms of computer trading for bonds and equities. Numerous techniques have been devised to carry out portfolio management. For example, they include complicated calculations to provide detailed information on future income flows, given certain combinations of bond holdings. This in turn helps banks synchronize returns with known future liabilities. Computers have also been applied for selecting investments in equity. The process is executed in a number of ways. Longer term investments are based on sophisticated calculations comparing balance-sheet performances with stock-market valuations. Computers allow the investor to trawl the exchanges for potential bargains. In the shorter term, computer power and faster communications permit banks and investors to arbitrage, when securities are differently priced across markets. This is becoming especially important with the growth of equity futures and options. Programmes have been developed to give automatic buy or sell orders depending on the divergence of current and future stock prices.[19]

To be sure, such technological advances are not without risk. The intensity of Black Monday's Crash has been blamed in no small part on the use of programme trading and arbitrage between the New York stock market and the Chicago financial futures market. In the wake of the Crash, numerous critics of deregulated markets have called for tighter controls on such operations, and beyond this stricter surveillance of market movements including the possibility of introducing trading shutdowns when stock fluctuations exceed certain levels — the so-called circuit-breakers. At the time of writing, it seems highly unlikely that the latter controls will be brought in. On the other hand, future restrictions on programme trading appear to be more feasible. Significantly, four top US brokerage houses (Salomon Brothers Inc., Morgan Stanley & Co., PaineWebber Inc., and Kidder, Peabody & Co.) announced in May 1988 that they were suspending such trading on their own accounts. A more fundamental problem following from the shift into high technology arises from the massive overheads it generates. While these were broadly sustainable during the bull market, the current downturn in bond and stock prices, together with the contraction of trading volumes makes them a considerable greater burden.

Lastly, the US and New York especially have been strengthened by the creation of International Banking Facilities (IBFs) in 1981. The IBFs are tax-free zones for eurocurrency activity. They allow New York to carry out "offshore" eurodollar banking in the United States for foreigners and non-residents. Since their establishment in 1981 IBF eurocurrency markets have expanded rapidly, accounting for nearly $200 billion by the end of 1985 — or half US offshore holdings.[20] Their impact on world finance was first felt primarily in the Caribbean offshore tax-havens like the Bahamas and the Cayman Islands. More recently, however, the re-patriation of American funds has also affected London — although the Japanese have taken up the resulting slack. The long term implications of the IBFs are difficult to assess. But, they will probably continue to expand as a centre for eurodollar activity. They will then take a growing share of the eurobond market — as source of finance for US borrowers. Much will depend on the future of US de-regulation. Notably a repeal of the Glass/Steagall Act, which separates commercial and investment banking, could entail a major shift US activity back to New York.

Equally, if not more threatening to London and British domestic banking is the rapidly expanding power of Japanese banking. With the build up of foreign currency from accumulated trade surpluses behind them, the Japanese banks are aggressively expanding overseas. So far, the largest share of these funds has gone into building up holdings in US government bonds, although this began to change markedly in 1987. The big Japanese security houses (led by Nomura) are clearly striving to diversify their activity into all the basic areas of investment banking. As part of this strategy, they are setting out to offer services on the same basis as major domestic players. Thus Nomura, for example, has become a primary market-maker in US bonds and so can trade on the same terms as Salomon Brothers or Merrill Lynch. In London, Noruma, along with Daiwa, has recently applied for a primary dealership in gilts, having become a member of the stock exchange, with floor presence, at the time of the Big Bang. Similarly, the four major Japanese houses muscled their way to the top of the eurobond market in 1987.

Cross-industry comparisons must, of course, always be qualified. Nevertheless, the strategy and tactics of the Japanese drive into world finance resembles manufacturing penetration of foreign markets. The style is more imitative than innovative. Japanese houses are hampered by the tradition of collective rather than individual decision-making. It militates against the rapidity needed for high pressure dealing. A more ritualized, formal and hierarchical form of management may also impede the flexibility vital to quick, speculative trading. But, although these characteristics may have stronger disadvantages in finance than in manufacturing, they also facilitate an almost unique deliberateness of action.

111

This sense of purpose, which has been such a hallmark of Japanese industry, appears also to define Japanese financial market behaviour. Once an objective is set collectively, everything is thrown into achieving it. Typically, such a strategy means establishing market share, almost no matter what the cost. The Japanese are very price-competitive — just as they have been in industry. And, as in industry, it has led to allegations of product "dumping" — ie. providing services at less than cost price.[21] Given the capital backing of Japan's four largest securities houses they are in a better position to sustain such potential losses than their British competitors. Markets like eurobonds are likely to remain under intense pressure. Issue management is now hardly a profitable business, with many companies actually making a loss. Until the market structure has changed, the situation is unlikely to improve. If and when it does, competitors such as Nomura hope their expanded market share will yield returns.

The rise of the euro-yen has also helped the Japanese houses to expand their bond business. A further spin-off from Japan's trade success, the euro-yen, began to emerge as an expatriate currency at the end of 1984. Under pressure from the Americans to open up their currency markets, and so help bring the yen nearer to its market value (ie. help it appreciate against the dollar) the Japanese authorities allowed the currency to be exported. Since then, its overseas holdings have expanded dramatically, and this too must be to the advantage of Japanese finance as a whole. More recently, with the fall in the dollar since the spring of 1985, euro-yen issues have become important to the eurobond market, adding to the strategic position of the Japanese banks. A further point to watch: Japan's large commercial banks are hard on the heels of their securities houses.

The European challenge:

Given Europe's position in the industrialized, and its physical location between the North American and Asian trading zones, it will undoubtedly remain a major pole in international finance. The emergence of 24 hour global trading creates a need for a European leg (or legs) in the world capital market, to bridge the time zones of North America and the Far East. At present, London fulfills this need. The question is: will it maintain its role?

The future of London as a major world banking centre lies in its position as a centre for expatriate business. Even if Britain's growth in the mid 1980s has been faster than

112

that of some of its main European partners, the domestic base for an international banking centre remains limited. London will therefore only partly be able to rely on greater domestic wealth to hold on to its position. Like a merchant bank, it will have to look to its wits rather than its assets to earn a living. From this point of view, it will truly be a centre of service industries, whose chief assets are their workforce and not their capital equipment.

The City has frequently been accused of siphoning off Britain's best talent from industry. If this is true, then the City should have a comparative advantage in manpower over those European nations where the task of manufacturing physical wealth is held in greater esteem. The City's accumulated experience as an international financial centre ought to perpetuate itself, and enhance its manpower advantage. There has also been a significant change in attitudes and work practices over the last few years allied with an infusion of commercial aggression, some would say greed, into the City, and especially the domestic markets. Gone are the days when banking and stockbroking were relaxed, gentlemanly professions. Instead, the domestic players in the London market are adopting the hard-nosed pragmatism, slavish working practices *and* rewards of their international brethren. Such a change of atmosphere, does not bring unambiguous blessings. It has made City life tougher, both mentally and physically. It has brought with it greater scope, and incentive, for fraud, as witnessed by the Guinness/Morgan Grenfell scandal. Such a change in culture is not something which the economist can measure and so evaluate in impact or justify by its results. It is largely a qualitative phenomenon, backed up largely by anecdotal evidence. But, this change in style will likely be as important as most other factors in determining London's future success.

More prosaically, the City's advantages stem from a combination of its relative openness, economies of scale, back-up services, and London's social infrastructure. Of Europe's main financial centres, London has traditionally been one of the least regulated, which has greatly encouraged foreign banks to work through the City. Yet, the passing of the Financial Services Act (FSA) has changed the regulatory balance. Although its effects have still to be judged, two factors stand out as particularly worrying for market professionals. First, the Act has brought in much tighter legislation, aimed at protecting the investors against bad or unscrupulous financial institutions. In itself, this is no bad thing. But the resulting paperwork slows the functioning of market, is likely to make it less flexible, and adds to transactions costs. Similarly, higher capital requirements for financial companies are likely to reduce the attractiveness of London as a business centre (especially for foreign firms).

That said, London remains by far the most cosmopolitan financial centre in Europe. If British finance's separation from British industry has been to the latter's detriment, it has helped the City in pursuing its international position. This is not just a question of cultural orientation. Instead, it has also been encouraged by the Conservative government. Thus, if the FSA has tightened regulation, the lifting of exchange controls in 1979, the deliberate attempt to place the shares of privatized companies overseas, and the admission of foreign dealers not just to the Stock Exchange, but into the market for government bonds, have all helped to create an environment conducive to international finance. Arguably, such measures may be to the detriment of British industry, when compared with the financial policies of many Continental countries. But, there can be little doubt that compared, for example, to the 20 percent limit on foreign ownership of former Prime Minister Jacques Chirac's privatization programme, or Germany's conservatism in adopting new financial instruments, Britain's more *laissez-faire* approach stimulates rather than discourages finance.

Indeed, a comparison with Germany highlights most clearly the advantage London has in competing for Europe's share of world financial services. The Federal Republic is Western Europe's largest economy — the third biggest in the free-market world. Like Japan, it too has a relatively thrifty populace providing a substantial domestic capital base for its banking sector. German industry has also produced strong current account surpluses since the early 1980s on which strong overseas banking sector could be built up. Nor can it be said that German banking lacks either the sophistication or the skills, let alone the means to with which to tackle international markets. By any conventional standard, the track record of Germany's universal banks in fostering domestic industry has been impressive.

But, the break-through into the big league has not been achieved. It is in part precisely because banking has been so strongly connected with domestic industry — representatives from the "house bank" frequently sit on the boards of industrial companies, in which the bank may also hold stock — that its international perspective has remained constrained. Banking at this level revolves more around the daily activities of clearing company transactions, and financing short term capital needs, through overdraft support etc. Large-scale financing is also more likely to be carried out through conventional lending, as the prevailing private ownership structure of companies confines equity issue to a relatively small number of firms. Corporate finance tends therefore to concentrate on commercial banking practices, far removed from the investment banking which has led the globalization of securities trading in the US, Japan and the UK.

This representation is, of course, schematic. German universal banks do also carry out securities business. It should be noted that Deutsche Bank is one of the most important issuers in the eurobond market. However, it is more than mere symbolism that it conducts this business out of London.

The link to industry is also one of the reasons behind the regional diffusion of Germany's banking industry. As Germany is a federation of states (Länder), financial services have developed across a series of state markets. Frankfurt may well be the epicentre of activity, but eight bourses with their attendant financial activities exist throughout the Republic. To a large degree the structure mirrors the geographical spread of manufacturing industry. Thus Düsseldorf, for example, with its proximity to the Rhur and hence traditional industry, has remained a crucial banking centre. More recently, as high-tech industries have shifted the balance of growth to the south, Stuttgart and Munich have risen in importance. As a result, no one centre has built up the necessary concentration, or achieved the critical mass which could make it a fully fledged challenger to London.

To these structural impediments to growth should be added the regulatory conservatism of the German authorities. The memories of history's traumas live on even today. Stable finance and above all stable money are still regarded by many as foundation stones not only for economic prosperity but for political security as well. This has fostered great caution with respect to the money markets and especially suspicion of anything that may reduce the Bundesbank's control of the monetary supply. Thus, if the government promotes the general idea of *Finanzplatz Deutschland* (literally Finance Centre Germany), its actions and those of the independent Bundesbank often belie its own propaganda. The most recent and spectacular example occurred when it was announced that a 10 percent withholding tax would be introduced on investments at the beginning of 1989.

A more concerted effort to open up domestic markets and meet the international challenge has taken place in France. It began under the Socialist government, when in 1983 a new banking law was setting out progressively to end credit controls, and so enhance competition. The impetus sharpened under the subsequent conservative government of Jacques Chirac. During its brief time in office — March 1986 to May 1988 — Finance Minister Edouard Balladur pushed through a number of measures aimed at substantially shaking up the structure of France's financial services.

The main thrust of this strategy has been to boost domestic stock and bond business, that has been spilling over into the London market. Privatization of France's huge state sector, and stock exchange reform were the two pillars on which this strategy was based. Following de Gaulle's bout of nationalization in 1946 and Mitterrand's in 1981/2, France's public sector had accounted for about one third of industry's output. It also had a virtual stranglehold on banking, owning not just major clearing banks but numerous other finance groups.

The privatization programme M. Balladur launched on entering office was highly ambitious. Nevertheless, it met with considerable early success. Favourable stock market conditions helped attract millions of private investors into the market. This in turn gave a further boost to the market. Thus, between 1976 and the market's all-time high in March 1987, capitalization jumped 700 percent to FF3,200 billion, while the volume of transaction grew from FF56 billion to FF2,200 billion.[22]

To underpin the expansion of activity and enhance Paris' position in the run up to Europe's single market in 1992, the government also initiated a major reform programme of the stock exchange. Aimed at eliminating the distinctions between securities trading and other services, as well as widening the international base of the exchange, French banks, insurance companies and stockbrokers will be permitted to carry out such trading along with other banking activities by 1990. To this end, legislation has been introduced abolishing the monopoly of Paris' 45 securities companies, as well as permitting outsider (both domestic and foreign) to acquire progressively 100 percent of these stockbrokers.

Unfortunately, subsequent events are stifling the whole reform programme. The stock market crash hit Paris badly, as a steep 40 percent drop offset a large part of its previously meteoric rise. This not just dampened general enthusiasm for the Bourse, but provided a hefty setback for the government's privatization programme — especially when shares of the Suez group fell 18 percent below their offer price, shortly after having been issued.[23] More recently, the re-election of President Mitterrand and the constitution of a centre-left government also bodes ill for privatization. Although there is no talk of renationalization, repeated statements by Mitterrand and the Socialist Party clearly show their scepticism, if not hostility, towards further privatization.

The termination of the programme poses two important problems to France's finance services. In terms of overall market size, the continued sale of state assets would have added to market capitalization and the depth of share ownership. Assuming the programme could have been reactivated at some point, despite the continuing fragility of the markets, it would have helped expand overall activity. With the re-election of M. Mitterrand this is now unlikely to happen.

On a micro level, the end of privatization means that two of France's main clearing banks, Crédit Lyonnais and the Banque Nationale de Paris, will remain within the state sector. Consequently, they have no recourse to the financial markets to raise share capital. This, in turn, is likely to put them at a distinct disadvantage in expanding their domestic business and forging international links as 1992 approaches.

Questions of size and/or economic nationalism will restrict the growth of other rivals. Thus, Luxembourg and Amsterdam are more likely to remain members of a constellation of European centres instead of emerging as rivals in direct competition with London. Similarly, despite the notable strength of its banking, Swiss finance's fragmentation between Zurich and Geneva limits its scope of large-scale concentration. Also, given the importance Swiss banking attaches to its discretion and secrecy, it remains cautious about exposing itself to the full attention of international activity.

The significance of size lies not only in economies of scale, but also in the range of services associated with it. This is one of London's strong points, without doubt. Although modern communications and transport have moderated the advantages of concentration, they have not negated them altogether. When the City developed as a multi-faceted market to service trade during the eighteenth century it incorporated all the necessary functions. Banks were developed and expanded to finance trade. Lloyd's and the insurance market emerged to service it, while the commodity exchanges and trading houses administered and executed it. The same remains true today.

First, the Stock Exchange has developed powerful dealing technology. Despite the teething problems of the Stock Exchange Automatic Quotations system (SEAQ), it remains one of the world's more sophisticated trading systems. In addition, market-makers and brokers have access to a wide range of independent information systems led by the giant financial information service, Reuters. Outside the immediate Exchange activities, the banking and securities market are served by all the other activities available in London. These not only include the modernized versions of traditional facilities like commodity broking and insurance. More important for banking has been the creation of a financial futures exchange. The London International Financial Futures Exchange (LIFFE) opened in 1982, permitting forward trading in numerous currencies and financial assets. Given London's importance in the world foreign exchange market, and the near certainty that the world's major currencies will continue to fluctuation strongly, futures activity in this area will become an increasingly important service in the London market.

Last, but by no means least, London has the advantage of being a world city whose mother tongue is English. It is served by a developed communications and transport network, with excellent inter-continental links. London's size also gives it the necessary facilities to handle a large traffic of business visitors. Though these are unquantifiable points in London's favour, they remain important. Nevertheless, they should not be overstressed. If London has a social infrastructure to service a transient or settled foreign community, it comes at a price. Office rents are higher in central London than in most other European cities. The same holds true for hotel and residential accommodation. Similarly, though the use of English may simplify life for many international bankers (especially from the United States) and may lower the costs of back-up services, in many continental countries a knowledge of English is widespread. Though such factors may be significant in tipping the cultural balance towards London, they have an essentially secondary impact.

The opening of the European market in 1992:

A big imponderable currently hanging over Europe's businesses, and especially its financial services is the European Community's plan to remove all remaining barriers to the free movement of goods, services, capital and labour by the end of 1992.

In principle the issue is simple enough. Under the second banking co-ordination directive put forward by Brussels in early 1988, credit institutions of member nations above a certain size are to be free to carry out a series of specified activities across the EC, including securities transactions. The legal mechanism for ensuring control and competition is based on the regulation of foreign activities/subsidiaries by "home" country governments. In other words, the overseas branch of a British bank in, say, Spain will fall under UK jurisdiction.

In practice, such freedom of movement is likely to run into serious difficulties. On the macroeconomic plane, the drive to free capital movement accepted by member governments, and so vital to the liberalization of services, still has to overcome considerable hurdles before it is realized. It remains to be see, for example, how a country like Italy — with its huge government debt mopping up a high level of domestic savings — will cope with capital flowing to other parts of the EC where it could earn higher returns. One way round this hurdle would be the full development of a common currency, issued through a common central bank. But, despite the increasing support for such a policy it is questionable whether a such super-EMS will materialize in the near future. Notably, the Bundesbank has voiced much scepticism, fearing a loss of control over the Deutschmark. Similarly, Mrs Thatcher's hostility to any monetary union hardly needs restating.

Even when this fundamental problem is assumed away, the potential for much nashing of teeth is still great. The whole ethos of regulation in the UK, under the present government, has been to lift controls and taxation. Granted, the Financial Services Act has imposed a number of statutory controls on activities. Nevertheless, the London market has been opened up with the aim of capturing as much international and offshore business as possible. It is this logic which the UK banking industry and the British Government are now applying to Europe 1992. Standardization of the EC is being equated with liberalization.

This, however, is not entirely the way 1992 is being viewed on the Continent. From Britain's point of view, this is likely to lead to two major clashes in the drive to a single European market. First, with its common law tradition, self-regulation has remained the guiding light of control over the money markets. To be sure, the FSA has backed up the powers of the new City watchdog (the Securities and Investments Board — SIB) by statute. But, it has also tried to maintain the principle of practioner control at the level of the self-regulatory organizations (SROs), which supervise the various areas of the market. Such comparative autonomy could conflict heavily with the much more formal restrictions that are common on the Continent where the legal system is codified.

Second, and tougher still is the likely battle over the freedom of foreign-owned banks resident in the UK, where they have been competing on exactly the same footing as British banks, since the Big Bang. Given the importance which such banks play in the London market, it is clearly in Britain's interests that they too are allowed to enter Europe on the same basis as domestic institutions. From the Continent such equality is far from obvious, with City-based subsidiaries being often seen as Trojan Horses.

Britain's partners in the EC are therefore likely to see the drive to a single market as including some degree of re-regulation, rather than just straight forward deregulation. Furthermore, their legislative goal may well include the introduction of some common tax system. In both cases, 1992 threatens to provide severe problems for the UK in its own backyard.

Nor is it certain that 1992 will prove an unqualified success abroad for British and UK-resident banks. Conventional City wisdom holds that its international activity is simply streets ahead of anything going on in Europe. This view is not without some foundation, at least in certain areas like securities trading. Nevertheless, it would be complacent to dismiss altogether either Europe's other centres or its banking institutions in the field of international banking. Significantly, the financial muscle of the large universal banks provides them with the capacity to expand into the British market (mainly through acquisition) should they so chose.

Furthermore, even if the British do have a strong comparative advantage in those activities which have traditionally been associated with investment banking, their success in the more conventional areas of commercial banking is likely to remain constrained. Past experience — like Citicorp's failed attempt to establish a retail network in the UK , shows how very difficult it is for commercial banks to crack foreign markets. Given the role such banking continues to play in Europe, both in the corporate and private sector, it will likely represent a major structural barrier to British entry. Acquisition or merger provides a way around this problem. Yet, even with all the Euro-enthusiasm currently surrounding 1992, it is difficult to image that any nation would be prepared to see one of its big commercial banks fall into foreign hands.[24]

Notes and references:

1. H. McRae and F. Cairncross, *Capital City: London as a Financial Centre*, Methuen, 1985.
2. W. Keegan, *Britain Without Oil*, Penguin, 1985.
3. Financial Times, various.
4. Bank of England Quarterly Bulletin, *International Banking in London*, September 1986.
5. ibid.
6. CSO Pink Book; and Bank of England Quarterly Bulletin, August 1987.
7. Bank of England, ibid.
8. Bank of England, ibid, Sept 1986.
9. Financial Times survey: *The City Revolution*, 27 October, 1986.
10. Barclays Bank Review, November 1986; and J. Walmsley, *New York's "Big Bang" - 10 Years After*, The Banker, March 1985.
11. Bank of England Quarterly Bulletin, *Change in the Stock Exchange and Regulation of the City*, February, 1987.
12. ibid. Barclays Bank Review.
13. H. McRae, *The Implications of an International Equity Market*, in Finance and the International Economy, The AMEX Bank Review Prize Essays, 1987.
14. The AMEX Bank Review, 24 March 1988.
15. Financial Times, 4 January 1988.
16. CSO press release, *UK Balance of Payments: Overseas Earnings of the City*, 30 July 1987..
17. The Economist and Financial Times, various.
18. Leon Nathans, *US Innovators still Ahead*, The Banker, March 1987.
19. The Economist, *Is your Stockbroker User-friendly?*, 25 October 1986.
20. The Banker, May 1986.
21. R. Cottrell, *No more an outsider*, The Far Eastern Economic Review, 3 July 1986.
22. Nigel Adam, *Echoes of Big Bang*, International Management, January 1988.
23. Financial Times survey, *France Banking and Finance*, 2 December, 1987.
24. A good general discussion of the impact of 1992, which provided an important source for this section, was a series of articles by Guy de Jonquieres in the Financial Times on February 19, 23, 29, March 1, 3 and 4, 1988.

Other references include:

A. Hamilton, *The Financial Revolution*, Penguin Books, 1986.
J. Plender and P. Wallace, *The Square Mile*, Century Hutchinson, 1985.
M.J.B. Hall, *Reform of The London Stock Exchange*: The Prudential Issues, Banca Nazionale del Lavoro, June 1987.

8 Insurance

The background to the British market:

When, on occasion, the public eye peers into the complex nature of financial services, it focuses above all on banking. In Britain, the Big Bang and the world stock and bond market booms, to say nothing of subsequent, spectacular crash in October 1987, have captured what little attention the man-in-the-street has for things financial. Given the overall turnover of international and domestic banking activity in the UK, this bias is to be expected.

Paradoxically, however, it is not from the money markets themselves that Britain receives its largest chunk of foreign service sector earnings. Instead, the biggest contribution to helping Britain "pay its way" in the world traditionally comes from the less glamorous insurance industry. For all the problems that have beset the London market during the 1980s, and for all the euphoria surrounding the globalization of banking, London remains the world's largest centre for international insurance, and the sector easily continues to be the main cash-cow for invisible earnings (leaving aside yields on foreign investments).

The weight of such revenues is all the more surprising given the nature of the world insurance business. Although a rising share of global activity is carried out on an international basis, the industry remains much more segmented in national markets than banking. There would seem to be two underlying reasons why this is so. On the one hand, demand can be more completely satisfied within a national framework. On the other hand, the industry is not subject to the same exogenous and autonomous factors which have affected banking. There has been, for example, no equivalent to the transfer of wealth to OPEC following the oil shocks that accelerated the expansion of an international banking system. As a result, governments have been able to limit foreign competition with the aim of controlling the funds managed by insurance companies, as well as protecting their national producers.

Consequently, the worldwide insurance industry is strongly shaped by the usual concoction of non-tariff barriers which affect industry and services in particular. These determine both the direct trade in insurance services and overseas provision through establishment trade, which accounts for the bulk of transnational supply. Licencing controls on foreign branches by host governments, additional administrative regulation, government procurement policies, discriminatory taxation, exchange rate controls etc. all play their part in preventing the free and equal production and sale of services.[1]

Lloyd's: London's specialty:

What characterizes the British market — and distinguishes it from others — is the large flow of earnings which accrue to direct trade. They not only make the UK one of the few surplus nations in insurance, but actually the world's largest creditor. The magnitude of these revenues is greatly explained by the existence of Lloyd's of London, a unique institution in the world market.

The significance of Lloyd's is not a function of its overall size. Indeed, it only accounts for about 1 percent of the world insurance market today. Instead, the importance of Lloyd's stems from its specialization in certain areas of insurance, and especially international insurance. Thus, for example, despite the retreat from Empire, the run down of Britain's share in world trade for most of this century, Lloyd's still handles approximately 25 percent of world maritime insurance. More recently, it has become one of the world's leading re-insurance centres. Lloyd's therefore, remains an international market place first and foremost, with about three quarters of its business still coming from overseas.[2]

The key to Lloyd's performance lies in its singular organizational composition. It is based on a structure which is essentially made up of a collection of separate and largely autonomous underwriting "syndicates", rather than a homogeneous insurance body. Lloyd's was, and effectively remains, an association of clubs, where individual members can band together to create syndicates aimed at suiting both their specific requirements as well as exploiting particular areas of the insurance market. By 1987 there were 370 syndicates, with over 32,200 members.

The crucial feature underpinning this system is the individual liability of members. Under the principle of "each for his own, not one for another", the individual member faces unlimited liability in meeting any claim filed under a policy he (she) has underwritten through his (her) syndicate. The advantages of this apparently brutal

124

arrangement arise in the way it prevents losses in one syndicate spilling over into the rest of the market, while at the same time guaranteeing the payment of claims.

To become a member or "Name" of Lloyd's, the applicant must be able to satisfy the Committee of Lloyd's that he has £100,000 in realizable assets, and agree to put a further £50,000 in the Lloyd's deposit fund as a preliminary guarantee to meeting potential losses.[3] These conditions may appear sufficient to deter any sensible private investor. But, they are generally believed to be greatly off-set by the considerable attractions of membership. The latter arise because the money invested in Lloyd's by the Names effectively generates a "double-return". The first is earned in the form of underwriting profit — the straight surplus between premium takings and payments against claims. The second source of profit lies in the interest earned on premium funds, plus the investment interest earned on the original stake put up by the member (including interest on the £50,000 deposit). Given that income earned at Lloyd's is subject to Capital Gains Tax (at 30 percent), rather than income tax, and given the three year lag between profit and taxation which allows inflation to cut the real level of tax, the overall investment advantages for the wealthy individual are substantial. Specifically, the inflationary 1970s, and the high levels of income tax under the last Labour government provided a very conducive environment for the huge expansion in of non-professional membership. For the first time in its history, wealthy individuals began to dominate Lloyd's, as passive investors taking no part in the actual business of insurance itself.

Preserving Lloyd's unique structure is its independent legal status. Unlike Britain's insurance companies, its rules for membership, investment, discipline and accounting are not governed by the Insurance Companies Regulations 1981. Instead, Lloyd's has managed to maintain control over its own affairs through a series of self-regulatory bodies, established by the 1982 Lloyd's Act. The purpose of this legislation is to ensure that the Lloyd's community is regulated in a way that preserves the market's flexibility. Historically, Lloyd's has been renowned for its accessibility, its innovativeness, its entrepreneurial flair and the speed with which new types of policy can be developed within the market. Its professional members claim that light formal regulation, combined with the loose regulatory structure of the syndicates and Names, are essential to maintaining the markets ability to adapt to, and exploit changing conditions. At the same time, the absence of a strict statutory framework has in the past also facilitated fraud by Lloyd's professional members, especially at the expense of non-practicing Names.

The companies and their big battalions:

In stark contrast to the specialized function of Lloyd's stand the insurance companies. All told, there are about 700 domestic companies operating within the British market, although a significant number of these are effectively under foreign control. There are an additional 170 foreign companies working in Britain.[4] But, the aggregate figures are misleading to the extent that they mask the degree of concentration of business in the company sector. Thus, it has been calculated that the 10 largest companies operating in the UK account for 80 percent of all activity.[5]

The cause for such concentration lies in the structure of the market. In the first instance, it follows from the economies of scale which the major companies derive from providing all the main forms of insurance. Most fundamentally, these can be divided into life and non-life insurance. The second category could be further subdivided into insurance provided to individuals and companies, although this separation is far from being absolute.

In examining the functioning of these forms of insurance, it is useful to address the business of life insurance first, due to its very distinct nature. Compared to other forms of insurance, life policies suffer only a small number of claims. Instead, payments usually occur at the end of a fixed period — often when the person taking out the insurance retires. Consequently, life-insurance tends not to experience the earnings fluctuations that otherwise affect underwriting. Instead, the onus of the business focuses on the investment of accumulated premiums. Effectively, this makes life-insurance an investment game, with company earnings deriving almost totally from spread at which it borrows money (ie. the interest paid on premiums) and invests it.

Given the social and political importance of this business, it tends to be heavily regulated, frequently through extensive government legislation. As a result, life-insurance markets are almost wholly serviced by domestic producers, with outside competition virtually non-existent or very strictly controlled. Government regulation tends also to be heavy in the other areas of personal and even company insurance. Most countries have stringent requirements on motor insurance, for example. Again, the provision of such services by foreigners is therefore limited.

126

Backing up such national compartmentalism are the straight forward logistics involved in providing general insurance cover. Unlike the business which flows through Lloyd's, and which tends to be geared to the highly specialized needs of corporate clients, the bulk of insurance is supplied through uniform packages. Mr X wants insurance for his house, holiday or car, so he selects one of the many standardized products offered by the large firms. Company Y wants to insure against fire and theft and it does the same. The provision of these services necessitates a physical presence near the customer. Consequently, the large insurance companies have to operate through extensive branch networks, in a way similar to the high-street banks. The high cost of establishing such networks in new markets acts as a strong disincentive to overseas expansion. They therefore underpin the national structure of the insurance industry, although merger and acquisition (where permitted) do provide ways around this.

The infrastructure and hence size dimension of the larger companies is enforced by a further characteristic which totally differentiates them from Lloyd's. As companies, they do not suffer the unlimited liability of the Lloyd's syndicates. Though they are consequently subject to considerable legal restrictions, they can enter the capital markets. As a result, they can expand their financial base and so take on more underwriting activity. This is a route not open to Lloyd's. The trade-off here, of course, is that the same size and diffuse nature of the companies, combined with the laws and regulations to which they are subject, also deprives them of the concentrated flexibility that so characterizes Lloyd's.

Yet, despite the manifest hurdles which the companies face in generating overseas business, British insurers have extensive ties to the American market. Of its non-life premium Commercial Union earns about 27 percent in the US, General Accident 40 percent and Royal Assurance a staggering 46 percent.[6] These figures highlight the strong ties which span the Atlantic, and contrast with the much feebler links that bridge the Channel to Britain's EC partners.

The middlemen:

More international still are the insurance brokers, the middlemen who put the clients and underwriters together, for payment by commission. The bulk of their activity is concentrated in the corporate sector. In the UK this means that over 90 percent of all domestic marine and aviation business passes through brokers, 80-85 percent of all insured pension business, and approximately three quarters of all non-marine business, excluding motor. By comparison, brokers arrange only about half all personal motor cover, 20-25 percent of ordinary life business and probably a similar amount for other household insurance.[7]

From an international standpoint, the brokerage of insurance was originally driven largely by the expansion overseas of American multinational companies during the 1950s and especially the 1960s. To provide their clients with worldwide cover, brokerage house too crossed frontiers. Given the comparative importance of multinational firms to the British economy, British brokers also moved abroad, capitalizing on the inherited experience gained during the age of Empire.

More recently, the outward movement of brokers has been encouraged by the development of the world re-insurance market. It has emerged as a way of spreading corporate risk (90 percent of re-insurance is in the non-life sector), and unlike direct insurance is lightly regulated. As a result, it has lent itself to internationalization, with broking activities being carried out across borders.

The last two decades:

As with many other commercial and financial activities, the rapidly changing economic conditions of the last two decades have caused fluctuations in the fortunes of insurers. The cyclical character of the industry has been underpinned by the problems connected with "long tail" insurance. It comprises any form of insurance where there is a significant time lag between the inflow of revenues and the payment of claims. For the insurer, such business offers opportunities because of the potential for capital gain on premiums. Yet, long tail business also carries dangers. They arise not only from the difficulties of assessing risk over the long term, but also from problems of exogenous financial factors, like the course of inflation, interest rates, stock and bond prices etc.

The 1960s and early 1970s were a boom period for the insurance world. As the world economies continued to grow, so did personal and corporate demand for insurance. With the expansion of multinational companies a global market developed, where skills, techniques and products became increasingly sophisticated. Measured in terms of premium paid per capita, insurance markets in most of the major Western economies doubled during the 1960s, and continued to expand well into the 1970s.

For the London market, however, this period of easy growth yielded mixed blessings. On the one hand, activity was buoyed up by general growth. On the other hand, this clouded the long term structural problems beginning to impede the effectiveness of British insurance. Generally, the British insurance business became locked into the relative but not absolute decline of the British economy. Such creeping retrenchment was compounded by the climate of complacency which prevailed over most of the City's domestic financial activities. Outdated administrative procedures were unable to cope with the growth in demand, while the technical efficiency of the market deteriorated due to a certain sloppiness in professional practices, notably in the procedures for drafting policies and carrying out claims. The net effect was to enforce the relative contraction of British business, while world markets continued to expand.

The reckoning came with the oil crisis of 1973. It brought the long boom of the post-war era to a crashing end. Its effects on the world insurance industry were no less marked. The downturn in global economic activity depressed demand for corporate and personal insurance, while boosting claims connected with industrial failure.

On the supply side, the slump in growth, the acceleration of inflation and the associated rise in nominal interest rates sent shudders through the world stock markets. The London exchange went into its severest bear market since the 1930s. In the insurance industry the result was a substantial rundown of capital assets. This in turn led to a substantial contraction of underwriting capacity.

The market reponse to these problems lay in the spectacular development of its re-insurance sector. Re-insurance takes place when the direct insurer lays off part of the risk on a policy to one or more re-insurers. The advantages of such a deal are numerous. Most obviously, it allows the direct insurer, and indeed the industry as a whole, to spread risk around by "atomization". Equally important, however, is the fact that re-insurance permits small and mid-sized firms to expand their activity above and beyond what their capitalization would allow in terms of direct business. The surge in re-insurance during the 1970s thus renewed the capital base of the industry and its capacity. Re-insurance was further encouraged by its relatively unregulated nature. This led to a lot of new companies entering the sector, and stimulated cross-border provision.

Lured on by the potential earnings of double return new entrants piled into the industry during the mid 1970s. Often these were "captive" operations set up by industrial and commercial companies, striving not just to cut their insurance costs but to gain high investment yields which premiums from third parties could earn on the back of rising interest rates. The lack of official regulation in the sector further stimulated the growth of such organizations in international tax-havens like Bermuda: which in 1983 boasted 1,200 registered captives and independent reinsurers generating $6.5 billion in gross premiums.[8]

Re-insurance became too much of a good thing. The exploding development saw the market boom from $5.6 billion in 1965 to $60 billion by early 1980s.[9] Such growth soon led to over-capacity within the market, and to a fierce price-cutting war. This, however, did not immediately bring about a contraction of capacity. Instead of withdrawing from the market as the combined ratio of claims to premium rose (above 100 — the level at which pure underwriting ceases to be profitable), re-insurers extended their commitments for the sake of investment earnings, notably on "long-tail" business.

The strategy, however, turned sour during the late 1970s as American legal decisions began to tilt in favour of consumers in the area of product liability. As a result, claims in this long-tail area mounted, further depressing the combined ratio of direct and re-insurance. On top of this, interest rates, which had peaked in 1981/2, began to fall thereafter, reducing investment earnings. More recently, a further contraction has occurred. The years 1984-5 proved disastrous for aviation reinsurance, crashes of American, Japanese, and Indian aircraft, leaving large insurance claims to be met.

In the wake of these shocks, the re-insurance industry has substantial undergone upheaval. To try to reduce future losses, underwriters have cut back capacity, notably where it is difficult to predict the size of future claims, for example, certain areas of product liability. As a result, it has been estimated that total re-insurance premiums have fallen to $40 billion, or by a third in nominal terms.

At the same time, clients became nervous, fearing that the emerging insurance operations would be unable to meet claims if and when they were made. So the insurance world has been experiencing a "flight to quality", with business shifting back to the old established centres. The insured started to return to the market places where they felt safe, and where adequate cover against a disaster could be guaranteed. The once popular

Bermuda operation started to lose its appeal. In 1984, for example, thirty independent underwriters had been working in the tax-haven. Within a year their number had been reduced to fifteen.[10]

A hardening of the market has followed since the mid 1980s. Yet, the position of the industry both for direct and re-insurance remains fragile. Despite rising profits over the last couple of years, certain areas of the market are far from healthy. The threat of claims resulting from old, long tail policies in liability continues. Secondly, there are signs that another price war is breaking out in the US property/casualty market, where premiums have only been rising since late 1985. Beyond this, the spectre of AIDS is posing a huge problem to the life-insurance industry of the whole world, while plans for the single EC market by 1992 are likely to cause turbulence in the structure of the European industry.

The British market: changes and international performance:

To compete in the changing world market, London too expanded its business during the 1970s. To raise its capacity, Lloyd's, the leader of international insurance in London, set about expanding its capital base. Being unable to enter the money markets, it began an ambitious recruitment drive of non-professional Names. Previously the market had been dominated by members who not only put up capital, but actually participated in it. By comparison the surge in membership initiated during the late 1960s and early 1970s was geared to tapping a larger pool of wealth by bringing in outsiders, for whom Lloyd's simply represented a form of investment for their private capital. The ensuing expansion turned out to be very successful, but it also stored up certain structural problems for Lloyd's, which took a while to reach fruition.

The introduction of non-professional members into Lloyd's was not catered for by the the 1871 Lloyd's Act, which continued to set the guidelines of the market. Though the Act covered the rules of admission to the market, the self-regulation of Lloyd's provided little or no protection for the non-working member. When the influx of members and wealth began to erode the intimate clubbism, it also paved the way for abuse of those outside the market — by those inside. As scandal and simple incompetence were dramatically revealed during the late 1970s, pressure mounted both within and without Lloyd's for reform.

131

The impetus for change also came from the rising penetration of U.S. brokers into the London market. The Americans began to buy up broking firms in order to take advantage of Lloyd's well established information channels and its international links. Specifically, they aimed at securing part of Lloyd's rapidly expanding reinsurance work. This area of activity had become fundamental to the market, accounting for 70 percent of all business in 1985. A large share also stems from the US market for direct insurance. Such growth of American interests added to the pressures for change if Lloyd's was to retain its independence, and its self-regulatory nature.

The first response to the clamour for reform was the creation of a working party (under Sir Henry Fisher) to consider the future of self-regulation at Lloyd's. It concluded that the 1871 constitution was inadequate to cope with the recent far-reaching changes. Its recommendations were taken up by Parliament, culminating in the 1982 Lloyd's Act. To protect outside investors, the Act called for a rigorous division of labour of Lloyd's various activities, to be implemented by July 1987. It required the separation between "brokers" (who seek out insurance clients and sell policies) and members' "agencies" (who manage the affairs of non-professionals). Previously, 70 percent of agencies had been owned brokers, thus creating a potential conflict of interest between the brokers' duties to his client (the insured) and the duty of the managing agent to the Names of his syndicate. The Act further provided for a council to introduce new self-regulatory measures and stamp out the abuses.

In the midst of the deliberations, the notorious Alexander Howden and the PCW scandals broke over Lloyd's. They centred on agents effectively stealing money from the names in their syndicates. In other words the scandals exposed another area of potential fraud, which would not be removed by the separation of brokers and agents. The resolution of this problem has proved equally difficult. Further measures have been introduced to codify the relationship between agents and Names, including a requirement for syndicates to produce audited accounts. Furthermore, the structure of the Council of Lloyd's has been altered so that outsiders make up its majority.

Foreign earnings by British insurers:

Overseas insurance revenues are made up primarily from four sources: earnings on underwriting (ie. trade income on non-factor services); repatriated profits earned by the insurance companies on their subsidiaries abroad; income from portfolio investment (ie. part of IDP earnings which are dealt with separate chapter) and earnings accruing to brokers (also part of NFS trade).

The export of underwriting services provides the most important contribution. By far the larger share of these earnings is generated by Lloyd's. During the early 1980s, however, the world slump in the industry, and especially in the re-insurance business, caused a contraction of nominal income, to say nothing of real revenues. As a result, Lloyd's underwriting income dipped below that of the companies in 1984. Yet since then these earnings have recovered strongly, rising from £220 million in 1984, to £730 million in 1985, and to £1.3 billion in 1986 (see Table 8.1).

Table 8.1:   INSURANCE EARNINGS ON SERVICES AND INVESTMENTS
(in £ million)

	1976	1980	1984	1986
Credits				
Companies				
Underwriting	44	94	256	426
Direct Investment Income				
Profits from Overseas Subsidiaries	190	177	104	723
Property Income	7	9	26	20
Portfolio Investment Income	70	132	654	702
Lloyd's				
Underwriting (overseas business written in UK)	279	188	220	1314
Portfolio Investment Income	57	153	344	422
Brokers	170	243	535	710
Total	817	995	2139	4316
Debits				
Direct Investment Income due to Overseas Affiliates	7	28	-34	56
Net Earnings by UK Insurance Institutions	810	967	2173	4260

Source: CSO, Pink Book, 1987.

By comparison, the underwriting income of the companies has grown more steadily over the last decade, ending up at £430 million in 1986. The big fluctuations experienced by the companies occurred in the profits of their overseas subsidaries. Determined particularly by events in the US market, these earnings oscillated around a downward trend from 1979 onwards, culminating in an abysmal profit of £40 million in 1985. Then in 1986, there occurred a meteoric recovery, with repatriated profits soaring to £720 million.

In the other main area of investment income, namely returns on overseas portfolio assets, both the insurance companies and Lloyd's have performed well. There has been quite rapid growth since the lifting of currency restrictions in 1979, which has enabled

133

the companies to place a larger share of their capital overseas. Given further encouragement by the bull market until the middle of 1987, the combined income of Lloyd's and the companies exceeded £1.1 billion in 1986.

Lastly, brokers' income since the mid-1970s has also grown steadily. Despite the world recession of the insurance industry during the first half of the present decade, these earnings only suffered one contraction (in nominal terms) in 1979. Since then, there has been growth every year, bringing broking income up to £710 million by 1986.

The future challenges to the London market:

The recent surge in overseas earnings provides grounds for optimism over the long-term development of the British insurance industry. It underlines the many advantages of the London market, which should ensure its role as an international centre. The rise in underwriters' earnings, after a five-year slump, is evidence not just of London's resilience, but also of the conservative nature of the international insurance markets.

The London market has a long record of being adaptable, flexible and reliable. Lloyd's record, that it has settled every claim made of it, has done much to build up confidence. The 1984-5 "flight to quality" underlined the strengths. In a cautious commercial environment, the reliability of London cannot be built up in another centre overnight. Any alternative would need to be tried and tested over a period before it could be considered a worthy alternative to London. Given the protectionist nature of the world insurance industry its seems unlikely that such an alternative centre can develop, even if the European market becomes totally free by 1992 and progress is made GATT on liberalizing service trade.

London also has the economies of scale of a large concentration of international insurance business. Despite the advent of mass telecommunication, ready personal contact between client, broker, and underwriter still remains an important factor. Similarly, there are the skill, reputation, and inventiveness of underwriters in London — Lloyd's was the first to insure satellites. The London market also benefits from the fringe services it offers. Contact offices, risk management consulting agencies, banking/insuring intermediaries, and Lloyd's worldwide information service all provide important back-up facilities.

The strength of Britain's overseas business is enhanced by the expanding capacity of Lloyd's. Despite the scandals, membership still grows. In 1987, a further 2,800 names joined, bringing the total to 32,200. With 8,700 existing names increasing their underwriting commitments, this brought about a 20 percent rise in premium capacity to £10.2 billion. It remains to be seen what the impact of the new regulatory measures on long term membership growth will be. The outlook for the present is good, although continued efforts will no doubt be necessary as investors are offered proliferating options in the financial markets.

The position of the London market, and Lloyd's in particular, has also been underlined by the continuation of the transatlantic merger wave affecting brokers. It began in the late 1970s when US broker Frank B. Hall took over Leslie & Godwin, followed by Marsh & Mclennan's acquisition of C.T. Browning. In taking over firms like Alexander Howden, Stenhouse and John Plummer, the Americans showed themselves especially keen to tap into Lloyd's re-insurance business, much of which was emanating from the United States. British brokers — increasingly squeezed out of US business — have responded by instigating their own ownership changes. Thus, for example, Sedgwick Forbes merged Bland Payne and later acquired US groups Fred S. James and Crump companies.[11]

The re-found optimism of the last couple of years is best captured by the spate of property development undertaken by the London insurance market, linked with the latest computer and telecommunications technology. The centre-piece is Lloyd's spectacular new building — the £160 million "refinery" which opened in 1986. But other developments include the Institute of London Underwriters' (I.L.U.) expansion with the opening of a new £6 million building, housing 50 separate underwriting units, permitting 110 member companies to operate under one roof.

Still, the British insurance industry faces hurdles. These can be divided into two, although there is an overlap between them. Thus, there are those problems which affect and arise out of the British industry and economy, and there are those connected with world activity and its composition. The most general weakness of Britain's international insurance industry must be the small base from which it has to operate, even if the UK is a relatively heavily insured market (see Table 8.2). Although the economy is out-performing its competitors for the first time in decades, the UK will never be able to match the size of the American, and more recently the Japanese, market.

The issue of bigness is more important in insurance than, say, in banking. The industry continues to be reliant on national markets to generate premiums and capacity. Insurance remains less international than banking, both in terms of capital flowing into and out of the industry. This would tend to limit not just the ability of British insurers to expand overseas, but also restrict the potential for London to expand as an international entrepôt for insurance, in the same way as it has done in banking.

Table 8.2: GROSS PREMIUM PAYMENTS IN 1985 IN U.S. DOLLARS

	Life	Non Life	Total	% of GNP
United States	156.2	145.6	301.8	7.6
Japan	65.6	23.0	88.6	6.7
United Kingdom	19.5	23.3	42.8	9.4
Germany	14.0	22.9	36.9	5.9
France	8.6	18.8	27.4	5.4
Canada	8.2	12.5	20.7	6.2

Source: OECD, Statistics on Insurance, Comparative Tables of Insurances Statistics for 1984, Paris 1988.

The fluctuating exchange rate of the pound also tends to impede international insuring. Since 1979 sterling has been subject to considerable market movements. At the turn of the decade its value soared against the dollar, and the EMS bloc. Subsequently, the pound settled into a downward trend. It until early of 1985 against the dollar, and until the spring of 1988 against the the EMS.

The effect of such instability is twofold. Much of the premium income which pours into London is paid in dollars. Sterling's erratic behaviour therefore creates uncertainty over earnings and claims payments, with the result that insurers become more cautious. This in turn undermines their international competitiveness. In addition, the depreciation of sterling creates problems in the premium/solvency ratio. Although a downward plunge causes a rise in the immediate sterling value of the premium, it will also cause the insurer's capital base to contract if the latter is largely denominated in sterling. Other things being equal, devaluation will therefore reduce the underwriters' capacity to insure. In the long term such a loss of scale will also erode competitiveness, as British insurance will not be able to meet foreign demand with the clear advantages represented by economies of scale. A sudden, drastic drop in sterling, in particular, would signal big problems for the London market.

The issue of long-term capacity is also important because it touches on some of the difficulties in customer service in the London. Customers recently appear to have experienced difficulty in finding the type and volume of insurance cover they desire. The underwriters have been accused of concentrating too hard on the short term gain, maintaining that a shortage of capacity is good, while a surplus of capacity is bad. Pressure has been building in the United States, where consumer groups are accusing Lloyd's of colluding with American companies in refusing to cover certain liability business with the aim of pushing up premium rates.[12] The withdrawal of cover from specific areas of business can be seen as a legitimate response to crushing losses incurred. Yet in the long run, if customers find difficulties in placing business in London it can but lead to the search for insurance elsewhere.[13] There have also been gyrations in contract, not just with respect to size but on price as well. As insurance contacts are usually long-term agreements, it should be to the advantage of all parties to work out more stable pricing and volume agreements than exist at present. It would enable them to plan more effectively.

London's reputation depends in the first instance on correct dealing. Though the scandals at Lloyd's do not appear to have reduced enthusiasm at home for membership, this is not shared abroad. For example, J. Lindbaek, (former managing director of Storeband Norden Group Oslo) warned the Insurance Institute of London in January 1986 that the long-term negative effects of professional malpractice should not be ignored: "seen from outside there is little understanding for the slowness and hesitation to prosecute and punish, [giving the impression] that for a gentleman the worst possible punishment is the loss of your good name and standing, and that this, in the view of many, is punishment enough".[14] The working practices of Lloyd's clearly do have an effect on business and on the reputation of London's financial services as a whole.

Beyond this, the professional reputation of the London market is linked to its position as leader in insurance know-how. This, however, is something that has to be fought for continually, especially in view of the innovations in American financial services. It is essential for London to keep ahead in insurance training and education. The orthodox principles of underwriting on which the London market built its renown, have already been exported, not only to other developed nations, but also to the Third World. London can only remain influential if its education keeps pace with the changing patterns of the world market, so that foreigners will continue to refer to London for the application of new techniques. Wlodek Zajdlic, in a study of British insurance education, criticized it for failing to appreciate that the industry was an "economic business unit diversified into many mutually independent transactions". There is a danger of concentrating too much on traditional principles of underwriting which fail to take into account changes in insurance.

Thus, while Britain retains a lead in the primary and secondary educational levels in the areas of motor, marine and fire insurance, training is wanting in the broader areas of managerial skills and portfolio policy, the importance of an overall market strategy, and the interdependence between investment and premium incomes.[15]

In the wider world, probably the most significant problem is the cyclical nature of the industry, due to largely to fluctuations in the US market. Accounting for about half the world's premium payments, gyrations in America have an immediate impact on British insurers. It has been estimated that US business amounted to 55 percent of the Lloyd's premiums in 1985.[16] Similarly, the larger UK companies are heavily committed to the US market. So a downturn on the other side of the Atlantic has substantial, direct repercussions on British insurers and invisible earnings.

The worry for British insurers dependent on the US must come from the price war which started in the US property sector at the beginning of 1987 and was spreading into casualty by the end of the year. At $190 billion (in 1985) this component of the US industry is by far the world's largest single market — representing about 75 percent of all US business, and approximately 55 percent of the global (non-Communist) property/casualty market.[17] A downturn after only two and a half years of rising premium rates threatens big problems, not only to direct underwriters, but also to global re-insurers for whom US property/casualty is a major customer.

Another question mark in the US is on-going battle concerning liability. Following the payments bout of the late 1970s and early 1980s, and the subsequent withdrawal of cover from the market, there has been a wave of initiatives to reform tort law. As the regulation of the insurance industry in the US takes place at the state level (due to the McCarran-Ferguson Act which excludes the sector from federal control) such actions have been both piecemeal and indeed limited. Yet, they may alter the regulatory climate.

Of more imminent impact are the developments surrounding liability payments on industrial pollution. The origins of the problem go back to 1980 when the "Superfund" law was passed. It demands that the Environmental Protection Agency (EPA) should clean up chemical contamination, recouping the cost from the companies responsible. EPA action accelerated from the end of 1986, the law having been renewed, this has led to a battle between manufacturers and the insurance industry over liability. Although court decisions so far have favoured the latter, insurers feel that a shift in the judicial environment could cost them dear.

Pressing from the structural point of view is the issue of anti-trust policy. The McCarran-Ferguson Act exempts the insurers from anti-trust regulation. In late 1986, however, the National Conference of State Legislatures called on Congress to scrap the Act, or specify more thoroughly its anti-trust policy towards the insurance business. If federal action does follow, and a more liberal environment is favoured by a number of government departments, then it could toughen competition. This could squeeze premiums and profits.

More direct competitive pressures are also developing within the American market from the New York Insurance Exchange (NYIE). Modelled on Lloyd's, the NYIE was set up in 1980 to provide similar underwriting services, to those which American companies were using in London. The size of the exchange remains small compared to its big brother in London. In 1985, there were only 45 syndicates operating, earning a gross written premium of $310 million. It suffered crushing losses during the recession the first half of the 1980s. In 1985 the exchange had a combined ratio of 160 percent, ie. it was paying out $1.60 claims for every $1.00 earned as premium. Yet, its mood was confident as the world industry embarked on its upswing.[18] For the moment, the NYIE and its fellow exchanges in Miami and Chicago do not seriously encroach on London's position. But over time such domestic exchanges may chip away at American business booked through London.

The two other main regional blocs in world insurance are the European Community and the Far East. Historically, both have been protected. Now, the market appears to be slowly changing. In Europe, the big Brussels project for the single, internal market in goods, services, capital and labour should enable more intra-community trade, especially in non-life insurance. Of course, it is probably unlikely that the scene will change overnight. When 1st January 1993 arrives, Europe will not suddenly wake up to the wholly unrestricted, pan-national provision of insurance.

Obstacles have to be negotiated before the legislative framework is adopted fully by the EC and then integrated into national law. Even when this has taken place, the retail nature of much insurance — with the physical market penetration it demands — is unlikely to lead to a quick proliferation of consumer choice. Still, the barriers and regulations will progressively come down. Both producers and customers will adapt to the changes. It seems likely that larger, corporate policies, as well as re-insurance will most readily crack the international market. In the longer term, transnational organizations will perhaps evolve as a result of merger and the acquisition of existing branch operations etc.

Quite how well the UK is placed to exploit a general opening of the European market is debatable. Received wisdom has it that UK insurers — along with other British financial services — will roll up cross-border business. After all, Britain is already the world's largest exporter of international insurance, and its companies are amongst Europe's largest (see Table 8.3). Such a gung-ho approach carries with it certain dangers. It perhaps overstates the ease with which British producers could penetrate other national markets, overlooking difficulties arising from language, culture preferences and the Continental legal system based on a codified law. Secondly, it might underestimate the expansionist desires and capabilities of Europe's larger insurance houses, who may find it simple to get into London's more open, international market. Thirdly, there is the danger that the market may be swamped with over-capacity as the existing national industries gear up to conquer their neighbours' turf, for example, by buying up smaller overseas companies and then pouring in money to expand them. This problem could be acute if the banking industry gets into the act. Links between banks and insurance companies already exist, both in Britain and on the Continent. As personal financial services proliferate Europe's major clearing banks could use their branch networks to sell insurance products.

Table 8.3: EUROPE'S 10 LARGEST INSURANCE COMPANIES BY GROSS CONSOLIDATED PREMIUMS IN 1986

	Gross Premiums	Life	Non-Life	Country
1. ALLIANZ WORLDWIDE	6.36	- -	- -	Germany
2. GROUPE ZURICH	4.64	1.17	3.48	Switzerland
3. U.A.P.	3.88	1.63	2.25	France
4. GENERALI	3.74	1.14	2.60	Italy
5. ROYAL INSURANCE	3.60	0.66	2.94	Britain
6. NATIONALE NEDERLANDEN	3.14	1.72	1.42	Netherlands
7. PRUDENTIAL	3.05	2.23	0.83	Britain
8. WINTERTHUR	3.02	1.07	1.95	Switzerland
9. COMMERCIAL UNION	2.62	0.68	1.93	Britain
10. SUN ALLIANCE	2.55	0.67	1.39	Britain

N.B.: British Companies' figures are for net premiums (ie. net of reinsurance).

Source: Le Monde d'Affaires, 21 May 1988 - from estimates by the Fédération Française des Sociétés d'Assurance.

Moving away from Europe, the major world market likely to develop for insurance (and indeed all other financial services), over the next years, is the Far East. Rapid economic growth with its attendant industrial expansion and rising levels of personal income make this part of the globe ripe for the picking. The two main problems for British insurers here are protection and the strength of local competition

Protectionism in insurance is rife even within the industrialized world, and only now is the EC trying to get rid of it, it is not surprising that developing countries are just as protective. True, services have at long last been brought onto the GATT agenda. But, it would take a brave man to state that progress will be quick. The vested interests are great, with the national industries wishing to ward off competition, and governments seeking to maintain sovereign control over insurance investments and restrict the outflow of capital.[19] So they will not make de-regulation easy.

Even if markets were opened up to foreigners, there is no guarantee that this would necessarily benefit either the British companies or Lloyd's. The absolute capacity constraints imposed by the size of the British economy have already been touched on. At the same time, the power of local producers is substantial. Top of the table are the Japanese. Helped by the appreciation of the yen, and based on huge domestic savings, the world's three largest insurance houses today are Japanese. With the creation of any international insurance market in the region, on must expect that it will be dominated by the Japanese, and then by producers in other regional markets, like Singapore.

The global securities markets may also affect the world insurance industry. From the middle of 1987, and especially since Black Monday, bond and equity markets have been fragile nearly everywhere, with the notable exception of Tokyo. Leaving aside the indirect effects this may or may not have on insurance through its impact on economic growth, the direct consequences on the capital value of investments and their earnings are significant. In Britain's case, the stock market slump is likely to have had a big effect on the overseas portfolio holdings of British insurance companies. Future IDP revenues will be smaller than they would otherwise have been. The contraction of investment capital is also likely to have an adverse impact on insurance capacity.

Other big areas of doubt centre on the future of the re-insurance industry, and the possible repercussions of the Aids epidemic on life-insurance. As has already been mentioned, the world re-insurance industry suffered a dramatic reduction in capacity following its excessive growth in the late 1970s, and the slump of the first half of the 1980s. Between 1984 and the middle of 1987, for example, 90 re-insurance companies

141

packed up, including many of the off-shore captives.[20] Since the downturn, however, premium rates have improved substantially, causing strong gains in profitability. The reintroduction of new capital into the industry and the likely development of capacity therefore again become pressing questions, given the ease of entry into this area of the insurance business.

It seems unlikely that history will repeat itself. Both potential producers and customers must be shy, but having been once bitten they see the scope for earnings on capital investment today as less favourable than in the 1970s. Unless there is a major resurgence in inflation, which cannot be wholly ruled out, interest rates seem unlikely to rise back to their previous levels. So the incentive to get back into the business to earn money on the investment of premiums has greatly diminished. The uncertainty surrounding the world capital markets at present can but enhance discouragement.

On the question of Aids (the Acquired Immune Deficiency Syndrome), the future remains grimly uncertain. Various estimates have forecast upwards of 1.5 million cumulative deaths from the disease in the United States by 1995 to 2000. If such figures are realized, and repeated with a lag in Europe and other regions of the globe, then it will change the whole nature of life insurance, which has for decades rested on levels of life expectancy in the developed world. It is hard to say what the reactions of the insurance industry will be. Obvious measures include extensive testing for applicants, differential policies for high-risk groups, higher premium rates all round and so on. The degree to which the industry will be able to enforce such measures is still unknown. It is clear, however, that unless a medical cure and/or prevention are soon developed, the impact of the epidemic on the world insurance industry will be severe. Furthermore, it is questionable whether the industry will be allowed to fashion its own strategy, independent of government regulation responding to social pressure.

Notes and references:

1. OECD, *International Trade in Services: Insurance*, 1983.
2. J. PLender and P. Wallace, *The Square Mile*, Century Publishing, 1985.
3. H. McRae and F. Cairncross, *Capital City*, Methuen,1985.
4. W. Zajdlic, *The International Future of the London Market (2)*, Policy Market, September 1985.
5. ibid H.McRae and F. Cairncross.
6. Vince McCullough, *Insurance*, The Economist, 6 June, 1987.
7. ibid H.McRae and F. Cairncross.
8. Financial Times survey, *Reinsurance*, 9 September 1985.
9. ibid.
10. ibid.
11. John Moore, *More Broking Mergers Likely*, The Independent, 3 July 1987.
12. ibid. Vince McCullough.
13. Philip Moore, *US liability business will not wait*, Policy Market, May 1987.
14. J. Lindbaek, *London _ World Insurance Centre*, address to the Insurance Institute of London, 20 January 1986.
15. W. Zajdlic, *Insurance Education _ too narrow*, Foresight, March 1984.
16. Financial Times survey, *Insurance and Insurance Broking*, 22 April 1988.
17. ibid. based on the Swiss Reinsurance Company — the percentage figure for share of total US market is also based on OECD statistics for 1984.
18. Financial Times survey, *Insurance and Insurance Broking*, 16 April, 1986.
19. ibid. OECD.
20. ibid. The Economist.

Other references:

Association of British Insurers, *Statistics Bureau, Overseas Earnings of the UK Insurance Industry*.

A.M. Baker, *Liberalization of Insurance/Services*, address to the ILL, 3 October 1984.

A.H. Bolton, *Maintaining London's position in the international aviation insurance and reinsurance markets*, address to the Insurance Institute of London (IIL), 21 November 1985.

G. Dickinson, *La Concurrence internationale dans les assurance*, Revue du CEPPI N 28, 4th Quarter 1986.

R.D. Hazell, *The Next Few Years*, address to the IIL, 31 December 1985.

D.V. Palmer, *Presidential Address*, to the IIL, 8 October 1985.

K.E. Randall, *The Development of self-regulation at Lloyd's*, address to the IIL, 24 October 1984.

R.M. Salter, *The 1986 Renewal Season _ Why place your business in London?*, address to the IIL, 13 February 1986.

9 The commodity, Baltic and Financial Futures Exchanges

Introduction:

As with insurance and banking, London remains an international commodity trading centre out of all proportion to Britain's position in the world league of economies. Though less important, and in recent years less dynamic than other City earnings, the commodity markets still provide a not insignificant boost to invisible revenues.

Part of the relative obscurity of commodity trading has been due to the fact that international and domestic changes in the other areas have far outpaced developments in the sector. This is linked to the discouraging global picture commodities have faced for most of the 1980s, compared with the progress of other financial services. However, it also stems from the esoteric nature of commodity trading in Britain. British commodity markets remain the preserve of a concentrated industry. In contrast to the US, big investment banks do not participate in the commodity markets through trading branches.

Similarly, the the London exchanges are not all open to individuals trading on their own account (so-called "locals"). Nor has the sector attracted the private investor in a way that equity and insurance markets have. Instead, the hard and soft commodity markets are dominated by three categories of professionals. There are the merchants who deal in physical commodities and so use the exchanges to hedge their real present and/or future holdings. Then there are the commission houses who deal solely in hedging instruments on behalf of clients. Lastly, there are the brokers who deal in physicals as well as futures and options.

The restricted nature of the pool of players arises for a number of reasons. It is partly the result of tradition, in markets originally organized to serve the specific commercial requirements of suppliers and customers, both being handlers of raw materials. It can be argued that membership remains restricted so existing traders on the main exchanges can exercise some, albeit very modest control on prices and volume flows. But the limited size of the markets also arises from the legal and tax structure which used to be imposed on individuals entering the market. Before the Financial Services Act, private traders in commodities were legally classified as gamblers. Consequently, debts owed to them were not recoverable through the courts, while profits were subject to income tax, rather than lower the Capital Gains Tax.

Only a small amount of trading on the exchanges is carried out in physical goods (about 2 percent for the London Commodity Exchange and 15-20 percent on the Metal Exchange), while the bulk of trading in physicals is carried out directly over the telephone or telex. Instead the focus of trading lies in the "futures" or "terminal" markets. These developed out of the forward contract, which permitted suppliers and consumers to protect themselves against short term price fluctuations. More specifically, the forward contract allowed agents in the market to "hedge" against price movements, by offsetting physical holdings against future contracts to buy or sell. The problem with this system was that it forced the trader to deal on a specific set of goods. By comparison, the modern futures contract allows dealers to offset their physical holdings in standardized grade trades, while their physical holdings are sold on the spot market. Similarly, the "options" market has been developed to permit hedging. In this market a dealer can take out an option (at a premium charge) to buy or sell a commodity at a certain point in the future. There are two main advantages of this instrument. First, it does not require the dealer to go ahead with the transaction should prices movements turn out to be unfavourable. Second, it allows for a high degree of market gearing, because the initial payment is only equal to premium. Hence the use of options expands market volume.

The importance of these instruments lies in the opportunities they present not just to the suppliers and end consumers of commodities to shield themselves from price fluctuations, but the potential for profits they open up for speculators. The latter may seem to outsiders to be largely parasitic traders, whose activities help destabilize the markets. But speculators actually provide a vital service in the markets. The benefits of their behaviour lie in taking up the hedges of the producers and users. They provide a crucial source of liquidity without which the exchanges could not be used as a buffer against fluctuations in the world market. That at least is the theory of how the exchanges should function under perfect market conditions. They do not do so all the time.

In market organization, the London commodity markets are dominated by a number of key institutions. Thus, the London Futures and Options Exchange (FOX — formerly the London Commodity Exchange or LCE) is the main market for "soft" commodities, dealing primarily in cocoa, coffee, and sugar. Parallel to it is the London Metal Exchange (LME) which deals in aluminium, copper, lead, nickel, zinc, and silver (tin trading having been suspended since the "tin crisis" of October 1985). The International Petroleum Exchange (IPE), which emerged in the early 1980s, has contracts in gas, oil premium, leaded gasoline, heavy fuel oil, and crude oil. The Baltic Exchange is primarily a market for chartering ships and aircraft but contains the Grain and Feed Trade Association (GAFTA). The latter provides a market for potatoes, wheat, barley and soya meal. In addition, the Baltic Exchange also offers a futures market for shipping contracts under the auspices of the Baltic International Freight Futures Exchange (Biffex).

The traditional mechanics of the various exchanges differ, although they are being brought together by technology, market developments and regulation. Notably, the London Metal Exchange was not linked to the International Commodities Clearing House (ICCH), until the Financial Services Act came into force. By comparison, both FOX and the Baltic Exchange were (as was the the recently created London International Financial Futures Exchange — see following chapter).

The ICCH is an association of all the main traders, which is owned by a consortium of the clearing banks. Its functions are varied, but crucial to the futures markets, where it checks, settles and reports each day's business on the exchanges. Its main role is to match buying and selling contracts. By becoming the principal in the contract, the ICCH enables other parties to enter and to leave the market separately, thereby increasing market liquidity. In the last resort, the clearing house as principal will meet the contractual obligations of defaulting members. The ICCH's main mechanism for regulating the market is the deposit system. It requires that when any member's client takes a speculative position in a market, the member has to make a down payment, or deposit (and sometimes an additional "margin") according to the market, the size of contract and subsequent price movements.

Other particularities which set the Metal Exchange apart from the Baltic and London Commodity Exchanges, include the absence of a *force majeure* clause to provide a let out in the case of an obstacle to delivery — a contract made on the LME must be carried out whatever the cost. There have been no fixed rates on commissions that members may charge, nor are there limits on the LME to the extent to which prices may fluctuate on a day before the Exchange closes the trading. On the other major exchanges if prices fluctuate widely up or down there is an automatic break in trading for a fixed period of time. The LME sanctions no such breaks in the belief the that members of the Exchange should be able to get in and out of the market whenever they desire. The LME argues

147

that it stops traders becoming locked into a market when prices are falling rapidly. Lastly, unlike the FOX and LIFFE, the LME has not admitted locals.

Downturn in the global commodity markets:

A look back over the last decade reveals a dramatic turnaround for international commodity trading. During the mid-1970s the markets for producers and dealers were reasonably healthy. The early 1970s were characterized by accelerating world inflation and a commodity price explosion. As a result, the financial rewards from taking market positions and income on commissions were significant both in hard and soft commodities. Investing in commodities seemed a safe way of protecting capital across the globe. In addition, the oil crises helped cultivate the belief that a shortage of raw materials would be a permanent feature in all world trade.

Yet, by the early 1980's the picture was changing and commodity prices started to decline. A series of factors was responsible. Inflation was beginning to fall in the major industrialized economies, while real interest rates reached historical highs. As a result, speculative investment in commodities as a safeguard against inflation became less attractive, while the lure of financial assets increased. Moreover, the expected crisis caused by a shortage of resources failed to materialize. If anything, quite the opposite occurred. Spurred on by the high commodity prices of the 1970s, many producers expanded output to boost foreign earnings, especially in the developing world. With protracted recession following the second oil shock, demand for raw materials was strongly depressed, causing substantial gluts in world markets. Consequently, prices began to fall almost uniformly across the commodity markets.

Since the middle of 1987, world markets have firmed. Indeed some, most notably nickel, have enjoyed a price explosion. In part, the present rise in prices is a response to the fall of the dollar since 1985. Given that many commodities are priced in the US currency, an upward adjustment in prices is a logical consequence of massive dollar depreciation. At the same time, firmer markets are also the result of evolving supply and demand functions. On the supply side, production has undoubtedly been streamlined since the recession. On the demand side, the continuing world economic growth, which if it has not been spectacular when compared with the 1960s, has nevertheless been fairly constant and is now leading to greater demand as de-stocking by industrial users comes to an end.

Despite these positive developments, it is almost inevitable that the fundamentals of the commodity markets will at some point reassert themselves, pushing prices back on their long term downward trend. This cannot but have a negative impact on the future earnings of London's commodity markets.

In addition, the 1980s have also witnessed an erosion of the physical barriers in the international markets. As in other financial services, de-regulation and globalization, enhanced by advances in communications and data processing have changed the nature of commodity trading. There are now opportunities to trade 24-hours a day from East to West across the globe. The different markets offer endless scope for arbitrage, swapping and holding re-arrangements. These changes have encouraged new agents to enter the market, many of whom have little time for the quaint traditions of the past. As a result competition has toughened, which has not been welcomed by all. As the Metal Bulletin (18 March 1986) noted, "few among the LME traditionalists are enamoured by the new boy on the market — Shearson Lehman — and the abrasive American way it goes about its business. But Shearson reflects tomorrow's world, owing no loyalty, giving no quarter, and asking none."

Crisis at the LME:

If these international trends have not actually borne down hardest on the London Metal Exchange, it has certainly been the most spectacular casualty of abundance. Incorporated in 1877, the LME gained world dominance in time of empire, and even today retains much of its international position. But competition is particularly strong from the American markets: not only do the Chicago exchanges make up the world's largest market for all commodities (though their soft commodity deals tend primarily to be geared to the US domestic market, while their most important business is in financial futures — see below) but the New York Commodities Exchange (Comex) is making a strong pitch at the metals market.

Significantly, the American challenge stems not just from the size and competitiveness from the largest commodity houses but it also follows from the greater diversity and

149

liquidity of these markets. Unlike the British markets, locals account for a large share of market activity. Their behaviour as speculators helps to boost overall capitalization of the market, and so enhances its strength. This comes on top of the stabilizing influence of New York's clearing house facility.

For the time being, however, the LME still offers the only market for lead, nickel, and zinc. It is also a leader in the copper market, having impressively fought off fierce competition from New York. Indeed, LME price quotations in copper are a major indicator of world supply and demand trends, and are frequently used as the basis of many contracts undertaken by producer countries. Furthermore, the Americans still have failed to make any impact in trading aluminium, which has become a key market in the LME. Nevertheless, with the slump in prices over the last few years and increasing competition from the US, the total number of contracts traded on the LME has fallen substantially from its peak of 4.5 million contracts in 1983, to 2.7 million in 1986. In addition to these underlying developments the position of the exchange has been greatly weakened since the tin crisis.

The crisis had its origins in the regulatory obligations undertaken by the International Tin Council (ITC). It was a body representing the governments of the 22 main producers or consumers of tin, who had a vested interest in restricting market fluctuations. To maintain market stability the ITC had established a system of trading through a buffer-stock. It had increasingly taken on the responsibility of buying up surplus tin as world production rose, thus putting a floor under world prices. In October 1985, however, it ran out of money, trying to meet its purchase obligations. As a result the price crashed, and trading on the tin market was suspended. The ITC was left owing millions to members of the LME, and to banks which had lent it money to pay for the tin supporting exercise.

The crisis deepened when the governments members of the ITC showed themselves unwilling to honour the debts of the Council. This directly threatened the LME with bankruptcy as members looked unable to honour their debts among themselves. In March 1986 the tin contracts left outstanding at the time of suspension, were settled by means of an imposed ring-out price of £6,250 per ton. This ring-out price was below the suspension price of £8,140 per ton but above the new March market price of about £5,000 per ton. Nevertheless, problems continue. In April 1988, a Court of Appeal decision backed the member governments of the ITC in their refusal to meet the debt obligations

150

of the Council, so that the £900 million in outstanding losses will have to be carried by traders and their financial backers. Further legal battles are still to be settled.

To some extent members have only themselves to blame. Many brokers knew that ITC was on the verge of bankruptcy but continued to do business in the belief that the member governments would bale it out. The gamble obviously did not pay off, and for a while the future of the exchange looked to be in the balance. Notably, in the immediate wake of the crisis the number of ring members dropped from 28 to 21, while business slumped by 50 percent.

The future success of the LME hinges very much on the reforms undertaken subsequently. These have been aimed at restricting scope for malpractice, while offering tougher safeguards when it does occur. Notably, the requirements of the Financial Services Act have led to the introduction of a clearing system operated by the ICCH. Apart from guaranteeing settlements, it is hoped that the presence of a clearing house will strengthen control in the credit system. With downpayments on trades, dealers will be discouraged from taking up positions they cannot match financially.

Still, there are reservations about the new arrangement. The LME fears a clearing house may prove too expensive for some trade clients and that they would simply cease to use its hedging facilities. The danger is that the reforms introduced to protect the very small number of private investors may well end up scaring away the much more substantial trade business which ensures the present liquidity of the market. Beyond this is the fear that the establishment of a clearing house will reduce the flexibility of the market, again acting to the disadvantage of long established trade customer. Furthermore, it is pointed out the clearing house system did not save Comex the embarrassment of the collapse of the Volume Investors Corporation on the gold market in 1985. Indeed, it is even argued that it was only the unique flexibility and inherent strength of the LME that enabled it to survive the tin crisis, so the establishment of a clearing house is definitely not the solution.

Reform at the LCE and the birth of FOX:

The LCE (which was re-launched as the London FOX or Futures and Options Exchange in June 1987) has also been affected by the weakness of international commodity markets over the last years. However, it has been fortunate to avoid the type of crisis experienced by the LME. Yet, sluggish domestic growth and mounting foreign competition have threatened the LCE's position as a world centre for soft commodity trading. At the same time, it has been faced with a series of internal problems, as markets fragmented, overheads rose and its membership appeared too restrictive and conservative in the face of change. The scandals at Lloyd's and the tin crisis at the LME gave the London markets in general a bad image, and helped fuel the popularity of the LCE's rivals in Paris and New York.

New York is the main rival in the LCE's struggle to increase its share of international business. The market is regulated by the federal government and gives private investors the safety and confidence they require. The large domestic market and the presence of locals increases the liquidity of the New York market, making it more attractive. It competes fiercely with London in the cocoa, coffee, and raw sugar futures contracts. The French have a much smaller commodity exchange but have in recent years been mounting an effective campaign to lure business away from London, especially by introducing a dollar conversion system for off-shore transactions. This allows traders in Paris to hedge against changes in currency rates as well as fluctuations in commodity prices.

Although the early to mid-1980s proved to be very sluggish for the LCE, it finally addressed itself to the need of a more competitive environment. In October 1985, Mr. Saxon Tate was appointed the first fulltime chairman, and set about tackling the administrative problems. In particular, unlike the Terminal Market Associations (TMAs) in various commodities which have always been independently capitalized and run under the umbrella of the LCE, the LCE itself has never been independently capitalized and lacked centralized executive power. Saxon Tate replaced the TMAs with a centralized profit-making company in which the various LCE trading members held shares. This has helped to reduce the fragmentation of the market.

The centralization has also made possible the evolution of an effective marketing and business strategy for the entire market, whereas previously each TMA had to promote its own contract separately. The LCE has adopted a more positive attitude towards selling itself. However, there are criticisms that brokers who operate on the market are still not doing enough. Few firms employ professional marketing personnel, and there seems to be no coherent marketing policy for attracting business in Western Europe especially, where the potential is significant.

Also, attempts have been made to reduce overheads. The LCE succeeded in reducing its clearing fee payments to the ICCH. Furthermore, the problem of declining membership and diminishing liquidity is being tackled. As a result, the LCE has introduced locals. They are granted licences to trade on whatever market they want, but they can only trade on their own account, and are not allowed to carry out any client business. It is hoped that locals will bring significant liquidity to the floor and help shoulder the risks of all other players, as has occurred on the London International Financial Futures Exchange. It was also noticed, that the presence of locals on the New York Exchange cushioned the exchange from the effects of the commodities slump in 1984-85. The hope is that the existence of locals on the London Market will have the same effect.

The LCE has been joined at Commodity Quay by the International Petroleum Exchange which will operate on the same trading floor, while maintaining a separate pit trading system. There have been attempts to woo the LME to Commodity Quay in the hope that a concentration of commodities, both hard and soft, will attract more business for both.

The LCE has also introduced traded options, which look set to be of increasing importance to the market. A traded option is a right a buyer acquires to buy or sell a futures contract, at one of several fixed base prices, for a fixed delivery month. Traded options have proved popular in the United States and have helped to boost liquidity and business — and the exchange. It is hoped that the same will happen in London.

But, the main thrust of the LCE's drive to obtain new business is centred around the private investor. The hope is that some of these investors can be tugged away from the allure of the Stock Exchange and the safety deposit accounts. The LCE noted that marginal returns from private investor business in the United States are becoming more valuable. Furthermore, under the Financial Services Act, the private investor will have considerably more protection. Still, the fear remains on the LCE that the determined drive to recruit private investors may fail, while the new market structure may turn away commercial traders.

It is too early to predict what the effect of these reforms will be on the LCE's competitiveness. The fact that the LCE has at last bitten the bullet may well lead to an improvement in performance, but success will depend on the amount of private investment attracted — especially if commodity prices remain on a long term downward trend. Even so, the increase in business over the next few years is likely to be restrained, and profits will continue to be affected by the current global price weakness of the commodities themselves.

The Baltic Exchange:

Compared to the dramatic events and reforms of the LME and LCE, the Batlic Exchange has maintained a low profile. The bulk of its business remains shipping, although the exchange also houses the Grain and Feed Trade Association (GAFTA) — with futures contracts in grain, potatoes, and (since 1984) meal and soyabean meal. The Baltic Exchange is the only international shipping exchange in the world. If Hamburg, Tokyo and Milan have shipping exchanges where a ship can be found, only at the Baltic can up to thirty quotes for the same type of ship be found in any one day. Partly as a result of the conservative nature of the shipping world (and probably more because of its depressed state), the exchange is confident that its international position is unassailable.

However, since the early 1970s, the world shipping industry has gone from recession to depression. Rates for freight shipping have been declining almost uniformly, so that by the mid-1980s they were at their lowest for 40 years. This is the result, on the one hand of over-capacity in supply. Smaller and less developed countries have been building up their fleets even though the international market continues to suffer from the glut of ships commissioned before the 1973 oil crisis. On the other hand, world trade has slowed down. Consequently, tanker freight rates collapsed after peaking in 1973, while bulk carrier rates contracted dramatically in 1980-81. It is only recently that any signs of a recovery have begun to emerge. Yet, even if the market continues to harden, growth is unlikely ever to return to what it was before the first oil shock.

To try to maintain its earnings, and fall into line with exchange developments across the world, the Baltic Exchange established a futures contract in freight in May 1985 — and the Baltic International Freight Futures Exchange (BIFFEX) was set up. Its purpose is to provide the shipping trade with price protection by reducing the financial risks of buying or selling large quantities of freight space. The specific impetus to establish this futures market came largely from the grain shippers who were concerned to protect their profit margins.

The greatest problem facing the launch of BIFFEX was educating the shipping market in the principles of futures trading. Some of the broker-owners seemed unable or unwilling to grasp the vulgarities of such trading. Still, despite initial worries BIFFEX appears to have been a success. In the first nine months of trading over 50,000 contracts were made, yeilding a total contract value of approximately £460 million. Since then, growth has continued, so that in 1987 172,700 were carried out.

Nevertheless some criticism persisted that the broker-owners have been slow to grasp the value of BIFFEX. Also charges have been made that floor members were not contributing sufficient funds to the marketing of BIFFEX, which concentrated too heavily on its hedging value, while neglecting its speculative benefits. Speculators are needed to increase the liquidity of the exchange. Such problems were borne out by the short existence of the Tanker futures contract. Launched in February 1986 to complement the Dry Cargo contract, it was cancelled at the end of the year because excessive volatility in the index and low liquidity.

Financial futures:

In stark contrast to the struggling performance of the traditional exchanges has been the explosive development of the London International Financial Futures Exchange (LIFFE — pronounced "life"). Unlike the other exchanges which deal in tangible commodities or shipping space, LIFFE trades in money and financial assets.

The origins of this form of dealing date back to the early 1970s. Under rising inflationary pressure, the dollar was forced off the gold standard in 1971, and began to float. This brought about the final collapsed of the Bretton Woods system of fixed international exchange rates, which had prevailed since the end of the war. Suddenly, the world was faced with the spectre of intense currency volatility, as the relative value of national monies was determined by the fluid markets.

The Chicago monetarist Milton Friedman pointed out that currencies, financial assets (like government bonds), and interest rates have effectively become commodities in their price behaviour. Consequently, they too could be traded as such. Trading in "financial futures" could therefore provide the same benefits to those seeking to hedge their risks, as future trading does for those operating in the physical commodity markets. Friedman's

155

theoretical analysis was quickly put into practice by the Chicago Mercantile Exchange (CME), which set up its International Money Market in May 1972. By the end of the year, its financial trading volume totalled 144,000 contracts, made up of six contracts in sterling, Canadian dollars, Deutschmarks, Japanese yen, Mexican peso and Swiss francs.[1]

By the end of 1982 the monthly turnover had reached 1 million contracts. The CME had been joined by other US exchanges in trading financial futures. Its historical rival, the Chicago Board of Trade (CBOT) had become the world centre for trading in US Treasury bond (T-bond) futures. By the mid-1980s T-bonds had become by far the world's largest futures market, dwarfing all other contracts, with an average daily turnover of 150 000 contracts during the first half of 1985.[2]

To try to tap into this booming market and broaden its services available to the international financial community, the City set up its own futures market (in the Royal Exchange). LIFFE opened on 30 September 1982, initially trading in two contracts: 3 month eurodollars and the sterling/dollar exchange rate, with trading volume merely averaging about 4,000 contracts a day during its first six months. Since then, however, business has proliferated. Not only has the volume of contracts expanded markedly, reaching about 60,000 contracts a day during the first quarter of 1988, so has the range of contracts. By the beginning of 1988, 13 future contracts were being dealt, including trades on: short sterling, the eurodollar, US T-bonds, gilts, Financial Times 100 Share Index, and currencies. LIFFE has also followed world trends in setting up option trades on its major contracts. These were first traded in June 1985, and are currently available on seven contracts.[3]

To enhance its position, notably with respect to its European rivals (the Parisian Marché à Terme d'Instruments Financiers and Amsterdam's European Options Exchange) but also against the giants across the Atlantic, LIFFE has established links in the East and West. In October 1986 it opened up trading with the Sydney Futures Exchange on contracts in eurodollar and US T-bond futures. By the end of the year these were each supplemented by an options contract. Similarly, in February 1986 LIFFE announced it had linked up with the Chicago Board of Trade to trade in US T-bonds, Japanese government bonds and eurobonds.

The advantage to the trader of such link-ups is that they permit a position to be opened in one market and then held throughout the day. As a result, the dealer is not obliged to "re-open" a position as trading crosses the time zones, but can carry it over, thus saving transactions costs. The link with the CBOT in particular should provide significant benefits to LIFFE in boosting its international business. Clearly, the London exchange hopes to strengthen its futures trading for the London-based eurobond market, while at the same time locking into the CBOT's hold on the US T-bond market. However, international experience in such link-ups has so far been rather inconclusive, and there is no guaranteeing that the bridge to Chicago will prove a boon for LIFFE.

Indeed, if anything it could even take business away from the London market and British traders in particular. Moves are being made to extend trading hours on the Chicago and other American exchanges. The CBOT, for example, has launched and evening session, running from 6.00 pm until 9.00 pm. There is serious discussion of moving to 24-hour trading. Were this to take place it would clearly wipe out the time-zone advantages of London and all other European centres.

There are, however, obstacles. Most important for the Chicago exchanges is the problem of persuading of traders and especially locals to work in the middle of the night and ensure sufficient market liquidity. A partial alternative to 24 hour trading lies in the development of electronics. Here, the CME has been especially prominent. In September 1987, it announced that it would set up a Post (Pre) Market Trade system (PMT) with Reuters, which would permit screen trading around the world. But it too raises difficulties. First, the issue of regulation has to be tackled, in particular, how electronic trading will be integrated into the market with open outcry. Linked to this is the second major problem of convincing the locals on the CME that the PMT will be to their advantage, and will not just benefit the large (international) broking houses.

If Chicago does succeed, either with 24 hour conventional or electronic trading, it could put a squeeze on the much smaller LIFFE. The Chicago exchanges alone already account for 70 percent of the world's business in futures and options. LIFFE by comparison takes about 5 percent of the world market in financial futures.[4] LIFFE with its 373 seats and less than 70 locals is not big enough, simply cannot provide the the necessary pool of participants or liquidity to match its American rivals.

Still, there are some signs of hope. Most obviously, this lies in the way LIFFE breaks down the traditional barriers of the City. Previously, commodity exchange dealing in Britain was separated from the other financial services and in particular from the investment banking. In America, the tendency is for the large investment banks to be connected with or own commodity trading houses. Given its financial nature, trading on LIFFE was bound to be different. Consequently, most of the major London banks (both British and foreign owned) are represented on the exchange. This should open up trading to much more of the financial community. The Big Bang has been a boon for LIFFE in the gilts market. Where the market was previously dominated by two jobbers, it is now in the hands of 23 market makers, many of them foreign owned. They are increasingly using LIFFE to offset their currency and interest rate risks on gilts using LIFFE.

Unfortunately, the popularity of long gilt futures is leading to a drain of liquidity from the other trading pits. This comes back to the problem of size, which will have to be solved by extending seats on the exchange, through a rights issue. Holding up such an extension is the legal structure of the exchange. As a limited liability company without issued share capital, the issue of new seats would result in a 15 percent VAT payment on existing members. To get round this obstacle, LIFFE plans to convert itself into a company with share capital, and so issue seats enabling holders to deal in less active, and newly created instruments. Such seats would then probably be convertible into full seats after a period of time. The hope of this strategy is that overall market capacity will be boosted, especially through the attraction of locals who could then more easily afford to enter the exchange. At present, seats cost about £220,000 which clearly creates a severe deterrent to individuals seeking to deal on the exchange on their own account.[5]

Beyond such immediate considerations, are the macro questions looming over the whole financial futures industry itself. Continuing currency and financial asset volatility seem set to remain a feature of the world economy for the foreseeable future. Despite repeated efforts by the G7 governments, there appears to be little likelihood of a new international monetary agreement on fixed exchange.

This is itself the product of factors which have created the further demand for financial futures. The desire by national governments to exercise sovereign authority over economic policy is a vital force in generating disequilibria between fiscal and monetary policies across the world. Of course, such sovereignty is not absolute, if indeed it ever, and governments are never entirely free from external constraints. Still, policy differences do occur, and these do affect interest rates, bond values, stock market performance and so on. The need for hedging instruments thus continues. If anything, it is likely to rise given the ever greater flow of capital across frontiers. Originally, such movements had been largely tied to physical trade and/or foreign direct investment. Today, however, world capital flows are increasingly dominated by the search for portfolio investments. Unless there is a concerted international movement to reduce such flows (eg. through the imposition of exchange controls) the demand for financial futures will continue to rise, probably substantially.

There are, however, some dangers in this development. These were demonstrated by the recent world stock exchange crash. The 508 point plunge of the Dow Jones index on 19th October 1987 has sparked a live controversy over the potential destabilizing role of financial futures. Specifically, the use of stock exchange index futures, programme trading and portfolio insurance have been cited as significant contributory factors to the speed with which the New York Stock Exchange crashed. This has led many, both inside and outside the markets to question the desirability of the unregulated use of such instruments. Should regulation eventually follow, it would doubtless encumber the development of the financial futures markets.

Foreign earnings by the traders:

Official statistics for the earnings of the exchange traders do not break down precisely in the same manner as the sector has been treated here. In particular, there are no figures given for LIFFE. This is probably due to the fact that the exchange is both a newcomer to the London market, and a composite organization whose members are spread across the City's traditional institutions.

The information available, therefore, is broken up into two main income series. One covers the net earnings generated by British commodity brokers. These arise from services which included brokerage in respect to physical trade conducted between foreign countries; as well as transaction charges in the futures market and premium earnings on traded options carried out by UK residents for foreigners, less UK business undertaken on foreign exchanges. The other income stream, given in the CSO Pink Book, covers the earnings of the Baltic Exchange for brokerage services rendered in respect to "chartering, sales and purchases of ships and aircraft, and miscellaneous associated activities".

Beginning with the commodity markets, two main features stand out. First, the decade until 1986 was defined above all by very strong fluctuations in foreign earnings, in many

159

ways mirroring in the state of world markets. Second, the real level of these revenues diminished in the process. Having peaked at between £200 and £210 million in 1975 and 1976, the foreign income stagnated for the rest of the decade, only picking up again in 1982 and 1983. Subsequently, revenue has fallen again, virtually returning to its level of the mid-1970s. Given the strength of inflation during the period, this represents a significant contraction of real earnings.

The performance of the Baltic Exchange is not that much better. Until 1981 nominal income rose in every year, except 1980, peaking at £287 million. Then, revenues on the exchange entered a two-year dip, but recovered somewhat in 1984, although to a lower level than previously. In the two following years, however, a renewed slump set in, with income falling to £221 million. Again, these figures are in current prices, so real income has fallen considerably more since its 1981 record.

Notes and references:

1.   Financial Times, September 13 1982.
2.   Financial Times survey, *Financial Futures and Options*, December 11, 1985.
3.   LIFFE.
4.   Financial Times survey, *Financial futures and Options*, March 10, 1988, and Euromoney.
5.   Financial Times survey, 1988 ibid

H. McRae and F. Cairncross, *Capital City, London as a Financial Centre*, Methuen, 1985.
C.W.J. Granger (editor), *Trading in Commodities*, Woodhead-Faulkner, 1983.

 Numerous articles from the following journals:
Futures World.
Metal Bulletin Monthly.
Shipping Journal.
The Economist.
Far Eastern Economic Review.

The Bank of England Quarterly Bulletin.

The information offices of the Baltic Exchange, FOX, LIFFE and LME.

PART 4

10 Consulting engineering

Introduction:

The world market for consulting engineering is in a bad state. For most of this decade it has been wracked by volatility and slumping markets. Since its 1981 record of $130 billion, international contracting has fallen to just under $75 billion dollars, the downturn in real activity (ie. after inflation and exchange rate movements) being even greater.[1]

The retrenchment of the 1980s contrasts sharply with the world boom in overseas work during the 1970s. Ironically, however, the causes of the recent decline are a reaction to the causes that led to such substantial growth previously. More than anything else, the construction boom of 1970s was sparked by the surge in commoditiy prices early in the decade, culminating in the first oil-shock in 1973-4. This had a multiple effect on the world economy, with consequences for international contracting.

In the first place, the supply shock of the quadrupling in oil prices plunged the industrialized world into recession. Overall demand crashed. At the same time, the long boom had already ensured that most major infrastructural work had been carried out in the OECD, notably the massive re-building of post-war Europe and Japan. With new opportunities limited and capital curtailed, construction was reined in.

But, the sudden switch of huge revenues to OPEC (and to some degree other commodity producers) unleashed a vast wave of demand in the Third World. Development programmes were initiated, aimed at creating an economic and social infrastructure in the shortest possible time. Projects for roads, bridges, airports, irrigation facilities, hospitals, schools or even whole cities were launched to develop the barren wastelands of Arabia and Persia. Further plans were launched to build up heavy industry, most obviously in petrochemicals. Elsewhere, construction was also fostered by the re-cycling of oil revenues. Latin American, in particular, soaked up capital that was being funnelled through the international banking system. There too the pursuit of western, concrete modernity helped underpin global contractors.

When the second oil shock occurred at the turn of the decade, the picture altered. It is true that the renewed flood of funds to the oil producers helped strengthen demand in the

Middle East especially. In addition, the higher price of oil generated production in fields previously uneconomic. This too will have led to new construction spending in the developing world. Mexico stands out as the notable example.

But other events were beginning to undermine global growth for the industry. Some were political, like the Iranian Revolution. Its bitter reaction to the Shah's modernization (to say nothing of his oppression) placed a severe question mark over future development projects, as did the Iran/Iraq war.

Yet, worse was to come. The second oil shock lasted longer than the first. Activity in the industrialized world remained weak until the end of 1982. Consequently, international trade slumped and the demand for commodities stagnated. Given that many producers had greatly expanded their supply capacity since the heady days of the early 1970s, prices went into a tail-spin. The resulting current account crunch was then further tightened as world interest rates soared, under the impact of US fiscal and monetary policies. There followed the unleashing of the Third World debt crisis in 1982, as borrowers were no longer able to meet their obligations.

The macroeconomic implications of these balance of payments difficulties for all Third World demand, including that of the construction industry, are obvious enough. From a micro-perspective this sector was also subject to particular pressures. The rise of interest rates has had the effect of making many projects uneconomic, especially where they involve a long pay-back time. This has been a growing problem not just for national governments or private banks, but also the international development agencies. With the financial capacity of the LDCs reduced, the relative role of the World Bank and its regional counter-parts has been enhanced. They, however, are facing rising difficulties in finding profitable projects, while at the same time not being able to subsidize projects in a way that national governments can.[2]

For such reasons, the absolute level of activity (expressed in current dollars) of the world's largest 250 international contractors fell 9 percent in 1982. This was followed by a plunge of 24 percent in 1983 and 14 percent in 1984. A respite in 1985 proved temporary, as the logic of commodity market strangulation finally hit oil. Since their surge at the turn of the decade, petroleum prices had been weakening gradually. Nevertheless, it was not until Saudi Arabia abandoned its role as "swing producer" in late 1985 that the rout took place. As the cost of crude halved, international construction tumbled another 9 percent in 1986. All told, overseas earnings by the world's top 250 have therefore fallen by over 40 percent between 1981 and 1986 (see Table 10.1).[3]

Table 10.1: **FOREIGN BILLINGS OF TOP 250 CONTRACTORS WORLDWIDE, BY CONTINENT - in current US Dollars (billions).**

	1981 US$bn	%	1986 US$bn	%
World	130.6	100	73.9	100
Mideast	47.2	36	16.1	22
Asia	21.4	16	17.3	23
Africa	23.9	18	13.1	18
Europe	9.8	8	11.9	16
North America	10.9	8	10.4	14
Latin America	17.4	13	5.2	7

Source: Engineering News Record, 15 July 1982 and 16 July 1987

The evolution of "design" trade has been less tumultuous. In the first place, it did not reach its peak until 1983, and then when the contraction came it was not compounded year after year in the same way. Instead, the 1984 downturn was followed by a partial revival the year after, though 1986 did also witness a renewed fall, so that nominal earnings were down 8 percent on the 1983 record.[4]

To be sure, design work is a relatively minor facet of the overall world construction industry. International turnover during the 1980s has fluctuated between a "mere" $3.5 to $4 billion — as opposed to gyrating between $130 and $75 billion in contracting. Nevertheless, its importance to service trade is considerable because the output of design work is exported directly and so contributes most of its earnings to the current account. By comparison, contracting tends to involve heavy expenditure on physical inputs to a project. These can either be supplied locally, as is the case of manpower, or they can be imported, as for machinery etc. Either way, the such inputs represent the largest share of project expenditure, so that the pure (traded) service component is relatively small.

The changing nature of the international market:

The shrinking size of the cake has had a marked effect on its partition and composition. Not surprisingly, the market is no longer dominated by the Middle East. From a high point of 42 percent of all billings, the region just slipped into second place behind Asia, in 1986. The other main contracting market has been Latin America, where the share crashed in 1982. The weight of Africa has fluctuated considerably, but without revealing any discernible upward or downward trend. In contrast, the relative positions of Europe and North America have improved, as these regions have more or less maintained their (nominal) spending levels.

From the point of view of the supplier, the shrinking world market has greatly toughened competition. This is especially so given the historical trend of new contractors emerging from within the Third World. Numerous developing countries (eg. Brazil and Singapore) have acquired the technical ability to carry out their own contracting, as part of a broader movement of into services. Others, South Korea and Turkey, have even become aggressive overseas producers, relying on the access to cheap manpower to enhance their cost advantages. Equally serious to traditional exporters in North America and Europe is the growing market share of Japan. It rose from 7.6 percent of the world total, in 1982, to 12.7 by 1986.

A factor in this Japanese success stems from the changing nature of competitive tender in large overseas contracts. Spurred on by the financial crisis of the LDCs, a vital component of any deal has become the financing package which the supplier can offer. In practice, this frequently means that loans on projects are "soft", or carry comparatively low interest rates. In turn the latter are increasingly supported by government subsidy, often linked to official aid. The Japanese have been particularly successful in harnessing such government support to their overseas contracting business.

The Japanese have also shown themselves to be adept counter-traders. Also known as barter-trade, this occurs when payment on a project (or any import) is made with physical goods. Typically these are commodities exported by the developing country, especially when the project itself is geared to raising output of oil, metals, agricultural products or whatever. Clearly such payments are difficult for the recipient. First is the problem of selling the commodities and converting them into cash, but this is accompanied by the danger of price fluctuations altering the revenue value of payment. Fortunately, the risk factor can often be reduced through hedging in the futures markets, or the creation of an "escrow" account. The latter is an account into which the income from sale of the commodities is placed by the producer, until the agreed price of the construction deal has been reached. In this case, the risk of any price fluctuation falls entirely on the customer of the project.[5]

Not surprisingly, the issue of counter-trade has become significant as the Third World debt problem has grown, and commodity markets have remained weak. In placing orders, a developing country will obviously favour contractors who will accept payment in physical goods, taking the responsibility for their subsequent sale. The capacity for handling such deals built up by the Japanese trading houses helps explain the growing importance of Japanese contractors.

Lastly, there has been a qualitative shift in the services required of the foreign contractor. It arises as the emphasis of consulting work moves away from design and construction alone, to include the more efficient use of resources once as the project nears completion, and indeed beyond. Greater capacity utilization, more stringent cost control, tighter planning and the general strengthening of the business management are unfolding as key functions of consulting work.

Along with this trend to the provision of general technical assistance, has been the emerging desire of the host countries to see more work carried out locally. This enables governments not only to reduce the current account expenditure of a project, and also nurture domestic talent in such high-skill service activities. The implication for international consulting companies is the need to exploit overseas markets through the establishment of subsidiary organizations. Again, it entails a substitution of trade through export by trade through establishment.[6]

The UK — fighting to maintain its position:

Not surprisingly, the UK too has suffered with the downturn of the world market. Nevertheless, it has strengthened its comparative position. Thus, whereas UK firms accounted for only 6.1 percent of all international contractors' billings in 1982, by 1986 their share had risen to 9.5 percent. Unfortunately, this still represented a reduction in current dollars of $0.5 billion — down to $7.0 billion in 1986. In the area of design, Britain's relative position scarcely changed. Over the same period, the share of international awards fell marginally, from 13.8 percent of the total, to 13.6 percent. However, the greater resilience of this sector meant that dollar earnings by British companies actually rose from $481 million to $514 million (see Table 10.2).[7]

In terms of Britain's trade account, the effect of such market share maintenance has been a relative stability in sterling earnings. Rising until 1982, Britain's foreign income for consulting engineering oscillated in a fairly narrow band for four years, between £560 and £580 million. It was not until the disastrous fall in 1986 that a noticeable retrenchment occurred, when revenues slumped by nearly 10 percent (see Table 11.4 in next chapter).[8]

Table 10.2: RELATIVE POSITION OF BRITISH CONTRACTORS AND
DESIGNERS IN WORLD'S TOP 250/200 IN 1986

	Contractors		Designers	
Nationality:	No of firms	% of Billings	No of firms	% of Billings
American	43	30.6	49	25.9
Japanese	29	12.7	12	6.2
Korean	14	3.5	4	1.5
European	126	45.5	106	55.3
Italian	35	10.0	-	-
French	18	9.6	15	8.6
British	17	9.5	26	13.6
German	17	7.5	21	8.0
Other	39	9.0	44	25.1
Turkish	9	3.0	-	-
All other	29	4.7	29	11.1
TOTAL	250	US$ 73.9bn	200	US$ 3.54bn

Source: Engineering News Record, 16 July 1987 and 6 August 1987

Turning to the regional distribution of Britain's foreign activities, it is interesting to note that British contracting companies are not necessarily strong in the same continents as British design firms. Also, the pattern of relative strength has changed in the period 1982 to 1986. In the Asian, African and Latin American markets contractors improved their comparative ranking, while in the Middle East it declined. Design firms, on the other hand, more or less maintained their relative position in all the major Third World regions, except Latin America.

Taking the longer perspective, conventional wisdom about overseas construction and design work holds that British firms are being squeezed across the Third World in general, and especially in the old colonial markets. To some extent, this is application of the economic retreat-from-Empire theory. Whilst Britannia still ruled the waves, British products from Lancashire wool to Sheffield steel had captive markets in every corner of the globe. As political imperialism ended with World War II, the existing international pattern of trade still gave the United Kingdom a substantial advantage in exporting or servicing these markets. This structure has, however, been slowly but surely eroded through the growth of domestic production and the penetration of these markets by exporters from other developed economies.

Although hard statistical evidence is hard to come by, there can be no doubt former colonial markets for consulting engineering have been similarly besieged or even conquered. Early competition was certainly led by the United States, as corporate America went global in the 1950s and 1960s. Even today, the Kelloggs, Parsons and Bechtels dominate the contracting league table (with the US still taking 30 percent of foreign billings in 1986).

More recently, the challenge has been led by regional producers. Thus the Japanese have emerged as the major contractors in the Asian market, as have the Koreans. In the Middle East, the Turks have become a force to be reckoned with, having not only a cost advantage in manpower, but also a greater cultural affinity to the Islamic world. In Latin America, a higher level of development, together with a tradition of economic nationalism, has led to considerable self-sufficiency in this as in other services.

As a result, Africa remains the continent which perhaps offers most to British companies — at least in relative terms. But here too, competition is also fierce, not just from the heavyweights of the US and Japan, but also from the other main European countries. In France, Britain has a tough colonial rival with continuing strong links to West (francophone) Africa. A more concrete factor is the economic aid which France and Italy especially are prepared to use to gain consulting works.

The growing importance of financial assistance, through soft loans, direct grants and other forms of development aid has already been pointed out above. It is in these areas that British contractors and designers face one of their toughest hurdles. Unlike other governments which accept and are prepared to support overseas contracts through the use of such subsidies, the Conservative government of Mrs Thatcher has been very reluctant to do so.

To be sure, the institutional vestiges of interventionism still exist. Under the Fixed Rate of Export Finance (FREF — introduced in the 1960s) the Export Credits Guarantee Department (ECGD) has a mechanism whereby private banks financing a project are reimbursed when market interest rates exceed the fixed payment rate agreed for the project. Unfortunately, the world recession of the early 1980s greatly damaged the

169

financial position of the ECGD. In addition, FREF has come under increasing scrutiny from the House of Commons Public Accounts Committee which is concerned about the cost-effectiveness of the scheme, as well as the foreign share of sub-contracting generated by projects.

Implications for the future:

Given both the present government's ideological hostility to state intervention, and a general lack of interest in development as reflected in the tight rein on official aid, it is to be expected that British consultants will continue to suffer a competitive disadvantage in the financial sphere. Recently, the loss of the contract for a second bridge over the Bosphorus became a *cause célèbre* for the industry. The order went to a Japanese-Italian consortium, rather than Trafalgar House, because the Japanese government put up a soft loan for the deal.[9]

More generally, the pressure on foreign work, and hence foreign earnings is likely to remain in this sector. Despite the relative strength shown by British contractors and especially designers over the last few years, the limitations of the international market make it highly unlikely that there will be a substantial rise in overseas income in the foreseeable future. Indeed, the best British producers are likely to be able to do, is to maintain their foreign income, although even this could turn out to be a tall order.

Although Asia just pipped the Middle East as the world's leading market in 1986, and the overall development of this region is substantial, it seems unlikely that it will replace the huge demand which once flowed out of the Middle East. In the first place, the continent will never experience the cash injection that accrued to the oil states with the the two price explosions. Building up a cumulative current account surplus as part of a process of export-led growth is not the same thing. It does not trigger a comparable surge in spending. Directly linked to this, is the fact that Asia does not exist as a bloc in the international trading system in the same way as OPEC did in 1973. Thus, if there are some countries whose balance of payments permit substantial construction, others are quite clearly not in this position. Also many of the more prosperous Asian states — like South Korea and Taiwan, but also Malaysia and even Thailand — already have sufficient domestic expertise not to have to import consulting services on a large scale. Where they do not have certain capacities themselves, it seems more likely they will turn to regional suppliers, especially Japan. Asia, therefore, appears unlikely to be the future bonanza for Western and hence British companies.

Nor is there much joy likely to come out of the Middle East. Unless global supply and demand conditions change radically, it seems unlikely that the petroleum market will improve dramatically. Indeed, at present OPEC is having enough trouble just holding prices firm in between $15 and $20 dollars. This puts a ceiling on spending in the region. Furthermore, much of the basic development of the region, at least in the major oil exporters is already complete. Exceptions are Iran and Iraq, who will no doubt need reconstruction if and when the war finishes. This leaves the poorer nations of the region (notably Egypt). They could generate demand, but they lack the necessary resources to translate need into purchasing power.

Lack of resources, or more specifically a crucial shortage of foreign capital arising from the debt burden, will also continue to constrain demand in the rest of the Third World. This is not just the case for Latin America where the absolute size of debt is largest, but also in Africa where the weight of debt relative to national GDP and exports tends to be even greater. In the absence of a definite solution to the debt question demand for imports of any sort, including consulting, will be severely limited.

The upshot of these factors is likely to be a growing introversion by contractors. They will be increasingly forced to look to domestic markets and those of the other industrialized nations. However, competition in this market too will be exceedingly tough, given that demand is likely to remain restrained due to slow growth.

Notes and references:

1. The source for these figures are successive annual surveys (1981 to 1987) carried out by the *Engineering News Record*, on the overseas work by the world's largest 250 international contractors. They are printed every July.
2. Jeff Ody, *Multitechnology Engineering: the borderlines get hazier*, Civil Engineering, August 1985.
3. ibid Engineering News Record.
4. Again, the *Engineering News Record* conducts an annual survey of the performance of the world's 200 largest design firms. They are published each August.
5. Alan Dickey, *Selling aeroplanes for peanuts*, The Engineer, 4 December 1986.
6. ibid Jeff Ody.
7. ibid Engineering News Record.
8. CSO, *"Pink Book", United Kingdom Balance of Payments*, HMSO, 1987.
9. Contract Journal, 6 November 1986.

11 Business services

Introduction:

More than any other sector, business services are an American phenomenon. With its huge accounting houses, its schools of management science, legions of lawyers and batteries of advertising agencies, the American market represents half or more of the world turnover in these industries. Not surprisingly, therefore, the United States government is at the forefront of pushing for the global liberalization of service trade. It is a policy, exemplified by the introduction of services on to the GATT agenda at the start of the "Uruguay round".

How is this American domination explained? At its base is the size and the economic development of the United States. With the advent of the Second Industrial Revolution, the harnessing of science and technology to industrial production and consumption, the US rapidly moved ahead of Britain as the world's largest economic power. This ascendancy no doubt owed much to geographical providence. America's national hinterland is continental, its natural resources are abundant, and war has stimulated economic development, rather than destroying it. But the strength of the US economy also owes much to cultural factors.

Primary amongst them is the fluidity of American society. Founded in the revolution of free men against autocracy, the United States set out to be a community upholding the equality of opportunity. In its pure sense, the goal of course turned out to be Utopian. Nevertheless, flawed though the American Dream may be, it has always been vital to society and distinguishes the New World from the Old. Even today, a visitor from Europe cannot but be impressed by the individual mobility — in its geographic, social, or economic form — which remains so much part of the United States.

A corollary to the Dream, the belief that anyone can attain anything by his or her own effort, is an equally strong faith in the perfectibility of self, notably through the application of reason and science. A trivial manifestation of this is the huge number of "how to" books sold in the American market. Texts on how to be a hostess, a writer, or a salesman cover every aspect of human behaviour, social, creative, or the all important commercial. Such books, and the psychology behind their appeal, assume that the secret

173

of success, if not genius, can be disaggregated into its constituent parts, communicated and taught to the reader, who can adopt and re-assemble them, and so too be successful. Combined with such social mobility and self-improvement, the comparative youth and immigrant nature of American society, lend themselves to a willingness to experiment, to seek out the new. And then communicate it.

It is, of course, very difficult in any social science, if not incorrect, to draw specific conclusions from cultural phenomena. Causality, even where it exists, is almost never unilinear. At the same time, it does seem probable that the character traits of American society mentioned here do have a direct bearing on the economy. The political philosophy of individualism on which the American constitution is based, for example, is directly translated into economic philosophy. Thus the legal framework of the US deliberately seeks to uphold the free market and limit the concentration of power either in the hands of government or private monopoly. Beyond this, the characteristics go a long way to explaining the continuing entrepreneurial drive exhibited by the US economy, measured in terms of the number of small businesses set up each year, the proliferation of venture capital and the huge success in creating jobs, etc.

It is the contention here that they have also been important in shaping the growth of business services. For example, it could be argued that the mobility and openness of American society, helped foster the development of publicly listed companies, and contributed to the separation of ownership and control. It did not in Germany, where the real thrust of industrialization occurred at the same time as in the United States. Even today, the importance of publicly listed companies to the German economy remains limited. Similarly, industrialization in Japan was also led by a small number of family controlled *zaibatsu*. Their economic power was only broken up after the war by the US occupation.

The separation of ownership from control goes a long way to explaining the development of business services. The evolution of accountancy was determined by a need for managers to explain their activities to company shareholders. Similarly, the separation has gone hand in hand with the drive to technocracy, which has become so much part of the world economy, but perhaps the United States in particular.[1] The application of reason and the scientific process has affected not just the technical side of America's economic mechanism but also the business side. The belief that management could be treated like a science, which can be progressively developed and perfected, has been instrumental to the rise of management consultancy. So too has been the willingness to accept outside advice. It has been underpinned by mobility, as managers constantly move in and out of jobs and companies. Even with America's economic power now in relative decline, many parts of its economic system, and especially its business management, are still seen as models for the rest of the world.

Given the importance of cultural factors in the development of US business services, it is not surprising to find that they also play a vital role in shaping the international supply of these services. Their provision frequently entails the establishment of foreign operations, because of their culturally specific nature and the restricted legal environment within which they have to operate. Unlike a physical item, services cannot be wrapped up and posted off to a customer, even in the home market. Instead, their supply involves a degree of local, or on-site production. Alternatively, their distribution itself becomes part of the productive process. And both may be subject to local legislation. This is especially the case for legal and accountancy services in which practice tends to be severely regulated. Statutory government regulation, backed up by supervision through official, non-governmental bodies, greatly circumscribes their free, competitive provision.

Additional restrictions arise from immigration control and government procurement. Governments, especially where they are nurturing industries, try to protect domestic producers as much as possible, and strict controls of working papers are one form of non-tariff barrier that can be used. Similarly, governments often employ nationalist procurement policies when consuming business services themselves. Accordingly, it has been estimated that direct export contributes only 8 percent of US foreign accounting earnings, 15 percent for advertising, 45 percent of management consultancy earnings, but more than 95 percent of legal earnings.[2]

Accountancy, the background:

Accountancy is a prime example of a service industry dominated by international firms, but in which production predominantly takes place in national markets. Thus, if the world's major firms are multinational partnerships, the individual national components are largely run by local partners.

175

The cause of this structure for is the regulatory and licensing framework within which accounting, as a producer service, functions. Following the legal requirement of firms to provide annual audited accounts (in the UK this came into law with the 1948 Companies Act), the industry is highly country-specific. Enforcing this system are the professional bodies which regulate the detailed execution of accounting, and especially auditing. Accordingly, in the UK, the profession is governed by six national institutes, each incorporated by Royal charter. These comprise the three national institutes (the Institutes of Chartered Accountants of England and Wales, of Scotland and of Ireland), two international institutes and one geared to the public sector. Only members of national institutes may call themselves "chartered accountants", and only they, together with the members of the Chartered Association of Certified Accountants are licensed to carry out legal audits.

Total fee earnings from audit work in the UK have been estimated at about £1 billion.[3] Furthermore, after the hard times of the 1970s and early 1980s growth is presently running at around 20 percent per annum.[4] Nevertheless, the key phenomenon to have affected the industry over the last two decades has been the shift into other business services. As a result, audit revenues today only represent about half all earnings.

This transition has occurred in response to a series of push and pull factors. With the decline of the British economy during the 1970s and into the early 1980s the operating environment for accountants also became much harsher. Competition has toughened considerably, as was lately reflected, for example, by the profession's acceptance of advertising in 1984. Consequently, the industry has been progressively propelled to seek other sources of revenue.

At the same time, the possibilities for offering new business services also expanded. Already by the 1960s the international expansion of US multinational companies, which began after World War II, was leading to the proliferation of new producer services worldwide. As this process continued, and especially as the large US accounting firms increasingly came to dominate the British market, UK accountants developed their expertise in numerous areas of management and finance. New services became integrated into the package of products the large accounting houses could offer their clients. They cover such areas as: acturial work, litigation, "start-up" consulting for small firms, corporate finance management buy-out, and public flotation advice for larger companies, to say nothing of management consultancy.

176

Paradoxically, a key advantage to the accountants in their quest for generating new services has been the role as company auditors. Being able to look into the guts of any commercial organization clearly provides accountants with a high degree of exclusive information and so provides a excellent base for carrying out other duties. An additional advantage arising out of their audit work has been the long experience accountants have gained in Information Technology (IT). Due to its repetitive and rigid legal structure, book-keeping was one of the first office functions to be computerized. Consequently, capacity in the profession for dealing with IT emerged early on, and this has given accountants a comparative advantage in the areas of IT systems consultancy.

The impact of these factors on the structure of the industry has been significant. Above all else, it has led to a domination of the British market by the large, multinational, American firms. The world's "Big 8" companies are also the leaders in the British market. Furthermore, the mega-merger between Peat Marwich McLintock and Klynveld Main Goerdeler (KMG) in 1986, which formed the world's largest accounting firm with over 5000 partners, suggests that the tendency to concentration and domination by the international giants is set to continue. Not surprisingly, this is creating a tightening squeeze on medium sized firms (ie. those with an income of between £7 and £20 million pounds). Specifically, these firms are being pushed out of the audit market on the one hand, whilst not having the size to match the large firms' expansion into newer services on the other (see Table 11.1).

Table 11.1:   TOP 8 INTERNATIONAL ACCOUNTANCY FIRMS

	Turnover 1985-86	Growth %	Partners
KMG[1]	2600	n/a[2]	5200
Arthur Andersen[3]	1924	21	1847
Coopers & Lybrand	1700	22	3075
Ernst & Whinney	1492	26	1640
Price Waterhouse	1488	21	2291
Arthur Young	1427	23	2572
Deloitte Haskins & Sells	1188	20	2192
Touche Ross	1151	18	2600

(1)   Merged of KMG and Peat Marwick McLintock.
(2)   Created by merger of Peat Marwick and KMG. No comparable figures available.
(3)   Andersen reports fees up by 20 percent to US$2.315bn in year to 31.3.87.

Source: Financial Times Special Survey, Nov 20, 1987.

Again, audit work is playing a key role in such structural change. This follows from the evolution of the company audit as a standardized commodity which firms are increasingly prepared to purchase through competitive tender, rather than simply placing their business with the company accountant. Competition on price alone is, therefore, becoming more important, which in turn favours the larger accounting houses. They have the economies of scale and the financial backing to offer substantial discounts (up to 40 to 50 percent) on audit work, with the aim of securing customers for their other services.[5]

Current and future challenges:

The movement to ever bigger companies, however, does have its disadvantages. From a managerial point of view, it throws up the question of organizational control over international partnerships, whose partners run into the thousands. More concretely, size is running into the problems of capital shortage as these partnerships seek to expand. There has followed an intense debate within the profession over the acceptance of incorporation (ie. the introduction of outside ownership). To date, the Institute of Chartered Accountants in England and Wales (ICAEW) has officially come out against such measures, arguing that it would jeopardize the independence and hence professional integrity of firms, and could even lead to outright abuse when clients own shares in the auditors.

Complicating the question are present plans by the Department of Trade and Industry to implement the European Community's eighth Company Law Directive by 1990. It will provide the basis for the next UK Companies Act, with the aim of bringing UK legislation more into line with the rest of the EC. Significantly, the eighth Directive allows for 49 percent outside ownership of accounting firms as well as limited liability — measures which are both known on the continent where the division between statutory auditors and other accountants is much stronger.

Limited liability would answer another rising concern of the accountants. It follows from the insurance crisis facing firms, sparked off by the surge in litigation against accountants (acting not just as auditors but also as management consultants) during the first half of the 1980s. On both sides of the Atlantic accounting houses have suddenly found themselves facing charges of incompetence and negligence from failed clients (eg. the DeLorean motor company's suit against Arthur Andersen). This explosion in legal

178

action has not only caused a substantial rise in the cost of premiums, but has also threatened to lead to a loss of cover as insurance companies have withdrawn from the market of professional liability. One obvious way out for the accountants is therefore to seek the implementation of some form of liability limitation.

If limited liability and incorporation are accepted, it is possible that statutory measures will be undertaken to ensure against abuse. Notably, the eighth Directive sets out to separate audit work from other consulting, thus paving the way for stricter demarcation between the various aspects of the industry. This again, however, underlines the complexity of reform, especially where it is conducted within a multinational forum.

The problems surrounding the directive, together with the existing structure of the international industry, indicate the severe limitations on trade in accounting services. Even if statutory regulations, licensing agreements, as well as training and qualifications are harmonized within the EC by 1992 (or indeed later on in the 1990s), it is far from clear that direct trade in accountancy will grow significantly, given the continuing prevalence of differing business traditions. Furthermore, the big move to internationalizing the supply of services — through the creation of international partnerships — has already provided a structure in which overseas markets can be exploited successfully. It therefore seems unlikely that the industry itself will feel the need to foster radically new and extensive ways of crossing national boundries; that is to say, that the share of trade earnings out of total foreign earnings (ie. trade and repatriated profits) will rise much beyond its present 25 percent.

What does seem more likely is that the concentration of services will continue. The dominance of the "Big 8" seems set to go on — with perhaps one or two additions or subtractions arising through merger or organic growth. As multinational partnerships, or even incorporated companies, they will be able to expand their hold on the global market, no doubt profiting from de-regulation and standardization measures, such as the EC's drive to a single market by 1992.

Management consultancy:

Compared to accountancy, management consultancy is a far more open, fluid and sometimes nebulous *métier*. Where accounting is government-regulated, institute

179

controlled and audit-determined, management consulting is carried out by free spirits combining professionalism and charade. From the perspective of trade, it is a far more marketable commodity, with direct exports representing a far higher share of foreign revenues than in accounting.

The reasons it differs from accounting lie in both the supply and the demand side of the market. Most obviously, and in absolute contrast with accounting, management consultancy does not fulfill any specific legal requirements for firms. It is therefore not subject to statutory or other official regulation. Nor does it have the barriers to entry which exist for accounting. What licensing does occur is limited, providing a quality guarantee rather than a permit to practice.

Beyond these factors, the causes for the extreme openness of the industry stem from the large diversity of activities that have evolved over time. Consulting as such, arguably began with the invention of time-and-motion studies during the latter part of the 19th Century. They comprised of analyses of the physical production process, with the aim of rationalizing the flow of functions — effectively bringing greater efficiency to bear on the division of labour.

At the same time, Arthur D. Little spread the appliance of science to the management end of business, so that the service activities of production were also subordinated to a rationalized, controlled process. The next new element to enter consulting was the focus on financial control. Pioneered by James O. McKinsey in the mid 1920s this aspect of consultancy has emerged as a major part of the business, helped especially by its close association with accounting. The most significant post-war development in the industry has been the emergence of strategy consultancy, first formulated by Bruce Henderson, who launched the Boston Consulting Group (BCG) in 1963.

Triggered by these innovations and promoted by the expansion and rising sophistication of the world economic mechanism since 1945, the growth of the industry has been spectacular. Thus, for example, the number of consultants in the United States rose three times from the mid 1960s to a approximately 50,000 by the late 1970s. In the UK the largest indigenous company, PA, had only 6 consultants in 1943, 370 in 1963 but over 1300 (in 22 countries) by 1984.[6] All told, it has been estimated that there are currently about 100,000 consultants worldwide, generating an annual fee income of $10 billion.[7]

Propelling this growth, and at the same time derived from it, have been the vast changes. These can be grouped as follows:[8]

1. The diversification of services in response to new areas of commercial activity, as well as environmental changes in the social, political and economic framework of the industrialized and developing world.

2. The emergence of new technology, in particular the rise of IT technology and its effect on all parts of production and management.

3. The rise of more aggressive business promotion strategies.

4. Entry of the "Big 8" accounting firms into management consulting in the early 1960s. By the 1980s they had become major players in a field which in turn was contributing between 15 and 20 percent of their earnings.

5. Growth of internal consulting with industrial and commercial companies.

6. Progress in the methodology of consulting, in particular a growing emphasis on client's participation.

7. Heightened customer competence, in defining the types of consultancy and hence supplier required.

The effect of these changes has been to broaden the services available under the generic heading of management consultancy. Despite the drive to specialization which has affected the industry (as it has all other parts of the modern economy), strategy consulting still remains an important part of the industry. More concretely, however, consulting has increasingly focused on general and specific areas of management, company finance, the organization of production, marketing and sales networks, as well as the development of personnel and human resources.

An important result of the very diffuse nature of services offered by the industry has been the strong fragmentation of its structure. To be sure, the mega-firms dominate the top end of the market (see Table 11.2). They are huge, international organizations, with representation across the globe facilitating the service of multinational clients etc. At the other end of the scale, are the thousands of small consultancies, frequently little more than one-man-bands. They too can find a niche in the market, precisely because of its diversity. Notably, their advantage lies with specializing in particular areas of consultancy, limiting themselves to a restricted geographic catchment area, and in developing more intimate client relations and customizing their service.

The basis for the demand of business consultancy has always been the desire to secure independent and technical knowledge not available within an existing company. The objectivity which the outside advice should provide rests on numerous factors. First and foremost, the consultant is financially independent of the company and to some extent the decisions or recommendations he/she makes. (This is not always the case, notably when fees are linked to performance improvements.) Beyond this, and in many ways of greater importance, is the administrative independence of the consultant. As an external adviser he does not have a political or emotional stake in how the company runs and ought therefore be able to provide his service in a totally impartial manner. (Such independence and the potential for change and disruption are also the indirect cause of much employee friction which often arises when consultants are called in.)

Table 11.2: INTERNATIONAL MANAGEMENT CONSULTING, 1986

Rank	Name of Firm	Type*	Revenues $m	1982 Ranking
1	Arthur Andersen	A	640	1
2	McKinsey	G	400	2
3	Towers Perrin Forster & Crosby	H/G	370	3
4	Mercer-Meidinger	H	360	6
5	Booz Allen & Hamilton	G	340	5
6	Peat Marwick	A	340	7
7	Coopers & Lybrand	A	305	8
8	Ernst & Whinney	A	280	10
9	Wyatt	H	270	-**
10	Arthur Young	A	200	11
10	Bain	G	200	17

* A=Accounting Firm G=General Consultant H=Human Resources Specialist
** Not in the top 20 in 1982

Source: Consultants News, the firms, Economist estimates,
          The Economist; as quoted in A Survey of Management Consultancy, Feb 13, 1988.

The technical need for using outside management help is linked to the accelerating sophistication of all areas of economic activity. Scientific knowledge grows exponentially, and with it all functions of industry, commerce and finance become ever more complex. This in turn is accompanied by a deepening division of labour, which extends into all areas of the service sector. As was pointed out in Chapter 2, the tertiary economy in the post-war era has been extensively shaped by the externalization of producer services. These activities previously carried out in-house, but which have steadily become cheaper to farm out as they have developed their own economies of scale. To them must be added the newer services which effectively emerged as independent parts of the economy. Many parts of management consultancy fall into this category, with demand being spurred by the desire to acquire specialist skills, either temporarily, or where possible, permanently through training by outsiders.

The role of government and international trade:

Ironically, government has long been a crucial player in the industry which is geared to the more efficient working of capitalism. The significance of public work can be traced back to World War II. The huge management challenge which total war imposed on society and the creation of a vast war economy in the United States, in particular, created a substantial market for management consultancy.

More recently, the drive to greater efficiency in public sector spending that has swept the industrialized world, in the wake of general disillusionment over government, has provided a renewed source of demand for consultancy. Based on absolute intervention by the state sector the case is clear enough. Despite years of rhetoric but limited action, the public purse still accounts for upwards of 40 percent of GNP in nearly all major economies — although this also includes transfer payments over which the state has limited control.

In Britain, 43 percent of GDP is allocated through government, with actual spending on goods and services accounting for just over 21 percent. Great wads of spending go into social security programmes (transfers of £41 billion), defence (£18 billion), health and personal social services (£17 billion) and education (£14 billion).[9] According to the Management Consultants Association (MCA), income from government represented nearly 30 percent of the total earnings of its members. The largest chunk of this is accounted for by central government. Demand from this sector has risen strongly in recent years, not solely because of the Thatcher government's desire to raise efficiency, but also in response to cut backs in civil service employment which mean that the necessary in-house expertise no longer exists. (Again, the process of externalization is at work.) In tune with political developments, consultancies are also intensifying their efforts in local government, and the NHS and education. These are areas on which the government's campaign to control spending and make it more efficient is presently focusing. They should therefore provide a fruitful source of demand.

From an international perspective, the role of government and other official organizations also plays an important part in how trade in consulting flows. The World Bank, for example, is a significant user of these business services for the evaluation and implementation of the development projects it funds. The same is true for other such multinational organizations. This contrasts with the impact of government. Through their power of procurement, governments can act to block international trade by favouring domestic suppliers. There can be little doubt that this goes on. Notably, it arises where nationalist policies are pursued not just for reasons of prestige and independence, but as governments try to nurture domestic expertise.

That such policies are adopted stems no doubt partly from the overwhelming dominance of the US in the international market. With an estimated 60,000 consultants turning over $7 billion per annum, US suppliers represent 60 percent of the world's practitioners and 70 percent of all earnings.[10] This gives the Americans a commanding position in the world market, which is clearly reflected in the nationality of the world's main consulting houses.

Furthermore, because of the nature of consultancy, national markets when open are far more liable to foreign penetration by trade, than are accountancy markets, say. This stems from the diffuse nature of consultancy, the fact that it is not normally bound to fulfill legal obligations, and the way work can be commissioned to meet specific requirements which do not necessitate the existence of local production. Accordingly, it has been calculated that about 45 percent of foreign earnings for US firms are from direct trade.[11]

For the UK the share of international work is considerably less. According to the MCA, only 12 percent of all earnings in 1986 came from abroad. Of this, the EC provided the most important regional share, representing approximately a third of foreign revenues (ie. 4 percent of all earnings).

Law:

The international trade in law is restricted. This follows from the very high degree to which law services are, by definition, specific to the national market. Consequently, such markets are dominated by local producers, at all levels. This phenomenon is manifested in

184

the United States, which once again is by far the world's largest producer and consumer of legal services. Notably, the American industry is also being affected by the same competitive forces affecting other business services. In a drive to realize economies of scale and scope, the top end of the market is increasingly dominated by mega-firms.

In England a similar structure exists. The market is also shielded from outside competition because English law is based on precedent and not code — as opposed to European law which is constructed from a Roman and Napoleonic heritage. Furthermore, it has been suggested that the closed nature of these two anglo-saxon professions stems greatly from the traditional links which local practitioners have with the banking and insurance sectors in the major centres where they operate: notably New York and London.[12] Therefore, although there are a considerable number of foreign firms represented in the City, have had limited success in staking out a substantial share of London's business.

National exclusiveness derived from the actual law itself, and structural barriers to entry exists elsewhere too. Thus in Germany, for example, the development of large, independent commercial law firms has been a comparatively recent phenomenon. Traditionally, bigger industrial and financial companies have relied on in-house departments to carry out much of their work, restraining demand of outside services. Similarly, entrance into the profession in Japan is very restricted. Indeed, the whole business of law is conducted in a very different environment from the aggressive litigation so strongly associated with the American industry. As a result, the overall size of the legal sector is small, proportionate to the economy.

What cross-national supply of legal services there is, tends to be very specific and carried out by direct trade. It frequently arises when overseas customers come into the domestic market, seeking the services available there. This is especially so for the UK. Far from being generated in the distant corners of the globe, foreign earnings by the law profession overwhelmingly accrue to the activity of solicitors and barristers in the City of London. There the latter carry out an essential back-up function to all the main financial service industries. The trade in law benefits from the concentration of activities which has developed in the Square Mile, and the international participants it has attracted. They too are fostered by the independent climate in which the City has thrived. The historical independence of the English judiciary has been of paramount importance.[13]

The main sectors from which these earnings generated are, not surprisingly, banking and insurance. In particular, the global shift to securitization has led to rapid growth in revenues since the beginning of the decade. In this process, solicitors are involved in drafting and issuing prospectuses, trust deeds and subscription agreements, as well as other documents determining the interaction between debt issuers, managers and the purchasers of the securities. London's position as the home of the Eurobond market has therefore greatly helped boost earnings since 1980, up by about 100 percent in real terms.[14]

Business also arises from the more established forms of banking, as in the syndicated loan market, which expanded rapidly during the 1970s. Again, details of negotiations and the drafting of agreements and contracts are carried out by solicitors servicing the various parties acting through the London market. So it is also with individual, international project finance. Such packages tend to involve co-financing by private and public investors. The attendant legal work is often very complex because there are no ready made models to follow.

A further substantial activity of the legal profession in the City is derived from Lloyd's and the international market in maritime insurance. With a refined and sophisticated case law, specialist law firms provide advice to underwriters, insurance brokers and the insured. The advantage the English legal profession has in this area is directly tied to the history of Lloyd's and the position it has built up and maintained as the world leader in this form of insurance.

Future growth:

The long term prospects for foreign earnings by Britain's legal profession are therefore linked to the health of the City as a major world financial centre. As long as the euromarkets and other offshore activities continue to be based in London, then the demand for legal services is likely to rise. Accordingly, two particular areas stand out. The first centres on the development of the triangular relationship between New York, Tokyo and London. If and when, for example, the separation between commercial and investment banking is terminated in the US and Japan, this could lead to a further rise in offshore banking conducted "at home". Were banking business to flow away from the London market, it would obviously reduce the demand for legal services.

Second, is the question of the single European market, to be established by the end of 1992. Even if exact deadlines are not met, there can be little doubt that this initiative will alter the whole framework of European financial and business services in the 1990s. To the extent that London's position as the continent's main financial centre is reinforced, the foreign demand for legal services undertaken in the City of London will grow. However, as Europeanization progresses, it must be asked whether the present market domination by British firms will be maintained. Notably, the principle whereby foreign financial institutions are regulated by the laws of their home country could well act to stimulate activity by outside companies.

Advertising:

Like accountancy, management consultancy, and even law, advertising is dominated by the United States. Not only is it the world's largest economy, but as a proportion of GNP it spends more on advertising than any other country. As a result, it accounts for upwards of 55 percent of all world spending. (It is important to note that the fluctuation of the dollar over the last decade has repercussions for the relative size of international spending.[15] Leaving size aside, the development lead which the United States took over Europe during the first half of the 20th Century, and the move to a mass-consumption society did much to accelerate the growth of advertising relative to the rest of the world. The early spread of television and its emergence as the main, single vehicle for advertising did much to underpin the growth of the American industry.

Reflecting this early expansion has been the emergence of the post-war world industry, with the creation of overseas branches of American producers. Foreign direct investment in local agencies has been the main vehicle for the international supply of this producer service.

The reliance on such establishment trade arises from the necessity of providing a service within cultural parameters that can be very specific. Thus, for example, American advertising tends to be direct, often putting on what Europeans would see as the excessively hard sell, especially where products are placed in immediate comparison. British advertising aims frequently to be more subtle, with a heavy accent on humour. It is arguably more diverse. In France, the emphasis is very much on the stylish and chic, often resulting in an odd blend of not-so-covert sex and hi-tech. The Germans, on the other hand, are marked by a certain correctness in their publicity. It is geared to being deliberately informative, almost didactic.

The few examples given here are not all-embracing. Exceptions are as frequent as the norm itself. Nevertheless, distinct cultural differences do exist, and are maybe even fostered because of the need to appeal to the mass market, the average man in the street, rather than the individual. Consequently, the national component to international advertising remains important, and foreign supply linked strongly to local production.

That said, things are changing. Without falling subject too much to the alarmist theories of cultural imperialism, there can be no doubt that consumer tastes in the developed world are converging. A trivial recent example has been the rise of the Yuppie. As a socio-economic phenomenon, the Young Urban Professional may have originated in the United States, but he/she has quickly spread elsewhere. Working in the financial service industries especially, the Yuppie has created a distinct trans-national image, associated with the consumption of high-performance, German motorcars, Swiss or French watches, English shoes and raincoats etc. Whether this amounts to Europeans aping Americans, or Americans aping Europeans matters little. The important point is that consumerism is being internationalized. The same is true down-market, as the poorer profligates chomp their way through "Big Macs", watch Dallas in every major European language, and take off in a Volkswagen in search of the Mediterranean summer sun.

Such shifts in consumption (facilitated partly by image makers), and the continuing internationalization of production in which European and Japanese companies have joined the Americans, are now creating the pressure for structural change within the advertising industry. It is leading to the emergence of "mega-firms". These arise through merger and acquisition. Their aim is to provide advertising services to multinational companies in all their main markets. By becoming so-called one-stop-shops that can satisfy General Motors all the way from Detroit to Düsseldorf, these multi-agencies are seeking to pre-empt national suppliers.

One consequence of this trend has been the tentative development of international advertising campaigns. A classic example is the "Malboro Country" cigarette advert which had astonishing success not just with an American public nurtured in the tradition of wide, open spaces, but also in a much more congested Europe. More recently, Saatchi &

Saatchi has launched a transnational campaign for British Airways, featuring a series of ads that can easily be dubbed into the requisite languages.

Equally significant is the changing structure of national ownership in the industry. Here the most noticeable feature of the last few years, has been the insurrection of the colonials in London, as they have turned the tables on their American masters. This is a story that has been largely shaped by the enigmatic brothers Saatchi. Setting up as a small London agency in 1970, Saatchi & Saatchi has become the world's largest advertising company in less than two decades. The performance is the most dynamic in the industry (see Table 11.3).

Table 11.3: TOP 10 ADVERTISING AGENCIES, 1986

Rank	Agency	Billings in £m	
		Own figure*	MR figure**
1	Saatchi and Saatchi	223.00	161.89
2	J. Walter Thompson	200.54	157.14
3	DFS Dorland	190.00	149.04
4	Young and Rubicam	142.00	92.65
5	Ogilvy and Mather	130.92	103.35
6	D'Arcy Masius Benton and Bowles	105.00	95.16
7	McCann Erickson Advertising	103.19	91.40
8	Lowe Howard-Spink Marschalk	102.20	62.16
9	Boase Massimi Pollitt	93.60	59.28
10	Grey	93.20	37.78

 * Own figures: all media and other activities
** Media Register figures: press and TV

Source: Financial Times Survey, Advertising, 29 October 1987 from
Campaign 20 February 1987.

The first great leap forward for Saatchi & Saatchi came in 1976. At the time, the agency was number 26 in the UK league, little more than a London-based shop. Then, the acquisition of Compton Partners (UK) catapulted the company to fourth place in the national market. The next landmark year was 1979. Saatchi's brilliant campaign for the Conservative Party brought the firm nationwide attention. In terms of market share, it captured the top spot in the UK. Next came the drive to global power with the purchase in 1982 of Compton Communications — the American cousin of Saatchi's UK acquisition. Finally, came the takeover of Ted Bates in 1986, which brought the agency to the top of the international table. As a result, the Saatchi & Saatchi empire presently takes fully 5 percent of world advertising, employing 14,000 people in 58 countries.[16]

The formula, if one exists, for such tantalizing growth is hard to define, let alone explain. At its origin undoubtedly lies the fertile yet opaque partnership of the two brothers, who appear to combine both technical advertising genius and startling business acumen. Thus Saatchi & Saatchi has so far been able to maintain the creative sharpness of its products. Similarly, the company has managed to get the financial support from the City to carry out its ambitious policy of expansion through acquisition. A more concrete reason lies in the highly innovative, yet very effective, financial strategy employed by the agency. Like many great ideas its basics are quite simple, and centre on splitting up a purchase into an initial downpayment, followed by stream of completion payments that are subject to future profitability. This has the advantage not only of extending the cost of acquisition, but also making it responsive to the ability to pay.

Much of the credit for executing the financial side of Saatchi's expansion must go to Martin Sorrel — former financial director of the company. He too has now emerged as a raider in his own right. Leaving Saatchi's in 1986, he became chief executive of a supermarket-trolley company called Wire and Plastics Products, now renamed WPP Group. This seemed a strange move for such a successful ad-man, but all was revealed in 1987 when WPP raided J. Walter Thompson. One of the traditional "greats" of Madison Avenue, JWT, though maintaining its creative talents, had slid into mismanagement. In many ways it offered the perfect opportunity for takeover by a hard-headed businessman, with an inside understanding of the industry.[17]

The issues and problems of internationalization:

It would, of course, be wrong to draw too many conclusions from these spectacular examples. Nevertheless, they point out that the world advertising industry is in a state of flux. This is already leading to other re-alignments, and could have further implications for the international ownership of the industry.

Yet, the shift to "mega-firms" brings with it a degree of instability. Industrial and commercial clients tend to switch agencies when acquisitions bring together advertising companies whose customers are competitors. When Saatchi's bought Ted Bates, the latter lost its long-established account with Palmolive-Colgate because Saatchi's already held a larger account with Procter & Gamble. Similar ructions affected WPP when it took over JWT. Led by clients like Burgerking, Sears and Roebuck, Goodyear and PepsiCo, JWT lost $400 million in billings, although it did manage to attract $350 million in new business. In this case the cause of departure was connected with growing long term discontent by the customers — the acquisition by WPP providing the trigger — and perhaps a degree of chauvinism in reacting to the intrusion of a foreign owner.[18]

Mergers can also generate considerable trans-national management problems. The dramatic bust-up which occurred in March 1988 between WPP and Lord Gellar provides an example of how high finance and high creativity do no always mesh well. Lord Gellar had been a small, independent, élite agency belonging to JWT. It included IBM amongst its prestigous clients, and was best known for the Charlie Chaplin ad campaign carried out for the computer giant. As it too came under the tighter business control of WPP, tension within the company rose. This led to a walk-out by the agency's top executives, to set up their own. Given the small size of Lord Gellar (billings prior to the breakup were running at $250 million) the damage to JWT is minor. Nevertheless, the affair demonstrated the dangers of aggressive international expansions.[19]

The emergence of a pan-European market is one of the most important factors facing British advertisers. It is being driven simultaneously by technology and legislation. The spread of cable and satellite television in Europe is opening up the possibility of multinational viewing and so a demand for multinational advertising. It is open to question how quickly the age of satellite dishes receiving ads for French yogurt or German butter will be realized. So far, Rupert Murdoch's Sky Channel continues to lose money, while the performance of the newer SuperChannel (jointly owned by ITV and the Virgin Group) has yet to be gauged. Nevertheless, it does not seem unreasonable to presume that European-wide programming will be part of the future of both television and advertising, all the more so given the emphasis the EC is placing on the free flow of services by 1992.

Another unknown of the international industry is the likely course of the Japanese market and its main producers. In absolute terms they are both big. With 1 percent of GNP, the Japanese advertising market is the world's second largest by a long shot.[20] A concentrated structure in which Dentsu and Hakuhodo respectively hold about 25 and 10 percent of the market, makes these two potentially formidable players on the international scene.[21] Nevertheless, what characterizes the Japanese advertising industry is its high degree of insulation.

This can partly be explained by the obvious cultural differences between Japan and its main economic partners. The issue of language alone creates enormous hurdles which scarcely exist between parent and subsidiary organizations in the US and UK, though more so between these two and the other main European markets. The same is true for differences in style and taste etc.

Added to this is the structure of the Japanese industry. Dentsu, which dominates the market, has been strongly connected with the emergence of the post-war radio and television industries, owning a small stake in Japan's commercial TV networks. As a result, the agency has a big advantage in securing advertising space. This is at a premium not just in TV, but also in radio and the press. Constrained accessibility amounts to a substantial entry barrier to both domestic and international competitors.

Given the importance of establishment trade to the earnings of advertising, changes in international ownership will be reflected on investment earnings. Repatriated profits will be flowing in both directions across the Atlantic. Again, given the statistics available it is hard, if not impossible, to calculate what these flows are. By comparison, it can be stated quite categorically that direct earnings on the trade account are very small. Globally it has been estimated that these account for only 15 percent of the direct/establishment trade total.

The foreign earnings of business services:

Two main factors stand out from the crude statistics on overseas earnings by Britain's business services (CSO figures give three income streams for: 1) solicitors and barristers, 2) management and economic consultants, covering accountancy, and 3) advertising). First, when compared to other branches of the service sector, the foreign contribution of these activities is marginal. In 1986 overseas revenues amounted to £322 million, up from and estimated £74 million in 1976.[22] Second, though the relative contribution is limited, it is constant and growing steadily (see Table 11.4).

Table 11.4: FOREIGN EARNINGS IN CONSULTING ENGINEERING AND BUSINESS SERVICES

	1976	1980	1984	1986
Consulting engineers	214	423	577	508
Solicitors and barristers	29	61	120	190
Management and economic consultants	17*	34	48	54
Advertising	28	48	64	78

* estimated figure, see note 22.

Source: CSO, "Pink Book", 1987

192

The most consistent performance was put in by management and economic consultancy. Its aggregate earnings expanded from an estimated £17 million in 1976, to £54 million in 1986, with each year clocking up a small nominal rise. By comparison, advertising revenues fluctuated slightly, suffering a recession between 1982 and 1984 inclusive. Nevertheless, overall nominal performance was positive, with earnings rising from £28 million in 1976, to £78 million by 1986.

The star achievers of the group were solicitors and barristers earnings. They exhibited spectacular revenue growth during the 1980s, tripling their nominal income between 1980 and 1986. As a result, the share generated by this sector within the business services total rose from just under 40 percent in both 1976 and 1981, to just under 60 percent in 1986. Management consultancy and advertising earned respectively 17 percent and 24 percent of the aggregate in 1986.

Notes and references:

1.   J.K. Galbraith, *The New Industrial State*.
2.   T. Noyelle and A. Dutka, Chapter 6,*Business Services in World Markets: Accounting, Advertising, Law and Management Consulting, lessons for trade negotiations*, for the conference on "Trade in services and the Uruguay Round Negotiations", Centre International de Conférences de Geneve, July 1987.
3.   Financial Times Survey, *Accountancy*, 15 December 1986.
4.   Financial Times Survey, *Accountancy*, 13 November 1987.
5.   ibid.
6.   M. Kubr *et al*, *Management Consultancy: A guide to the profession*, International Labour Office, Geneva, 1986.
7.   The Economist, *Management Consultancy Survey*, 13 February 1988.
8.   The classification given here is based on the main factors put forward by the ILO, ibid.
9.   Financial Times Survey, *Management Consultancy*, 26 October 1987.
10.   ibid The Economist.
11.   ibid. T. Noyelle and A. Dutka.
12.   ibid.
13.   D. Mullock, *The Overseas Earnings of the Legal Profession*, for the British Invisible Exports Council, Sept 1986.
14.   CSO nominal figures deflated by a price index implied from volume changes.
15.   W. Burger and R. Henkoff, *The Message Merchants*, Newsweek, 21 March 1988.
16.   ibid.
17.   D.K. Subramanian, *Les Anglais colonisent New York*, Médias, 12 Février 1988; as well as J. Buchan and N. Tait, *Moving out of the glass palace*, Financial Times, 9 March 1988.
18.   ibid Financial Times.
19.   ibid Financial Times.
20.   M. Waterson, *Surprise findings of new comparative study*,Focus, June 1986.
21.   Financial Times survey, *Advertising*, 2 October 1984).
22.   The 1976 figure for management and economic consultants is an estimate. When statistics for this activity were separated out of a residual "other consultancy" category, they averaged 19.5 percent between 1979 and 1986 of this aggregate. Thus it is calculated here that the income in 1976 was £17 million, or 19.5 percent of £87 million.

12 Film and television

The global market:

Along with Coca-Cola and MacDonald's, Hollywood and the US TV networks are the strongest exportable manifestation of the American way of life. Ranging from "Gone with the Wind" and the "Sergeant Bilko" to "Rambo" and "Dallas", American popular culture of the big and small screen has penetrated all corners of world. The crude statistics are dramatic enough. It has been estimated that the household market for audiovisual (AV) services in the OECD was about $26 billion in the early to mid 1980s. The lion's share of this is swallowed network television ($18 billion), followed by cinema ($6 billion) and lastly "new media" (like pay TV, video etc. — $2 billion). The US alone accounts for half this market. Similarly, of the 500,000 people employed in the sector within the OECD, 210,000 work in the US.[1]

American domination turns to near absolute hegemony in trade. Total OECD trade flows in film and television were reckoned to be about $1 billion annually (in the early 1980s). Of these, American TV and film respectively earned $350 million and $450 million (in 1980). Way behind, the UK took second place in TV earnings with $22 million, and France earned $15 million on films.

This overwhelming strength of the US is indirectly borne out by an earlier UNESCO study which concluded that in 48 countries over 90 percent of consumption in each domestic market went on imported films. In a further 14 countries, imports accounted for between 70 and 90 percent of demand, while only five countries consumed more domestic than foreign film.

Yet, despite the US weight in the audiovisual industry, these gross trade figures also show up two major features of the sector which have substantial effect on its trade, and beyond this the international supply of services. In the first place, the share of trade in overall consumption is very small, slightly less than 4 percent. As will later be shown, this stems largely from the cultural and regulatory barriers that affect TV products.

Secondly, the trade in audiovisual "software" pales into insignificance when compared to the exchange of hardware. Although the OECD calculates that consumption in the household sector for both product groups is roughly similar, trade in goods has a volume of $20 billion, 75 percent of it stemming from the annual addition/replacement of the 350 million TV receivers owned within the OECD. When looking at future of the entire audiovisual industry — and to so to some extent the developed world economy as a whole — this imbalance between the flow of goods and services stands out as a crucial factor.

What shapes the international market:

Essentially two main factors are at work in determining the trade in film and television. On the supply side, the market is primarily driven by the economies of scale of the US domestic market. With half the turnover of the world industry, the US producers can achieve economies in production that are not available to other producers. More importantly, however, they can rely on a huge reservoir of domestic demand that is more or less culturally and linguistically homogeneous. This effectively underpins large-scale production — even if the unit cost of the product is greater in the US than its equivalent is elsewhere. Quite simply, Hollywood and the major US TV networks have the resources to pour into a greater number movies or television series than do their competitors. Once these have been sold to the internal market, any overseas takings provide the jam on the bread and butter. Only about 7 percent of all revenues come from abroad.[2] Significantly, the scale of the US industry allows the large production houses to spread losses when they occur.

Conversely, the individual European industries do not have the scale and hence resources to dominate their own markets in a comparative way. As a result, they are forced to rely on comparatively cheap imports. This is especially true for feature films, but it also affects television.

Preventing the absolute free-flow of US material into European (and most other) markets is the intervention of government. It mainly occurs with the aim of supporting national industry, in the hope that this underpins domestic culture. In the film industry, the general policy instruments of government centre on the use of taxes/duties and quotas on imports, combined with subsidies for domestic production. Classification is usually determined by the nationality of the producer, the source of finance, the actors involved, the location of filming and use of other production facilities etc.

Despite these barriers, the trade in films is relatively free, at least within the OECD. The same cannot, however, be said for television. When George Orwell made his "telescreen" the centrepiece for totalitarian control in 1984 he was perhaps only slightly overstating the case. There is no other medium with the same ability to shape peoples' lives, with comparable powers of propaganda. Quite how pervasive television's influence can be, is, of course, open to discussion. It would be excessively simplistic, if not downright wrong, to suggest that "the masses" are simply fobbed off by the goggle-box. Nevertheless, if the average West European watches 2 1/2 hours per day, and the average American 4 1/4 hours, then television is bound to have some hold on public opinion.[3] Furthermore, there seems little doubt that this capacity is stronger in television than in alternative forms of communication. It is reflected, amongst other things, by the advertising resources poured into TV.

As a result, television is almost universally under nationalized ownership or subject to strict government regulation. The main exception is the United States, where nearly all channels are private and the controlling legislation is very limited. Yet, as little public money flows into American television, it is the market that controls, primarily through the allocation of advertising spending. The ensuing ratings war amongst the networks (in which one percentage point per annum equals $80 million in revenue: pushes production in the direction of the mass-market.[4] Programmes are made to attract the highest audience. This is not simply a trade-off between high-brow and low-brow, or minority- and majority-interest television. Instead, it is a strategy geared at providing a minimum level of satisfaction for a maximum number of people. Programmes are made that will attract the biggest audience, even if each individual in that audience would really rather watch something else.

A particular consequence of this programming logic is the desire to create popular series, be they soap-operas, sitcoms, or police sagas. The huge advantage these have is that a successful series tends to guarantee audiences and hence advertising revenue. Again, given the size of the American market, the industry which has grown up around such series is immense by international standards. Consequently, the potential for exports is substantial, due to the comparative cost advantage which off-the-shelf American programmes have over domestic production overseas. It is, therefore, hardly surprising to find that over 40 percent of the fiction broadcast in Europe is supplied from across the Atlantic.[5]

That American penetration of other markets is not greater stems out of a mixture of popular preference for domestic programmes and government intervention. Despite the appeal of American TV, audiences still tend to favour home-grown entertainment. Domestic soap is more sought after than foreign soap. Supporting such preferences are the systems of restrictions on imports and support for local production which governments impose in most countries. Again, quotas and taxes or duties are used to discourage imports. Production, on the other hand, is underpinned either through direct subsidies, but more generally through competition control. By restricting access to the market (through state ownership, licensing or whatever) governments can ensure monopolistic revenues for national TV stations. They can, therefore, produce programmes which could otherwise not compete, be these national series based on the American model, or cultural and educative programmes that do not attract wide audiences.

Britain as a performer:

Perhaps it is the inheritance of Shakespeare, perhaps secret exhibitionism that occasionally escapes a normally expressionless nation. Whatever the reason, the dramatic arts have always been one of potent parts of Britain's culture. It is therefore not surprising to find that the UK is the world's second largest exporter of film and television material.

But, if the relative standing is impressive, the absolute performance remains modest. This is especially so for television. Total turnover for the BBC and ITV is about £2.5 billion — made up largely from licence fee payments and advertising.[6] By comparison, earnings on the overseas sale of TV programmes amounted to only £110 million in 1985 (see Table 12.1).

The single largest vehicle for these exports is the subsidiary of the BBC, "BBC Enterprises Ltd". Set up in 1959 within the BBC, it became a separate company in 1979, though continuing to be owned exclusively by the Corporation. Its foreign earnings in 1986 amounted to £40 million, of which direct programme sales contributed £32 million, with the difference being made up by co-productions.[7] Marketing at BBC Enterprises is conducted through a number of departments, each responsible for a global region, e.g. Asia, the Middle East, Africa, Latin America and the Caribbean. Canada and Australia are directly served through local offices, while distribution in the United States is run

198

through a wholly owned BBC affiliate company (Lionheart Television), due to the complexity of this market. The next most significant exporter from the UK market is Thames Television, which accounts for about 1/6 of foreign sales.[8]

Table 12.1: OVERSEAS TRANSACTIONS OF FILM AND TELEVISION (BBC and IBA) COMPANIES
(in £ million and percentages)

| | 1980 | | | 1985 | | |
	Film	TV	% of total Film & TV	Film	TV	% of total Film & TV
Receipts						
EC	19	8	16	42	14	15
Other Western Europe	9	3	7	12	6	5
North America	61	30	53	171	65	64
Other Developed countries	14	6	12	16	16	9
Rest of World	18	3	12	19	9	8
TOTAL	121	50	100	260	110	100
Of which receipts in respect of rights restricted to television	22			17		
Expenditure						
EC	11	5	18	25	13	18
Other Western Europe	4	4	9	6	4	5
North America	40	18	64	71	56	62
Other developed countries	1	1	2	4	4	4
Rest of the world	3	3	7	18	5	11
TOTAL	59	31	100	124	82	100

Source: British Business: Dept of Trade and Industry, 19 Sept. 1986

Not surprisingly, blockbuster series like "Brideshead Revisited" and "Upstairs Downstairs" are successful. They dish out to foreigners (and indeed the British public) a certain version of what England was like, all brought across in sumptuous style. Highly popular too, are situation comedies, notably "Yes (Prime) Minister". In the sitcom business, the British share a virtual world oligopoly with the Americans. Oddly, enough, markets for these programmes also extend beyond the English speaking world, with countries like Sweden, Belgium and Spain buying up such comedy, despite problems of translation etc. Wildlife and natural history programmes are also very popular.

Yet, the importance of such programmes remains limited by the overall size of the export market. In the United States, for example, screening on network TV remains very conservative. The smash successes of Brideshead and Upstairs Downstairs occurred on the non-commercial Public Broadcasting Service. Similarly, the sitcoms are largely sold to the networks as scripts alone, with production being carried out in the United States. The market is therefore very restricted. In Europe, and elsewhere, a major impediment to exports — in addition to the usual legal constraints — is the cost of translation. The viewers in the larger European countries prefer to watch dubbed TV, and this creates a considerable extra cost.

In terms of imports, the flow is also comparatively limited. In 1985, Britain's television companies bought productions worth £82 million. With an aggregate budget of £2.5 billion this represents a mere 3 percent of turnover. But, given the relatively low cost per hour of such imports their share in programming is considerably greater. Still, it has been estimated that British material represents just over 85 percent of all broadcast television.[9] Again, the reasons for such limitation stem largely from cultural preferences, backed up by a policy within the stations themselves of restricting imports. There are no specific government regulations, be they quotas or duties, aimed at curtailing the use of foreign products.

Turning to the film sector, it is perhaps not surprising to find that the flow of material into and out of the UK is much greater than in television. Cinema is generally much more international than television, as has been pointed out above. It is also the sector where America's comparative domination is strongest. Indeed, of all the "long films" shown in Britain (ie. films of 33 1/3 minutes playing time or more) between 70 and 80 percent are foreign and these are overwhelmingly American.[10]

This makes the earnings and receipts of the film sector by far the larger part of the combined film and television total. Notably, foreign earnings have risen substantially since the early 1980s. This has been due to the international success not so much of big hits like "Gandhi", but to a number of medium-sized films like "A Draughtsman's Contract", "My Beautiful Launderette", "Mona Lisa", "Room with a View" etc.

On top of the recent flowering of such films — for which the production strategy of Channel 4 must get considerable credit — the general rebound of cinema-going has provided important impetus to the market. Since reaching a post-war low of 53 million, attendances have recovered quite significantly, rising to 73 million in 1986 and probably 80 million in 1987.[11] But, the growth of demand has obviously not been entirely to the benefit of the British film industry. Huge foreign successes like "Rambo", "Rocky IV", and "Crocodile Dundee" have also helped double nominal expenditure on imports since 1982.

Another aspect of the film trade figures follows from production expenditure by foreign companies in the UK, and overseas spending by UK-resident firms. A substantial share of the latter is connected with the need to shoot on location. By comparison, production in the UK is also largely motivated by the availability of film services, which either do not exist elsewhere or are cheaper here. In certain special effects areas, for example, UK facilities are exceptionally good. On the question of expenses, the UK has also been a desirable location, especially when compared with the United States during the years of dollar strength, though this cost advantage has eroded more recently. Nevertheless, the importance of production earnings — especially from North American companies — continues. It makes up about half the receipts on the film account, and slightly more than half the expenditure.

Into the future:

In the immediate future, it seems likely that present trends in film and television will continue. This is especially so for the film industry. It has long undergone the transition to competition from television as the major alternative audiovisual medium. In the case of television, the situation is a lot more complex.

The issues facing British and European television are of potentially monumental consequence. At root they are propelled by technology, although the administrative drive to a single European market will likely also have a considerable impact on the industry. Specifically, the two most important forces affecting television today concern the distribution of material through cable and over satellite. In the international context, these are by no means new sources, in the sense that they have only just emerged from the laboratory. But, their proliferation in Europe has been slow. This is especially the case for cable TV, which has suffered not just from indecisive government, but is further discouraged by the substantial infrastructural costs entailed and their long pay-back time. Forecasters have estimated that by 1990 it will reach between 50 and 60 percent of all "TV households" in the United States, yet only just over 20 percent (or about 25 million homes) in Europe.[12]

Similarly, the expansion of satellite TV in Europe has been a lot tougher than was widely expected at the turn of the decade. Again, part of the blockage stems from the slow spread to cable, as this is one means for distributing satellite TV across the

Continent. It also arises, however, from the costs involved, the incompatibility of national TV systems, and the general uncertainty surrounding the emergence of a pan-European market that can be tapped by direct broadcasting. As a result, for example, the oldest English-speaking satellite network in Europe, SkyChannel (owned by Rupert Murdoch) was piling up annual loss in the order of £10 to £15 million during the mid-1980s.[13]

Nevertheless, it must be said that cable and satellite do almost certainly represent a considerable part of the future of television in Europe. This in turn is likely to cause a substantial change in the structure of TV services across the Continent. Overall, the main result will be the breaking of government's hold and regulation over the medium. It will follow from the fact that government will no longer be able to determine the provision of services — either directly through state ownership or indirectly through licencing. Satellite TV creates the possibility for transnational programming to be beamed straight into the homes of an international audience. The same is true for cable, albeit to a lesser extent. At the start of 1987, for example, the US network NBC launched a cable news channel, aimed at eventually reaching Western Europe's 340,000 to 500,000 hotel rooms.[14]

The financial impact on Europe's current television network in the future will be substantial. Most obviously, the break-up of national monopolies/oligopolies will likely impose severe pressure on existing commercial stations. They will find themselves without the restricted market for the advertising air-time they currently sell. Concern was, for example, already voiced by the ITV companies (to the Peacock Commission) about the possibility of introducing advertising to the BBC. The eventual arrival of, say, five or ten commercial channels broadcast via cable or satellite would undoubtedly generate even greater competition. The same is true for most of the other European national networks, where commercial competition remains largely circumscribed.

Difficult to predict in such a highly modified environment, is the future effect on foreign earnings. Indeed, the concept of neatly delineated foreign earnings as understood will be greatly altered, if it does not disappear altogether. How will the income and expenditure flows of a multinational satellite channel, screening TV programmes (produced in America and various European countries) at a pan-European audience, paid for by multinational adverts, be defined and allocated?

What can be said, however, is that British TV probably does have a comparative advantage over its Continental rivals. Not only is it widely respected across Europe, but its respect is built on the existence of an export industry which is not matched elsewhere. Furthermore, although problems of transmitting to different language groups will always exist — and may in fact represent the paramount obstacle to pan-European television — Britain has the advantage that English is increasingly entrenching itself as the world's *franca lingua*.

Notes and references:

1.   OECD, *International Trade in Services: Audiovisual Works*, Paris, 1986.
2.   G. Pineau, *L'Europe des Programmes*, Dossier de l'audiovisuel, N 13, Mai–Juin 1987, La Documentation Française.
3.   A. Gottlieb, *Television*, survey in The Economist, 20 December 1986.
4.   ibid A. Gottlieb.
5.   ibid G. Pineau.
6.   The BBC and the Financial Times survey, *Advertising*, 29 October, 1987.
7.   BBC Enterprises.
8.   B. Lalanne, *La Foire aux images*, Dossier de l'Audiovisuel, N 13, Mai–Juin 1987, La Documentation Française.
9.   ibid OECD
10. CSO, *Annual Abstract of Statistics, 1986 edition.*
11. ibid Financial Times.
12. ibid A. Gottlieb and G. Pineau.
13. ibid Financial Times.
14. Broadcasting, *NBC goes to Europe*, 6 October 1986.

13 Interest, dividend and profit revenues on overseas investments

Introduction:

A key component to the invisible trade income is the IDP earnings, or interest, dividend and profit revenue on all forms of overseas assets, predominantly held in the private sector. Such returns are generally a form of *rentier* income, and so a different type of invisible revenue from service sector earnings. As has been argued, the latter can legitimately be called products, to be sold in either the domestic or international markets. Such is not the case for IDPs. Instead they are the interest generated by accumulated capital. Thus, they constitute an unearned income — or return on the current account from investments registered on the capital account. Above all, this is the case for income generated by overseas portfolio investments (ie. by paper assets).

By comparison, the profits flowing from foreign direct investment (FDI) stem more from the commercial and industrial process. Traditionally, such investment has been geared to exploiting raw material sources, benefiting from lower foreign labour costs, as well as supplying local markets with domestically produced manufactures. It is generally a physical form of investment in plant and equipment, real estate, overseas offices, management branches etc. With the strengthening of international economic links, such FDI has also been increasingly aimed at developing foreign distribution networks, through which producers in the home country sell their output in the host country. This is especially the case for services. Indeed, as already pointed out, the nature of many services products often makes distribution an indistinguishable part of production. As a result, foreign markets can frequently only be supplied through the establishment of local producers/distributors. FDI is therefore a vital component of service sector trade.

The new Conservative liberalism:

Historically, IDP earnings have played a crucial role in Britain's economic development. Britain's heyday as a *rentier* economy came at the end of the 19th century, lasting until 1914. By World War I, Britain had accumulated £4 billion in foreign investments, generating £180 million in earnings.[1] By the end of World War II, however, the bulk of

205

this empire in overseas investments had been dismantled. Indeed, when lend-lease was cut off by the US in 1945, Britain suddenly found itself a debtor nation unable to meet its foreign liabilities.

Yet, even after the long boom of the 1950s and 1960s had restored the balance on the capital account to surplus (ie. overseas assets rose in excess of liabilities), Britain's role as an international creditor remained limited. This stemmed not just from her underlying trade position, but also from the maintenance of exchange controls by both Labour and Conservative governments. During the 1970s, the situation changed little. The deterioration of the trade balance after the first oil shock, and the ensuing recourse to borrowing from the IMF in 1976, coupled with of stricter exchange controls under the Labour government, meant that total foreign assets remained restricted throughout the decade.

Since then however, there has been a fundamental change. It has largely followed from two major factors. First, the newly elected Conservative government lifted all exchange controls during the second half of 1979, in line with its free-market politics. For the first time since the war, British residents were permitted to export capital in any capacity, and so hold unlimited foreign assets. Secondly, the termination of exchange was soon followed by the emergence of a surplus on Britain's oil trade. This shift in her economic activity engendered a dramatic turnaround in the trade balance, and so strengthened the current account. Under an inflow of current earnings, the UK was able to accelerate the outflow on the capital account.

Table 13.1: SUMMARY OF UK EXTERNAL ASSETS AND LIABILITIES IN £ BILLIONS

		1975	1979	1985	1986
FDI					
	Assets	18.6	31.4	74.8	90.8
	Liabilities	12.1	22.0	43.3	48.6
	Balance	6.5	9.4	31.5	42.2
PORTFOLIO INVESTMENTS					
	Assets	6.9	12.3	100.7	145.7
	Liabilities	6.1	10.4	32.4	42.9
	Balance	0.8	1.9	68.3	102.8
BANKS					
	Assets	61.6	126.4	369.7	438.2
	Liabilities	67.9	135.8	416.0	493.4
	Balance	-6.3	-9.4	-46.3	-55.2
OTHERS					
	Assets	11.6	27.7	50.2	56.2
	Liabilities	9.7	17.4	26.6	31.7
	Balance	1.9	10.3	23.6	24.5
TOTAL NET		2.7	12.2	77.2	114.4

Source: CSO, "Pink Book", 1987.

The subsequent build up of net foreign assets has been spectacular. Between 1979 and 1986 Britain boosted its net overseas assets from £12 billion to £114 billion (see Table 13.1). Though provisional estimates show these to have fallen by £20 billion in 1987 since the world stock exchange crash, Britain remains the world's second largest capital exporter. Only Japan has larger overseas holdings. The United States has recently emerged as the world's largest debtor, following several years of crushing trade deficits.

Britain's build-up of external assets:

Traditionally, overseas holdings have resulted from foreign direct investment in physical assets. These integrated mining, commercial agriculture, manufacturing and commerce abroad with the economic activities of the home country. In Britain's case, a history of international trade and then colonialism has made such links a crucial characteristic of its economic development. Even today, the number of large multinational firms operating out of the United Kingdom is disproportionate to the size of the domestic economy. Not surprisingly, FDI remains an important feature of Britain's activity and its capital account transactions.

Since the end of exchange controls, the aggregate overseas assets accumulated through FDI have risen from £31 billion to £91 billion by 1986. Over the same period, investment by non-residents in the UK expanded from £22 billion to £49 billion, yielding a net rise of £33 billion. This rise in asset values is not entirely attributable to the net outflow of capital. During the period, the latter amounted to £26 billion. The difference between these two figures is explained by the appreciation in value of existing assets. It is due predominantly to two factors. First, it follows from the fall in sterling. When this takes place it boosts the sterling value of assets denominated in the currencies against which the pound depreciates. Secondly, overseas assets may also grow in worth. Such has been the case for financial assets especially, as will be shown below.

It is beyond the scope of this report to look at the composition of FDI in any detail. But, as has been pointed out above, the overall, international trade in services is strongly linked to the development of overseas production and distribution outlets — the so-called establishment trade. For the UK, the service sector accounted for just over 30 percent of FDI in the decade to 1984.[2] Since then, there has been a large jump in banking investments overseas, so that services as a whole probably now represent closer to 35 percent of all FDI.

Despite this most recent expansion, service sector establishment trade (as measured by this capital outflow), and indeed the total performance of FDI, pales into insignificance when compared to the build-up of overseas portfolio assets. These consist of "all investment in securities with an original contractual maturity of more than one year as well as in corporate equities, bonds and other securities with no specified maturity". They do not include "investment in short-term instruments such as Treasury bills", the latter forming part of "other capital transactions".[3]

The growth of such assets has been little short of astounding. In 1979, portfolio investments amounted to little more than £12 billion — 7.4 percent of all overseas assets. By 1986, these had risen to £146 billion, nearly 20 percent of the total. The resulting net expansion saw such holdings balloon from £2 billion in 1979 to £103 billion by the end of 1986. This surge in the capital stock was led by a total net outflow of £72 billion.

Again the difference between the growth in stock and the cumulative investment stems from the depreciation of sterling and the rise in capital values. Between its average value in 1980 and February 1985, sterling tumbled by over 50 percent against the dollar. Against the Deutschmark it fell by a third, from its peak in 1981 to its unofficially pegged rate of DM3.00:£1, held through 1987. Such a heavy depreciation will have had a significant effect on the sterling value of foreign assets. Conversely, the fall of the dollar since the spring of 1985 will have acted to depress the sterling value of dollar-denominated assets more recently. Similarly, the rise of the pound against the Deutschmark, which began in the spring of 1988, will act to reduce the sterling value of assets held in Deutschmarks and the other EMS currencies.

The expansion of portfolio assets has also vastly benefited from the international bull market in equities and bonds. It was triggered through a combination of factors, which took hold in 1982. To begin with, the tighter monetary policy adopted in most industrialized economies (and especially in the US) at the turn of the decade, combined with the global recession, had dramatically squeezed world inflation while raising interest rates. The corresponding rise in real yields once again made financial assets an attractive investment — contrasting with inflation hedges like commodities and property that had prevailed in the 1970s. Then, the Federal Reserve began to ease monetary policy in response to the American recession. With inflation under control, the ensuing fall in nominal interest rates placed direct upward pressure on bond prices, which also spilled into the stockmarket. Add to this the switch away from syndicated lending to the Third World and into security investments due to the debt crisis, as well as the rising confidence that was welling up in the American economy, and the scene was set. The US securities markets began to move, Tokyo was already in a bull market in any case, and Europe soon followed. The resulting global rise in the capital value of financial assets also boosted the stock of Britain's foreign portfolio investments.

Last of the major flows on the UK's capital account are the asset and liability transactions made up by bank borrowing and lending. These capital flows represent by far the largest single item on the capital account — 60 percent of all assets in 1986 and 80 percent of all liabilities. But, by their nature these transactions are different to FDI and portfolio investments, because they are intrinsically part of the banking process. They arise from London's role as an international banking centre: as the home of the eurobond market, a major pole in the world inter-bank market, and as a key location for all other offshore banking activities. In carrying out this business vast sums flow in and out of the market, and hence on and off Britain's capital account. Between 1979 and 1986, transactions on this account have also risen substantially, with assets growing from £126 billion to £438 billion, and liabilities expanding from £136 billion to £493 billion. As a result, net liabilities have increased from £9 billion to £55 billion.

The IDP revenue stream from foreign assets:

The stream of IDP earnings on the current account — which has followed from these outflows on the capital account — has risen accordingly. Total net IDP earnings on net assets have risen from £1.2 billion in 1979 to £4.7 billion by 1986. A breakdown of the aggregate figure shows that the biggest rise in net earnings has come on portfolio assets. Given their build up since 1979, this is not particularly surprising. Nevertheless, it does stand out in marked contrast to the consistent deficits on portfolio investments recorded during the 1970s. Indeed, it was not until 1982 that current account earnings from the sector swung into surplus (see Table 13.2).

A noticeable feature of the returns on these portfolio assets, has been the consistency of the yield — calculated as percentage of income/assets in each year. Only once during the last decade has it fallen out of a narrow band between 3.6 percent and 4.4 percent. (The exception occurred in 1985 when the return moved up to 5 percent.) Such a steady rate of return on portfolio assets contrasts quite strongly with the higher, but more erratic income generated by FDI. From 1976 till the end of 1986 the yield on physical investments overseas averaged 11.8 percent, but fluctuated between 8.6 percent (in 1986) and 18.5 percent (in 1979). The oscillations in the rate of return are also reflected in the debits on foreign investment in the UK, and hence the net earnings of this sector. In the trough of 1982, net income on FDI fell to a paltry £137 million, subsequently rising to a record £2.3 billion in 1986.

Table 13.2:   SUMMARY OF INTEREST DIVIDEND AND PROFIT EARNINGS
ON UK EXTERNAL ASSETS AND LIABILITIES IN £ BILLIONS.

		1975	1979	1985	1986
FDI					
	Receipts	1.95	5.82	8.08	7.81
	Expenditure	0.60	4.00	7.41	5.56
	Balance	1.35	1.82	0.67	2.25
PORTFOLIO INVESTMENTS					
	Receipts	0.27	0.54	5.05	5.70
	Expenditure	0.43	0.84	1.78	2.29
	Balance	-0.16	-0.30	3.27	3.41
BANKS					
	Receipts	4.00	9.82	35.87	31.00
	Expenditure	4.16	10.44	37.87	32.60
	Balance	-0.16	-0.62	-2.00	-1.60
OTHER					
	Receipts	0.34	1.35	3.36	2.87
	Expenditure	0.49	1.05	2.30	2.23
	Balance	-0.15	0.30	1.06	0.64
TOTAL BALANCE		0.89	1.19	2.99	4.69

Source: CSO, "Pink Book", 1987.

The divergent earnings profile by each form of overseas asset can be explained by numerous factors. FDI earnings, or the profits earned by ICCs, tend over the long term to be greater than returns on financial assets. This follows from the dynamics of the market. The sector is not only locked directly into the productive process, but its profit has to compensate for the greater risk it carries. Furthermore, its return has, by definition, to exceed any interest or dividend payment on capital borrowed or equity issued.

But, if this is the long run picture of FDI, its performance in the short run can very poor. It is much more likely to experience earnings fluctuations, being in the front line of all activity. Events since the first oil shock have borne out dramatically the potential for such changing fortunes. They have been reflected in FDI earnings, although it is

210

difficult to say what exact profit levels resulted from sterling's currency oscillations. Nevertheless, there can be little doubt that two main phases stand out. The first centred on the recovery of profits following the 1973/4 oil shock, culminating with the yield of 18.5 percent in 1979. The second major phase has been that of lower profits, associated with the world recession of the early 1980s, and the subsequent absence of strong, stable and widespread growth.

The apparently lacklustre, though very dependable, yield on portfolio assets is perhaps surprising, given the great boom of world securities which lasted from 1982 until the middle of 1987. It sits oddly with the variations that have affected world interest rates (both nominal and real) since the mid-1970s. There is less doubt, however, about the spectacular performance of such investments in terms of their capital appreciation. Between 1979 and 1987, the UK's overseas portfolio assets rose from £12 billion to £146 billion. Only £69 billion of this expansion can be attributed to new acquisitions. Consequently, the total capital gain on all portfolio holdings during the period amounted to no less than £65 billion (ie. £146 – 69 – 12 billion). As explained above, this capital growth has been largely due to the depreciation of the pound and the bull market in financial assets.

Net bank earnings on borrowing and lending also show by strong fluctuations. In 1981 they generated an exceptional surplus of £81 million. In 1985, a record deficit of £2.0 billion was chalked up. This deficit follows directly from the fact that liabilities have tended to exceed assets — given the way bank activity is disaggregated in balance of payments statistics. In the reality of banking, this division between traditional business and securities transactions etc. does not properly reflect banking activity and so the overall IDP performance of the banking industry. Still, a crude calculation of returns on overseas lending gives an average yield 8.8 percent during the period of 1976 to 1986. The rate of interest paid over the same time was 8.3 percent, suggesting that the average spread earned by the banks was 0.5 percent.

The Crash of '87, the rising current account deficit, and the politics of foreign investment:

The scale of IDP earnings, and above all their huge capital gains, provide a retort to the criticisms of the government's liberal exchange rate policy. More than anything else, these have centred on the belief that the windfall of North Sea oil could have been used to re-vitalize British industry. Instead, it is argued, the government simply allowed much of this wealth to be invested abroad, at a time when Britain experienced a slump in capacity utilization and a massive rise in unemployment. The latter entailed not just widespread social misery, but also swallowed up huge current sums through the payment of unemployment and social benefits — as indeed still occurs. So resources were frittered away in an unforgivable way.

Given the dire straits through which the British economy passed during the early 1980s, and a level of unemployment which is still very high by post-war standards, the appeal of this argument is obvious enough. A domestic investment strategy which would have boosted competitive industrial output, as well as creating new jobs, might have justified the continuation of exchange controls. However, it begs the question of whether yet another government-initiated, if not executed, growth policy would have worked. It does not take a dyed-in-the-wool Conservative to see the obvious problems of the Alternative Economic Strategy (AES), put forward by Labour at the time. A Keynesian fiscal expansion, protected with trade barriers, supported by renewed industrial policies and nationalization, would have caused political problems with the EC. Beyond this, it would probably have led to a severe misallocation of resources as industries like steel, coal and shipbuilding would almost certainly have received high levels of state aid.

The case against the huge capital exports since 1979 is therefore ambiguous, when looked at from the point of view of domestic output and employment. It is, however, less ambiguous when approached from the financial standpoint. Given the growth of capital assets, the investment of oil revenues overseas just cannot be portrayed as wasting resources. Instead, it can be strongly argued that undertaking such investments while the price of oil was high (and sterling was strong, at least at first) was the best way of converting this finite resource into permanent assets yielding permanent returns.

Furthermore, the move into a current deficit which began in 1987, accelerating strongly during the first half of 1988, will likely help redress Britain's net asset position. Although the causality between the current and capital accounts is complex, the UK is likely to suffer a rise in foreign liabilities to finance its imports, and hence a closing of the capital account surplus. Again, to the extent that this reversal of balance of payments flows is due to rising investment, the allocation of capital by market forces will probably be more efficient than if it had been imposed by government.

But, there are a number of fundamental qualifications to this more positive interpretation of the build up of foreign assets. Just as the Lord giveth, so the Lord taketh away. There is nothing to suggest that favourable currency and market movements, which have so benefited the capital value of assets, cannot be reversed, perhaps substantially. Indeed, this has already happened.

US Secretary of the Treasury, James Baker, may have been full of good intentions when he went on a further bout of talking down the dollar in the early autumn of 1987. Another effort to boost American export competitiveness and hence reduce the trade deficit was, and remains, a worthy cause. Unfortunately, his timing proved less than opportune. The US stock and bond markets were shaky. In response to rising inflationary pressures, the new Federal Reserve Chairman, Alan Greenspan, had already raised interest rates during the summer, squeezing bond prices. At the same time, Japanese investors were becoming increasingly wary of US bonds, given the currency losses they had suffered on their dollar investment. As a result, their purchases were slowing down significantly, putting further downward pressure on prices and upward pressure on interest rates. By August 1987, the weakness in bonds was beginning to spill over into the stock market, though to a limited degree. Then came Baker's public spat with the Germans about the value of the dollar, and on Monday, 19th October, Wall Street plunged a record 508 points. In the subsequent days, all the world's leading exchanges followed.

Since the crash, neither the prophets of doom nor optimism have proved founded. On the one hand, after five months the markets did not go into a further downward spiral — as occurred after the Great Crash of 1929. Nor is the world economy threatening a Great Depression. On the other hand, the instability of all markets, with the notable exception of Tokyo, would suggest that a sustained rally is quite a way off. Such hesitancy is justified by the ambiguous nature of real activity. Thus, if Japan has succeeded in switching to domestic demand-led growth, considerable worries still centre on the US economy. These focus on the continuation of the twin deficits. Despite repeated efforts, it remains questionable whether Washington will seriously get to grips with the Federal budget in the immediate future. Indeed, it is almost impossible for any substantive measures to be taken before the new president is inaugurated in January 1989. Even then, the deficit reduction is likely to remain long and arduous. On the trade account, change is more likely to occur. In fact, it already has. Export volumes rose by over 15 percent in 1987, while personal saving has risen by about 1 percent of GNP since the crash. This is slowly being translated into a closing of the current account gap, although at a slower pace than dealers would like to see.

As a result, Wall Street and the currency markets remain nervous, and the danger remains that they are increasingly reinforcing eachothers' fluctuations. Thus if the dollar falls, it puts the Dow Jones index under pressure because of the threat of rising interest rates, and raises the incentive for foreigners to liquidate assets and so avoid further currency losses. Similarly, falls on Wall Street are reflected in the currency markets, when foreign investors pull out of the market and the dollar. The Japanese having so long poured billions into US T-Bonds, cut back their bond purchases in 1987, and have virtually ceased to invest in American equities since the crash.[4]

It has been provisionally estimated that since the world stock market crash, Britain's net foreign assets have fallen to £90 billion. This figure is probably largely due to the capital loss of the crash itself, and subsequent currency losses on the dollar. At the same time, the contraction also results from a substantial run down of portfolio investments which occurred during the last quarter of 1987. Outflows on this account had already slowed greatly since the end of 1986. During the first three quarters of 1987, new overseas portfolio investments amounted to a "mere" £2.3 billion, compared to £18.7 billion for the same period in 1986. In the wake of the crash, these flows reversed dramatically, as an estimated £10.3 billion was repatriated.

Beyond this, uncertainty over sterling also threatens both Britain's net foreign asset position and so IDP revenues. This is not the place to indulge in excessive speculation on the future of the pound. Nevertheless, there would appear to be a number of important factors presently affecting sterling. Unfortunately, these are contradictory, and are different for the rates against the dollar and the Deutschmark/EMS block. With respect to the dollar, it seems most unlikely that the pound will experience significant change within the immediate future. The US currency has probably reached its trough. At the same time, a major rebound must be regarded as improbable.

Against the European currencies, the picture is more complex. The persistence of higher inflation in the UK than in West Germany, and even France, together with Britain's burgeoning current account deficit would suggest that sterling has to fall. Set against this is Britain's comparatively successful economic performance. Over the long term it ought to raise the pound. For the present, international confidence in Mrs

Thatcher's policies is holding up the value of sterling. Simultaneously, the Chancellor of the Exchequer has made known his preference for keeping the pound close to DM3.00, even though his neighbour at No.10 has more readily bowed to market forces.

On balance, it therefore seems that sterling will continue to fluctuate in the markets for the foreseeable future, but that such oscillations will be limited. The effect on overseas assets, denominated in pounds, and on IDP revenue earnings will therefore also be restrained. Some currency gains or losses are likely, but there will probably not be a massive shift in either direction, as has occurred over the last years.

Altogether, it therefore seems probable that the pattern of the IDP flows which has prevailed since the turn of the decade, is set to change. The stock exchange crash, with its effects on capital values and investment behaviour, together with likely rise in liabilities due to Britain's expanding current account deficit, suggest that the net asset build up experienced between 1979 and 1986 will has probably come to an end. For the intermediate future, it is appears likely that IDP earnings growth will slow below expenditure growth. This will return the IDP account back to the behaviour it experienced from the mid-1960s until 1980.

Beyond this strictly economic picture, lie the political constraints facing foreign investments and their returns. Mrs Thatcher took a bold step when she abolished all exchange controls in 1979. Given that both Labour and Conservative had operated some form of exchange control throughout the whole of the post-war period, her action then stood out as controversial. To the critics of the policy, who feared a flight of capital, events in the interim will only have strengthened their arguments for some form of control. Notably, the Labour party has argued that the capital which went into foreign investment could have been better invested domestically. Should Labour be returned to office at the next general election it cannot be ruled out that an attempt will be made to repatriate at least part of Britain's overseas investments — although this would probably fall foul of EC efforts to ensure free capital movement by 1992. To the extent that legislation and/or taxes would be used to penalize future foreign investment, or lure existing capital back to the UK, it will obviously affect Britain's net asset position and its IDP earnings.

Notes and references:

1.   H. McRae and F. Cairncross, *Capital City: London as a Financial Centre*, Methuen, 1985.
2.   D. de Laubier, *La percée des services dans les investissements internationaux*, Economie Prospective Internationale, for the Centre d'Etudes Prospectives et Information Internationales (CEPII), to be printed in 3rd quarter 1988.
3.   The CSO Pink Book.
4.   The Amex Bank Review, 24th March 1988.

The main statistical source for this section is the CSO *Pink Book*. In addition, Bank of England *Quarterly Bulletin* reports on Britain's overseas assets were extensively used to provide explanatory information about the variations in capital stocks and their income flows. These appear annually, usually in the second or third quarter issues.

PART 5

14 A tentative forecast

Introduction:

The difficulty with forecasts is that they are nearly always wrong. This is so, even when the environment within which the particular phenomenon to be forecast exists remains fairly constant. For example, nobody could blame the humble forecaster predicting growth at the beginning of the 1970s for not taking into account the effects of the first oil crisis. To be sure, world inflationary pressure was building up at the turn of the decade. Capacity constraints were pushing up commodity prices. But only a clairvoyant could have foretold that the Yom Kippur war would unleash a quadrupling of the oil price as the Arab world translated its political will into OPEC's economic action.

Less easy to explain away was the euphoria which surrounded the slump in oil prices in 1986. As the cost of a barrel of crude oil fell into the lower teens in *nominal* dollars, forecasters the world over were churning out optimistic prognoses of faster global growth at lower rates of inflation. In the event, the performance of the world economy changed little.

Despite, these obvious drawbacks and failures, the demand for forecasts persists, both at the macro and microeconomic levels. They continue to provide an essential part of the framework in which policy makers — either in government or private enterprise — plan their future actions.

This report too, aims at outlining a rough course for future invisible earnings. The basis for this prediction is, of course, the preceding industrial investigation. However, total income and expenditure flows on the invisible account go beyond the activities examined here. They include not only a number of other private sector services, but also government activity and transfer payments.

The methodology for this forecast is relatively simple. It combines both a basic statistical analysis and a qualitative prognostication of how earnings and spending are likely to evolve until 1992, after which the parameters of activity could change substantially, making longer term forecasting even more tenuous.

219

The statistical aspect of the prediction centres on breaking down the income and expenditure streams of each activity over the last two decades into four time periods: 1965-70, 1970-75, 1975-80, 1985-86. For each period a real growth rate is calculated. This is done by dividing the nominal credit/debit value in a particular year by a standard inflation index, and then calculating the average compound growth rate between the two end values in each period. A similar growth calculation for the entire time between 1965 and 1986 is also made.[1] The aim of providing these two sets of statistics is to show up cyclical earnings trends on the one hand, and long term or secular trends on the other.

The projection of future income and expenditure which is then made, is based on an evaluation of the relative importance of short and long term growth patterns, as well as factors likely to affect growth over the next few years. This evaluation is made in the light of the preceding sectoral examinations, and is used to furnish the rate of real growth which each sector is likely to exhibit over the coming years. From this growth rate, earnings and expenditure figures are calculated for 1990 and 1992. These are computed using 1986 as base year, and are given at the value of the pound in that year (ie. they are not nominal figures including inflation between now and 1990 or 1992).[2] Given the qualitative interpretation involved in determining future growth rates, these forecasts are partly subjective.

The main assumption on which this forecast rests is that the operating environment of Britain's service sector exports remains broadly similar to what it is now. In terms of the world economy the assumption implies an evolution corresponding to the "reference scenario" put forward by the IMF. The latter stipulates "unchanged [government] policies, constant real exchange rates, and the absence of financial market disturbances". Under these conditions, the IMF predicts 3 percent growth in world output through till the end of 1989. Thereafter, growth in the industrial countries will run at an average of 2.8 percent until 1992, this being about the same as the average forecast for the second half of the 1980s. For the ("capital importing") developing countries, growth between 1990 and 1992 accelerates somewhat to 4.8 percent. No aggregate figure is given for world output growth between 1990 and 1992. But the stronger performance of the developing countries suggests that world output will probably slightly exceed 3 percent.

The accompanying trade picture presented by the IMF states that volume growth will peak at 5.5 percent in 1988, then falling back to 4.3 percent in 1989. No further estimates are given by the IMF. However, on the basis of 3 percent world output growth,

220

it seems likely that trade volumes will expand by between 4.5 and 5 percent until 1992. Should trade growth stabilize at this level, it will represent a significant improvement on the poor and fluctuation performance of first half of the 1980s, though it falls short of the 6.2 percent average recorded during the 1970s.[3]

Looking at the British economy, forecasts by the IMF and the National Institute for Economic and Social Research indicate that the very rapid growth experienced in 1987 will give way to a more moderate expansion in 1988, and a further slowdown in 1989. Accordingly, the organizations expect real GDP in 1988 to rise by 3 and 3.5 percent respectively, while in 1989 both forecast a drop in the rate to 2.2 percent.[4]

Turning to the medium term (ie. 1990 and beyond), prediction once again becomes more difficult. Other things being equal, it is to be expected that UK growth will probably be sustained around 3 percent, or slightly less than the average rate experienced since 1983. Under these circumstances, it seems logical to expect Britain's invisible account to conform broadly with trends established during the 1980s.

But, all things are not equal, and the UK economy shows all the signs of overheating. Notably, strong domestic demand, bolstered by income tax cuts, is putting upward pressure on inflation, as well as sucking in further imports. As a result, Britain's current account deficit is rising sharply and seems set to continue to deteriorate throughout 1989. At some point, this is likely to lead to government action to depress activity, and so force down growth. The impact of slower UK growth on the invisible account is likely to be positive on the whole, as indeed it ought to be on the trade balance. It ought to reduce demand for service sector imports while making British services more competitive abroad.

Nevertheless, it is assumed here that the downward adjustment of the UK growth rate will be limited. Similarly, it is assumed that the current account deficit will drive down the pound gradually, and that this movement will be limited. Accordingly, the forecasts made for Britain's invisible earnings are as follows:

Sea transport:

Britain's overseas earnings on sea transport have experienced a severe deterioration over the last fifteen years. From displaying buoyant growth at 7.7 percent during the latter

221

half of the 1960s, credit expansion slumped to 1.4 percent between 1970 and 1975. Subsequently, this meager growth rate gave way to contracting real earnings. Between 1975 and 1980 annual income fell by an average rate of -4.5 percent. In the 1980s, the fall accelerated to -5.5 percent per annum.

The dramatic fall in real income stems from the reduction of freight transport revenues, as well as a drop in receipts from ship chartering. These two factors, in turn, follow directly from the rundown of the British merchant fleet which has occurred since the mid-1970s. It is most likely that this process is now coming to an end. The simple fact that the fall in tonnage has already wiped out so much capacity, the likelihood that certain large companies like P&O will not shift away from the British flag, the probable emergence of the Isle of Man as Britain's own flag-of-convenience registration centre, and political pressure on the Government to stop the shrinkage, make it likely that the slump is bottoming out. Consequently, it is expected that real earnings will fall at a much slower rate than they have been. Thus, at a -1 percent growth, income by 1990 will be reduced to £3.2 billion, and to £3.1 billion by 1992.

Similarly, change on the debit side of sea transport is also likely to reduced. During the 1970s debit flows suffered negative real growth, at first at a mere -0.4 percent, then at a more substantial -4.6 percent. Between 1980 and 1986 the rate of contraction slowed to -2.8 percent. It is estimated that this rate will slow down further, so that there will in fact be no real change on shipping debits between 1986 and 1992.

The resulting balance in sea transport, that emerges from these trends, shows the 1986 deficit of £940 million widening gently to £1.1 billion by 1990 and £1.2 billion by 1992.

Civil aviation:

Unlike sea transport, long term credit growth on the civil aviation account has been positive. Expansion between 1965 and 1970, and from 1975 until the end of the decade was especially strong. During the first half of the 1980s, however, real earnings stagnated. The subsequent fall in nominal income 1986 pushed down the real rate of credit growth between 1980 and 1986 to -1.1 percent.

222

Given the one-off nature of the fall in nominal receipts in 1986 — due to the massive slump in tourism from the United States — coming on top of the poor state of world tourism during the first half of the present decade, it is most likely that earnings will resume positive growth. However, compared to the long term average, future increases will probably be constrained due to capacity limits on the British fleet. Consequently, it is not expected that earnings will expand by more than 2 percent per annum. At this rate credits in 1990 will reach £2.6 billion, and in 1992 will rise to £2.7 billion.

By comparison, debit expansion is likely to be considerably greater. Over the long term, it has developed at an average annual rate of 6.9 percent, as opposed to 5.3 percent for credits. Furthermore, even between 1980 and 1986 an average increase of 4 percent was recorded. Given the anticipated expansion of British tourism abroad over the next few years (see below), it is most likely that debit growth will continue at 4 percent at least. This will lead to foreign spending of £3.9 billion by 1990 and £4.3 billion by 1992.

The resulting balance on civil aviation will therefore fall from -£450 million in 1986 to -£700 million in 1990 and -£1 billion in 1992.

Tourism:

Over the long term, there has been a secular decline in growth of real tourism earnings by the United Kingdom. During the late 1960s an annual expansion of 12.4 percent was recorded. This fell to 9.2 percent in the first half of the 1970s and to 4.9 percent from 1975 until the end of the decade. In manifesting such a progressive slow down, the UK was broadly mirroring developments within the world industry. Similarly, the global recession during the first half of the 1980s, followed by the catastrophic fall in US tourism to Europe in 1986, caused real growth to sink further to 3.8 percent.

In looking to the future, it is most likely that earnings will experience accelerated growth, as the world industry maintains its post-recession buoyancy. Accordingly, it is estimated here that annual increases will average 6 percent over the next years. (Taking out the unusually poor year of 1986, in itself already raises the growth rate to 5.4 percent.) Such growth will raise the total level of receipts in 1990 to £6.8 billion, and to £7.7 billion by 1992.

Debit growth, however, is likely to be even faster. Since 1975 UK tourist spending overseas has expanded briskly, averaging growth of 9.3 percent during the latter part of the decade. Outgoings remained buoyant even between 1980 and 1986, picking up strongly in the latter year as spending recovered from the recession of the early 80s. It is most likely, therefore, that future expenditure will continue grow at least at the 7 percent attained during the this period. Accordingly, foreign payments will equal £8 billion in 1990 and £9.1 billion in 1986.

Under these conditions, the net balance on the travel account is set to deteriorate substantially. Other things being equal, a deficit of £1.2 billion will occur in 1990, widening further to £1.4 billion in 1992. Of course, not other things are not always equal, and a significant fall in sterling especially could have a strong impact on the balance as it raises foreign revenues, while discouraging overseas travel.

Financial and other services:

Insurance: The earnings on insurance have exhibited extreme volatility over the last two decades. This stems above all from the wild income fluctuations experienced by underwriters. Having undergone explosive growth during the late 1960s, real foreign income by British underwriters fell throughout the 1970s. During the last time period of this study (ie. 1980 through to the end of 1986), revenues once again witnessed dynamic growth. It was led by the huge surge of income in 1985 and 1986 at Lloyd's, due the recovery of the world insurance after its deep recession in the late 1970s and early 1980s. As a result, the annual growth rate during this period averaged 27 percent.

Earnings by brokers have been less volatile, though they too have oscillated considerably. Notably, these jumped strongly from a 2 percent average during the second half of the 1970s, to over 12 percent in the 1980s.

Such massive variations in income, make it very difficult to predict future revenues of the industry. Accordingly, it has been decided to use the average long term growth rate as the basis for projecting future earnings. For British underwriters, annual growth between 1965 and 1986 averaged 5.2 percent in real terms. Assuming that the relative importance of insurance in world economic activity is rising, and that the international component of this activity is expanding due to expenditure technological and regulatory

224

phenomena (like the creation of Europe's single market by the end of 1992), average growth ought to rise. At 6 percent per annum, this would yield a foreign income to underwriters of £2.2 billion in 1990 and £2.5 billion in 1992. It must, however, be stressed that these figures are very tentative. If, for example, the US property/casualty market goes into recession and/or claims on industrial waste disposal are granted by the courts then clearly the whole picture for underwriters changes.

For brokers, the picture is a little more stable. Over the long term annual growth has been positive in each time period, averaging 6.6 percent. This makes the growth between 1980 and 1986 of 12.2 look unusually high. Accordingly, it is estimated here that annual increases over the next years will be at the lower rate of 9 percent, translating in an income of £1 billion in 1990 and £1.2 billion in 1992.

Banking: Foreign earnings growth by Britain's banking sector averaged 11.6 percent between 1965 and 1986. This figure, however masks significant changes. Notably, until the 1975, growth at just over 15 percent was very high indeed. Then during the latter half of the 1970s it slowed to 6.3 percent, only to pick up again to 10.2 percent during the 1980s.

Despite the stock market crash in October 1987, and the one-off effect of Big Bang, all indicators point to a continued rapid expansion of British and international bank activity in London. If the world's securities business has slowed down in the wake of the crash, it is likely to be replaced, at least in part by other forms of banking activity. There has, for example, been a renewed interest in the syndicated bank lending that dominated the 1970s. One way or another London seems set to benefit from this business, in addition to being the obvious focal point for financial developments connected with the European drive to 1992. Consequently, it seems likely that growth in the order of 10 percent will be maintained. On this basis, foreign non-factor service income by banking will amount to about £1.8 billion in 1990 and £2.1 billion by 1992.

Commodity traders: In contrast to insurance and banking, the fate of Britain's commodity trading is unlikely to be buoyant. Since the global surge of commodity prices in the early 1970s, which translated into average real growth of 13.9 percent in invisible earnings for the London market, commodity traders have had to put up with falling real earnings.

Although the depressed state of world commodity markets appears to be giving way to firmer conditions, it must be questioned whether substantial change will occur within the short to medium term, and whether this will be translated into higher income for the traders. In particular, it is doubtful that there will be the fundamental changes in demand and supply schedules that could trigger a sustained turnaround in prices. Whilst depressed markets are leading to a rationalization of global commodity production, moderate world growth rates are likely to constrain demand for the time being. Consequently, it is estimated here that real foreign earnings by the London market will show only modest growth to £250 million by 1990 and £290 million by 1992.

Other financial services: This amorphous group includes revenues by Britain's export houses. Their earnings are on brokerage services provided for third-country trade in goods that are not commodities. This income accounted for 35 percent of total in this category in 1986. Further income in the group includes foreign brokerage earnings by the Baltic Exchange (22 percent of the total), the Stock Exchange (15 percent), Lloyd's Register of Shipping (2 percent), and other brokers (25 percent).

Forecasting for such a diverse collection of activities is, of course, a hazardous process, all the more so because of the fluctuations experienced during the last twenty years. Notably, growth fell from nearly 8 percent during the early 1970s to -2.4 percent for the rest of the decade, before recovering to an average rate of increase in the 1980s of 5.4 percent, this latter figure being almost identical with the long term growth rate.

Over the next years, it is estimated that growth in this category should pick up, due largely to faster earnings by the stock exchange and trading in financial futures. Furthermore, a hardening, at long last, of the international shipping market should underpin the otherwise lacklustre performance of the Baltic exchange. Accordingly, it is predicted here that this residual category of financial services will experience growth in the order of 7 percent, pushing up total earnings in 1990 to £890 million and to £1 billion by 1992.

Consulting Engineering: Consulting engineering went through a very fast period of growth during the 1970s and very early 1980s. As the two oil shocks transferred massive funds from the industrialized world to the OPEC nations, and on to other Third World countries as part of these earnings were re-cycled back into the world economy, worldwide demand for international construction soared.

When, however, oil prices reached their peak in 1981, when the Third World debt crisis suddenly exploded in August 1982, and once much of the basic infrastructural work had been carried out in those countries with the means to afford such development, international demand began to contract. This market situation was reflected in Britain's foreign earnings performance, which experienced an annual average fall in real terms between 1980 and 1986.

It seems likely that this movement is now coming to an end. Once the collapse of oil prices in 1986 has worked its way fully through the international demand structure, the market should stabilize and may even witness the return to positive, if modest growth.

Yet, to what extent this will rub off on British earnings is questionable. On the one hand, British companies have done surprisingly well in limiting the fall in foreign income. In doing so they have increased their share of international contracting business. On the other hand, British firms appear to be coming under growing pressure on financial competition. Following from the present government's free-market philosophy, state aid for development and credit support is being severely squeezed. As a result, British companies are likely to find themselves in a growing competitive disadvantage vis-à-vis contractors and designers which do receive state financial backing. Consequently, it is estimated that earnings growth is unlikely to be much more than 1 percent per annum, yielding an income of £530 million in 1990 and £540 million in 1992.

Solicitors and barristers: On the back of London's international banking and insurance activities, this sector has experienced accelerating growth since separate statistics have been available. Thus the average rate of increase jumped from 3 percent in the first half of the 1970s, to 10.8 percent in the second half, to a vigorous 13.4 percent between 1980 and 1986.

Given the continuing general buoyancy of London's financial services, and the further internationalization of City business as British firms expand abroad and foreigners move into the British market, to say nothing of the demand boost likely to occur as European business gears itself up to 1992, earnings in this sector seem set carry on expanding at a fast rate. Thus it does not seem unreasonable to propose future growth running at 12 percent. This will lead to foreign earnings of £300 million by 1990 and £380 million by 1992.

Management and economic consultants: Consultancy work of this kind has exhibited reasonable but unimpressive growth of 4.4 percent, since separate statistics were recorded in 1975. This aggregate, however, masks the fast expansion which occurred during the late 1970s when foreign earnings were growing at an average rate of just over 8 percent. Subsequently, growth dropped off substantially to 1.4 percent during the 1980s.

Looking to the future, it seems likely that the healthier growth environment for the latter half of the 1980s, combined with the evolving structure of international ownership and transnational production, will lift growth once more, and bring it more in line with its long term average. At 4 percent, earnings by the sector will total £60 million in 1990 and £70 million by 1992. Clearly though, the direct trade in such consultancy work remains a peripheral activity on the overall services account.

Advertising: More or less the same thing can be said about advertising. Although the world industry has been dominated by large multinational companies for quite some time, the reliance on local production or establishment trade constrains greatly the foreign income of this sector.

Furthermore, real income growth has been especially lacklustre, averaging a mere 1.3 percent between 1975 and 1986. It is possible that as the economies of Europe, in particular, integrate, direct trade will become important. Indeed, international advertising campaigns are already growing in importance, so that growth could well rise to about 2 percent over the next few years. This would lift foreign earnings to £80 million by 1990 and £90 million by 1992.

Film and television: Since the mid 1970s British film and TV exports have undergone sustained real growth, first at the relatively fast rate of 9.8 percent until the turn of the decade, and then at a more modest 3.8 percent. This expansion stands out in marked contrast to the the declining trend which had prevailed between 1965 and 1975.

It seems unlikely that there will be any major changes in the foreseeable future to reverse the present growth pattern. If anything, the continuing international development of audiovisual services will raise the growth rate. The expansion of cable and satellite television across Europe, in particular, is likely to provide a further outlet for British products. At the same time, the revival of the British film industry over the last years is likely to continue, and so should boost foreign sales further. Thus it is estimated that foreign earnings will probably rise in the order of 6 percent, to a level of £390 million by 1990 and £440 million by 1992.

Spending on overseas productions will, however, probably rise at a faster rate. Having maintained steady growth at 3 percent during the 1970s, debits on film and television shot up during the 1980s at an annual rate of 8.8 percent. Given the cost advantage of the US TV industry in producing fiction, and given the expansion of television time which began in the early 1980s and which is almost certain to continue, it seems most likely that real level of imports will carry on rising more or less at a rate of 8 percent. This would lead to total debits of £260 million in 1990, and £300 million by 1992.

Telecommunications and postal services (not covered in the report): Transactions in this sector arise on telecommunication and postal services provided by British Telecom and the Post Office to foreign PTTs and vice-versa. The rates charged for such services are set by international agreement.

Over the last two decades, credits have been generally quite buoyant, showing very strong growth at 14.5 percent during the second half of the 1970s. Subsequently, growth fell to 5.9 percent between 1980 and 1986. Activity over the next few years is expected to be closer to the long term average, notably as international business links strengthen. Based, therefore, on a growth rate of 7 percent, credits will expand to £850 million in 1990 and £980 million in 1992.

Turning to debits, these have consistently experienced faster growth than credits over the last two decades, and it is expected that they will continue to do so in the future. In particular, the level of spending rose very strongly during the early 1980s, averaging 11.4 percent. If the rate of increase falls back somewhat towards its long term average, debits are likely to rise at a rate of 10 percent over the next years. This will produce spending levels of £1.1 billion in 1990 and £1.3 billion in 1992.

North Sea oil and gas companies (not covered in the report): Payment flows in this area arise from services conducted by UK resident companies to foreign drilling rigs in the North Sea and vice versa. Not surprisingly, the sector underwent astronomic expansion during the 1970s as the exploitation of gas fields in the North Sea was expanded, and oil production was brought on line. During the 1980s, this gave way to negative growth rates, on both the credit and debit side.

Given the state of the international oil market, coupled with the declining output of oil production which set in during the mid-1980s, future income and expenditure streams in this sector are likely to continue contracting. Accordingly, it has been estimated that credits will fall at an average rate of -4 percent, to £150 million by 1990 and £140 million by 1992, while debits will contract at a rate of -3 percent to £500 million and £460 million respectively.

Land transport — freight (not covered in the report): This comprises of credit payments to UK haulers for carriage outside the UK of British exports and imports, and debits incurred to "all overseas land transport operators for the carriage of UK imports between the exporting countries and the UK".

Quite clearly, the flows in this sector are directly linked to visible trade. Given the development of such trade over the last decade, it is not surprising to find that debits have manifested far greater growth than credits. Since 1975 the former have experienced average increases of 18 percent, while the latter only expanded at a rate of 6 percent. Significantly, the growth of debits accelerated during the 1980s while that of credits slowed down.

230

Over the next years, it is estimated that credits will advance at about 5 percent as British export growth rises above its level of the first half of the 1980s. This will produce earnings of £190 million in 1990 and £210 million in 1992. Debit growth on the other hand will probably slow down to 20 percent until 1990 and perhaps 15 percent thereafter, yielding substantial payments of £720 million in 1990 and £950 million.

Royalties (not covered in the report): Royalty receipts and payments have experienced very erratic growth over the last two decades, making future predictions especially precarious. Notably, both income and expenditure plummeted at average rates of -14 percent during the second half of the 1970s, returning to only modest growth during the 1980s.

Given these very wide variations in behaviour, future flows have been calculated using the long term average. Thus credits are forecast to rise by 4.6 percent per annum to £990 million in 1990 and £1.1 billion in 1992, while debits are predicted to expand at a rate of 3.2 percent to £610 million and £650 million respectively.

Other services provided by/to UK companies to/by related and unrelated concerns (not covered in the report): This generic category of transactions contributes heavily to both income and spending, comprising of all UK private sector corporate services sold to and bought from related or unrelated private sector companies overseas.

On the credit side, earnings have exhibited strong growth since the early 1970s, maintaining a steady average rate of 10 percent from 1975 onwards. Accordingly, it seems likely that growth will continue to be in the order of 10 percent over the next years, so that by 1990 credits will total £3.3 billion and £3.7 billion by 1992.

Debit growth has also been substantial, but it has fluctuated much more strongly than credit growth. In particular, the startling expansion of 40 percent per annum experienced during the early 1970s gave way to -1 percent growth during the second half of the decade. During the 1980s increases once more accelerated to 8 percent. Given such strong fluctuations, the forecast for future debits is based on the long term average growth rate of 12 percent, leading spending of £2.6 billion in 1990 and £3.0 billion in 1992.

Expenditure in the UK by overseas students, embassies etc., and US bases and forces (not covered in the report): On the whole, these sources of foreign earnings, aggregated here, have exhibited steady but low growth. During the first half of the 1970s annual increases did accelerate to just under 8 percent. Since then, however, growth has fallen back considerably, averaging a mere 2.1 percent during the 1980s.

Given the importance of public spending to this sector, and the general stringency currently exercised over government expenditure throughout the world, it seems likely that credits will continue to grow at a low rate. At best it may attain 3 percent, yielding an income of £1.8 billion in 1990 and £2.0 billion by 1992.

Residual earnings (not covered in the report): This is a residual basket of earnings. It comprises not just "commissions on UK imports" and "miscellaneous" credits, as well as "loss/damage to UK imports" and "miscellaneous" debits, but also other income and spending categories which have not been treated elsewhere, or have been separated out of other statistics over time. In particular, this residual income stream includes earnings by process engineers, chartered surveyors and other consultants.

The varying, and composite nature of this category makes any form of prediction highly tenuous. However, as the virtual lack of growth in credits has been consistently recorded between 1970 and 1986, it is assumed that this pattern will continue. Consequently, real income in 1990 and 1992 will be the same as in 1986, or £1.4 billion.

On the debit side, residual payments have fluctuated more strongly. Of particular note is the strong contraction in the early 1970s. But, in the two periods since 1975, outflows grew constantly by just over 5 percent. It is therefore assumed that this too will repeat itself, so that by 1990 debits will amount to £310 million, rising to £340 million by 1992.

Aggregate income and expenditure on financial and other services: The sum of all credits arising from these individual projections yields a total income in 1990 of £16.1 billion, and of £18.1 billion in 1992. This implies average annual growth for all financial and other services of 5.8 percent. At such a rate of expansion, credit earnings will grow slightly more quickly than they did between 1980 and 1986 (ie. 5.5 percent), and slightly less quickly than over the whole period between 1965 and 1986 (ie. 6.0 percent).

Debits, on the other hand, will increase at a considerable faster rate than they did in the last period, as well as over the long term (both average growth rates being 3.7 percent). Aggregate expenditure for 1990 is estimated here at £6.1 billion, and at £7.0 billion in 1992. This implies a rate of growth of 8.6 percent until 1990, falling to 7.1 percent. The cause for the slowdown in the rate of increase stems from the fall in spending growth on land transport — freight. It is estimated here that expansion in this area is likely to drop from 20 percent to 15 percent, between 1990 and 1991.

The principle sectors driving such an accelerated expansion are telecommunications and postal services, land transport—freight, and other services provided to UK companies by overseas firms. These three areas already account for a large share of debits, and given their fast rates of expansion will not only expand their proportion spending, but will push up the overall level considerably.

The resulting balance on financial and other services will be, therefore, £10 billion in 1990, and £11.1 billion in 1992. This represents a fall in the rate of growth of the balance to 4.4 percent until 1990 and then 5.5 percent thereafter, whereas previously the balance showed long term growth of 7.8 percent and short term expansion of 6.5 percent between 1980 and 1986.

Interest, dividends and profits:

Private sector and public corporations: Long term growth of IDP credits has been high, averaging 10.1 percent from 1965 through to 1986. During the 1970s the rate of expansion was particularly strong, led by the development of international banking within the London market. Thus, earnings increased by an annual average of 19.2 percent during the first half of the decade, and 13.4 percent during the second half. Given such credits were to a large degree simply the mirror of payments, it is not surprising to find that debits also surged. Indeed, they grew even more rapidly, recording 37.5 percent growth between 1970 and 1975 and then 18.4 percent growth until the end of the decade.

During the 1980s, both credit and debit flows slowed down considerably, as the re-cycling of oil wealth progressively ceased and the nature of international banking changed. Significantly, however, the rate of credit increase at 5.9 percent surpassed debit growth at

3.5 percent. This reversal in previous trends can largely be explained by the huge rise in net portfolio assets accumulated by the UK, in the wake of exchange control abolition.

Trying to predict future growth of IDPs is an extremely hazardous business. First, There are a very large number of variables likely to affect not just rates of interest payments on overseas assets and liabilities, but also the actual size of these capital stocks. Fluctuations of the pound against those currencies in which assets and liabilities are held, financial market developments, world interest rate movements etc. make any sort of forecasting excessively conditional to even minor changes. It is no coincidence that previous growth rates of earnings and payments have oscillated wildly. Second, the relative size of IDP credit and debit flows on the invisible account makes their performance paramount.

That said, certain key factors are likely to shape the future development of these flows, and the underlying capital stocks which generate them. Primary amongst these is the future build up of foreign assets by UK residents. It has to be asked to what degree capital can continue to leave the UK. After Japan, Britain is the world's largest net capital exporter. Given the relative size of the UK economy it seems most likely that net asset growth will slow in the future.

This is all the more likely due to turnaround in world financial markets, and the growing pressure on Britain's current account. It has already been estimated (see Chapter XIII on IDPs) that since the October '87 stock exchange crash net foreign assets have fallen by over £20 billion, due to capital losses and the repatriation of portfolio assets. Given the continuing nervousness of global financial markets, the incentive to carry on building up foreign portfolio assets has been reduced as the potential for capital gain is now much less than it was during the 1982 to 1987 bull market.

At the same time, Britain's widening current account deficit is likely to put upward pressure on foreign liabilities. Although the causality between current account flows and capital account stocks is greatly blurred by exchange rate fluctuations and financial market movements (for example, between 1979 and 1986 the UK's net foreign assets rose by £102 billion, the cumulative currency account surplus was only £23 billion), there is little doubt that if the current account stays in deficit over the next years this will put downward pressure on Britain's net asset position.

Consequently, it is estimated that the rate of growth in IDP credits will probably slow down further to 4 percent. At this level, it will produce earnings of £54.5 billion in 1990 and £59 billion in 1992. By comparison, debits growth is estimated to accelerate to 6 percent, so that payments in 1990 rises to £51.8 billion and £58.2 billion in 1992. Such figures will lead to a falling net balance, down from £5.6 billion in 1986, to £2.7 billion in 1990 and £800 million in 1992.

Government IDPs (not covered in the report): Government credits arise largely from interest on foreign exchange reserves and on the UK's holdings in Special Drawing Rights (SDRs) with the IMF. Other receipts accrue to long term loans to overseas countries, as well as interest paid on sterling export credit advanced by UK banks and the Export Credit Guarantee Department (ECGD).

These earnings grew rapidly during the 1970s, but suffered a sharp, real average annual contraction of -6.4 percent during between 1980 and 1986, as real asset growth fell to zero. Given the expansion of reserves since 1986, it is estimated here that credits will probably rise. Consequently, receipts in 1990 and 1992 will expand to £1 billion.

By comparison, debits did grow during the first half of the 1980s. These are predominantly interest payments on overseas holdings of British government stocks, foreign currency bonds, notes and Treasury Bills etc. It is assumed that future growth will continue at the same rate of 4 percent, so that expenditure in 1990 will equal £2 billion, and £2.1 billion in 1992.

Transfer payments:

Private transfers (not covered in the report): Credits in this sector stem mainly from the repatriated earnings of UK nationals working abroad, in addition to pension payments and other transfers like gifts etc. Since the mid-1970s these have experienced real growth of 4 percent per annum, and it is therefore expected that they will continue to do so for the foreseeable future. Accordingly, inflows in 1990 will amount to £2.0 billion, and in 1992 to £2.1 billion.

Table 14.1 INVISIBLE EARNINGS: CREDITS

	65/70	70/75	75/80	80/86	65/86	1986	%*	1990	1992
General Government	-2.1	8.6	3.3	1.6	2.7	508	2	550	570
						508		550	570
Sea Transport	7.7	1.4	-4.5	-5.5	-1.2	3339	-1	3200	3100
Civil Aviation	9.3	6.3	8.1	-1.1	5.3	2922	2	3200	3300
Travel	12.4	9.2	4.9	3.8	7.3	5419	6	6800	7700
						11680		13200	14100
Financial and other Services of which:									
Insurance Underwriters	(42.8}	-5.2	-4.6	27.1	5.2	1740	6	2200	2500
Insurance Brokers		4.8	2.0	12.2	6.6	710	8	1000	1200
Banks	15.1	15.2	6.3	10.2	11.6	1208	10	1800	2100
Commodity Traders	-	13.9	-9.2	-2.4	-1.5	223	0	250	270
Other Financial	11.1	7.8	-2.4	5.4	5.3	995	7	890	1000
Consulting Engineering	-	16.4	10.2	-2.8	6.8	508	1	530	540
Solicitors and Barristers	-	3.0	10.8	13.4	9.3	190	12	300	380
Management and Economic Consultants	(6.0	-2.1)	8.1	1.4	4.4	54	4	60	70
Advertising	-4.2	-0.4	0.9	1.8	1.3	78	2	80	90
Film and Television	6.7	4.0	9.8	3.8	2.0	281	6	390	440
Telecommunications and Postal Services	-	40.5	14.5	5.9	7.6	651	7	850	980
North Sea Oil/Gas Companies	-		30.5	-2.3	19.7	181	-4	150	140
Land Transport – Freight			9.4	3.2	6.0	159	5	190	210
Royalties	11.9	1.3	-13.8	5.9	4.6**	(2800}	5	990	1100
Other services provided by UK Companies	5.0	17.9	10.9	10.0	11.4**		10	3200	3700
Expenditure by Students, Embassies and Military	2.8	7.8	3.3	2.1	3.9	1637	3	1800	2000
Residual	9.0	0.8	0.2	-0.9	2.1	1389	0	1400	1400
						12804		16080	18120
Private Sector IDPs	3.6	19.2	13.4	5.9	10.1	46610	4	54500	59000
Government IDPs	2.1	22.1	13.2	-6.4	5.5	760	7/0	1000	1000
Private Transfers	4.2	-1.2	4.2	4.0	2.8	1705	4	2000	2200
Government Transfers	-	-	6.4	7.3	6.9	2135	7	2800	3200
						51210		60300	65400
Total	7.4	10.1	7.4	4.6	7.2	76202		90130	98190
Net Balance	29.4	3.0	-2.3	22.6	9.4	7483		5530	4490

*   Projected growth rate
** 1980-85

236

Table 14.2 INVISIBLE EARNINGS: DEBITS

	65/70	70/75	75/80	80/86	65/86	1986	%*	1990	1992
General Government	-1.7	1.6	-2.7	1.9	-0.2	1907	2	2100	2100
						1907		2100	2100
Sea Transport	9.0	-0.4	-4.6	-2.8	-0.3	4276	0	4300	4300
Civil Aviation	10.8	5.9	7.8	4.0	6.9	3371	4	3900	4300
Travel	1.1	5.7	9.3	7.1	5.8	6065	7	8000	9100
						13712		16200	17700
Financial and other Services of which:									
Film and Television	-6.7	3.1	3.0	8.5	1.5	191	8	260	300
Telecommunications and Postal Services	12.0	6.8	4.7	11.4	8.8	749	10	1100	1300
North Sea Oil/Gas Companies	-	70.0	-7.8	-3.3	12.0	593	-3	500	460
Land Transport - Freight	-	-	11.5	23.7	18.0	346	20/15	720	950
Royalties	11.0	2.2	-13.9	2.6	3.2	(2250}	3	610	650
Other services provided by UK Companies	4.5	39.1	-1.1	8.0	12.0		8	2600	3000
Residual	2.4	-13.6	5.1	5.2	-2.8	254	5	310	340
						4383		6100	7000
Private Sector IDPs	4.2	37.5	18.1	3.5	14.5	41016	6	51800	58200
Government IDPs	7.1	-2.9	-1.0	4.1	1.8	1668	4	2000	2100
Private Transfers	-4.3	18.0	15.2	1.5	6.7	4370	2	4700	4900
Government Transfers	6.5	3.7	2.3	0.0	2.9	1663	0	1700	1700
						48717		60200	66900
Total	5.1	11.1	9.3	3.5	7.0	68719	5	84600	93700

* Projected growth rate.

237

Debit growth, on the other hand, has decelerated progressively over the last two decades, so that between 1980 and 1986 no real change took place. This status quo is projected into the future. Thus payments in 1990 and 1992 will still be in the order of £1.7 billion.

Government transfers (not covered in the report): Government transfers comprise largely of grants to foreign countries, as well as subscriptions and contributions to international organizations. For the UK, credits are the payments received from Common Market institutions. These have been subject to rapid growth since the began in the mid-1970s, and it is expected that they will continue to expand at their long term rate of 7 percent. By 1990 this will lead to receipts of £2.8 billion, and to £3.2 billion by 1992.

Debit payments made by the UK government include transfers to the EC, military contributions to NATO and its agencies, multilateral economic assistance, and transfers as part of the membership of various international organizations. Such disbursements rose very quickly during the 1970s, notably due to payments to the EC. During the 1980s there was a very marked slowdown of growth, and it seems likely that this will continue in view of the Government's overall policy on public sector spending. At 2 percent growth, therefore, it is estimated that debits will rise to £4.7 billion in 1990 and £4.9 billion in 1992.

The aggregate balance on invisible trade:

Summing the credit earnings estimated above produces an overall level of receipts in 1990 of £90 billion, and £98 billion in 1992. In real terms, this represents an average annual growth rate for the invisible earnings aggregate of 4.2 percent. At such a rate of growth, credits will expand at a considerably lower pace than their long term performance (7.2 percent), but only slightly less quickly than they did between 1980 and 1986 (4.6 percent).

For debits, aggregate payments in 1990 will equal £85 billion, and £94 billion in 1992. At these levels, they imply an annual rate of expansion of 5.3 percent. Whilst this level of growth is also below the long term rate, it is above the average increase registered between 1980 and 1986.

238

Given that debits are thus set to rise more quickly than credits, it follows that the real balance on Britain's invisible earnings will fall from £7.5 billion in 1986, to £5.5 billion in 1990 and £4.5 billion in 1992.

This reversal is largely due to development of net private sector IDP earnings which are scheduled here to undergo a considerable fall of £2.9 billion by 1990 and £4.8 billion by 1992. At the same time, sea transport, civil aviation and especially tourism will also contribute to the reduction of the present invisible surplus. Combined, these three sectors are estimated to witness a further deterioration in net earnings of -£900 million by 1990 and -£1.5 billion by 1992. By comparison, financial and other services will expand their surplus by £1.6 billion by 1990 and £2.7 billion by 1992. Given the size of the other contractions and especially on IDPs, however, this positive performance will be insufficient to maintain the real level of net balance.

Notes and references:

1. The choice of index in calculating real values is complicated and always entails a measure of compromise. To establish real volume growth in the export and import of services, a specific services index ought to be used, largely because price inflation in services tends to be higher than for the whole economy, and manufactured goods especially. However, as the aim of the prediction here is not so much to determine the real, absolute level of volume output, but rather the comparative value of the income derived from overseas sales in relation to the current account, it was decided that the Consumer Price Index would be more appropriate.

2. Assuming an average annual inflation rate of 4 percent, nominal values can be easily calculated by multiplying the figure for 1990 by 1.1699 (ie. 1.04^4) and by 1.2653 (ie. 1.04^6) for 1992

3. IMF, World Economic Outlook, April 1988.

4. Figures for the National Institute are given in its latest Economic Review, and have been taken here from the Financial Times, 26 May 1988.

15 Conclusion

The main question posed in the Introduction of this report asked to what extent invisible earnings, and service sector exports in particular, would be able to replace visible exports as a means of earning foreign revenue on Britain's current account. The necessity for addressing this issue stems from the severe deterioration experienced by Britain's trade balance during the 1980s.

Two factors have been overwhelmingly responsible for this development. The first stems from Britain's shift into a manufacturing trade deficit in 1983. This was an historic event for the nation which not only pioneered the Industrial Revolution, but had remained a net exporter of manufactured products even throughout the 1970s, as her competitive position declined progressively.

The second major factor which has precipitated the rapid plunge into current account deficit has been the fall in oil revenues. The sudden collapse of crude prices at the beginning of 1986, combined with winding down of North Sea production meant that foreign earnings on the oil account halved from £8.1 billion in 1985 and to £4.2 billion in 1986.

Leaving aside the income effect of the oil account, a more precise examination of Britain's trade balance reveals that the rise in the deficit has been led largely by the rapid growth in import volumes, relative to exports. During the first quarter of 1986, Britain's import and export and export volumes were up 24.9 and 17.5 respectively on their 1980 levels. By the last quarter of 1987, however, the divergence had accelerated sharply, so that imports were up by 52.2 percent on their 1980 level, whereas exports had only grown by 34.8 percent.

The variation in the performance of exports and imports is, of course, due to a host of factors. To an important degree, these centre on the competitiveness of British industry. Although the last years have seen substantial strides in the productivity record relative to most of the postwar era, significant improvements have also taken place in Britain's main rival economies. Furthermore, the comparatively high pace of wage settlements in the UK partly offsets these positive developments.

241

Significant also is Britain's relative growth rate. The UK is presently in the unusual position of being near the top of the OECD growth league. Given the interaction between growth and trade, this alone will tend to cause imports to rise more rapidly than exports.[1] The fact that Britain's current expansion has also been greatly driven by consumer spending further enhances the import propensity of domestic demand, due to the historical preference the British consumer has displayed for foreign goods.

Most indicators suggest, that demand will continue to be buoyant, although it will slow down during 1989. During the first half of 1988, growth in disposable income accelerated to about 8.5 percent. According to the National Institute for Economic and Social Research, such a rate of increase, together with the wealth effect of surging house prices (far outweighing the negative impact of the stock exchange crash), means that consumer spending will remain a dynamic component of domestic demand and hence will carry on underpinning import growth. Furthermore, private, non-residential investment has also been growing more quickly since the beginning of 1988, so that it too is strengthening demand and hence imports.

As a result, all forecasts expect a continuing deterioration of both the trade and current account balances. The National Institute ranks among the more pessimistic, predicting a current account shortfall of £6.2 billion in 1988, followed by an even greater deficit in 1989 of £9.1 billion.[2] Other forecasters are a little more optimistic. The OECD predicts that Britain's trade deficit in 1988 will rise to nearly £14 billion, and just over £16 billion in 1989.[3] This in turn will lead to a current account shortfall of £5.7 billion in 1988 and £7.5 billion in 1989.[4] More recently, after a disastrous deterioration in May, predictions for the deficit in 1988 have been greatly revised, with some forecasters expecting a shortfall of between £8 billion and £10 billion already in 1988.[5]

Much will depend on the continuing growth differential between the UK and its main trading partners. If it narrows, especially if national incomes rise more quickly in Europe, then the trade and current account gaps may not be forced open so rapidly. Similarly, if surge in sterling which occurred during the first half of 1988 is significantly reversed then smaller deficits in 1989 especially are to be expected.

Yet whatever the exact outcome of Britain's external position, there can be no doubt that the UK does face rising pressure on its trade balance, and hence current account, until the end of the decade and possibly well into the 1990s. Quite what the consequences will be are impossible to tell. Conventional economic logic would suggest that at some point such deficits will self-correct, as market forces are brought to bear. This would lead either to a substantial depreciation of sterling or the introduction of a deflationary policy by the Government as it seeks to maintain internal and external monetary stability — or some combination of the two.

An alternative scenario suggests that Britain could sustain a current account deficit for a number of years, by simply running down its net overseas assets (as foreign liabilities rise to pay for imports). This could quite feasibly occur, especially if the pound more or less maintains its present value. Under these circumstances, the market perceptions over the long term prospects of the economy become paramount, over-riding short term balance of payments difficulties. If the markets believe that the present current account problems are largely a transitory phenomenon linked to healthy growth, they will probably tolerate a deficit for a while.

This was, for example, the case of the US economy until 1985. Surging domestic growth led to a huge deterioration of America's trade position, which did not affect the value of the dollar. Indeed, the US currency experienced a massive appreciation, as foreigners invested in paper and physical assets. Subsequently, of course, the crunch came.

It is quite possible that Britain too will succeed in benefiting from similar market optimism over its economic prowess — at least for the intermediate future. Overseas observers widely attribute the present buoyancy of the UK economy to Mrs Thatcher's government. As long as the Iron Lady remains in power, therefore, Britain and sterling are likely to be able to draw upon considerable reserves of confidence. Significantly, and in direct contrast to the American experience, the UK government is set to record a budget surplus in 1988 and 1989. Furthermore, if the Britain's savings rate has fallen dramatically since the turn of the decade and private consumption has played a major role in the boom of the mid-1970s, the acceleration in investment which began in 1987 should also dampen market fears.

The likely contraction of Britain's invisible earnings:

Yet no matter how exactly equilibrium is maintained on the balance of payments, the principle conclusion of this report is that Britain's invisible earnings will not be able to cover deficits on the trade account. Indeed, it is seems likely that real invisible earnings will probably fall between 1987 and 1992. Table I provides a summary of the predictions made in the previous chapter, and shows how total invisible earnings (expressed in 1986 pounds) will fall to £5.5 billion by 1990 and £4.5 billion by 1992.[6]

Table 15.1: NET BALANCES ON BRITAIN'S INVISIBLE EARNINGS:-
PRESENT VALUES AND PREDICTIONS FOR 1990 AND 1992
(in £ millions)

	1986[1]	1986[2]	1987[3]	1990	1992
Government Services	-1399	-1401	-1600	-1550	-1530
Sea Transport	-937	-909	-921	-1100	-1200
Civil Aviation	-449	-537	-653	-700	-1000
Tourism	-646	-646	-968	-1200	-1400
Financial and other Services	8421	9102	9850	9980	11120
Private Sector IDPs	5594	5962	6899	2700	800
Government IDPs	-908	-905	-1173	-1000	-1100
Private Transfers	42	59	-	300	500
Government Transfers	-2235	-2216	-	-1900	-1700
Total Balance	7483	8509	7946	5530	4490

(1)   Source: CSO Pink Book 1987
(2)   Revised Estimates in Monthly Bulletin, April 1988
(3)   Monthly Bulletin

Above all, this turnaround in the performance of the invisible account stems from a reversal in the fortunes of Interest, Dividend and Profit earnings in the private sector. They represent by far the largest flows in invisibles, accounting for about 60 percent of receipts and payments. Consequently, any change in the annual growth rate of either income received on British assets or payments made on foreign liabilities will have a considerable impact on the overall level of invisible earnings. The problem of predicting future developments on this account lies in the significant volatility displayed by receipts and payments, and hence their net balance. Between the mid-1960s and 1980, net IDP revenues were generally positive, exhibiting some fluctuation but also demonstrating no growth in nominal terms.

Since 1981, IDP revenues have grown substantially as Britain's net foreign assets have been built up. Triggered by the abolition of exchange controls and the shift to a current account surplus (as North Sea oil came on stream), the UK private sector embarked on a vast foreign investment boom, predominantly in portfolio assets. Until 1987 this movement was sustained by the spectacular global bull market in bonds and equities. The depreciation of sterling from its giddy heights in 1980/1 acted further to raise the pound value of both assets and their yields.

The collapse of the bull market in securities during 1987, culminating in the stunning 508 point crash of the New York Stock Exchange on 19th October, appears to have brought this investment wave to an end. Provisional estimates suggest that Britain's net foreign assets shrunk by over £20 billion in 1987. This figure is partly accounted for by immediate loss of assets due to the crash itself. However, it also stems from a significant turnaround in portfolio investment.

British investors had already reduced capital outflows substantially during the first half of 1987: down to £2.1 billion, from £11 billion recorded during the second half of 1986. Then, in the second half of the year, overseas portfolio investments were actually run down, as £10.3 billion was repatriated to the UK during the last quarter (ie. during and after the crash).

Coming on top of this fall in the capital value of assets, is the present likely rise in foreign liabilities, due to the rapidly growing current account deficit. To be sure, the causality between current and capital account flows is exceedingly complex. As was pointed out in the previous chapter, Britain's net overseas assets rose from £12 billion in 1979 to £114 billion by 1986, whereas the cumulative current account surplus during the same period only totalled £23 billion. Conversely, predictions of what effect a current account deficit will have on the capital account are highly tenuous. Nevertheless, it does seem probable that a sustained deficit over the next few years will act to cut further Britain's net foreign assets, and by definition this will reduce the IDP income stream from such investments. Under these circumstances, receipts and payments growth would revert back to the pattern which existed from the mid-1960s until 1980, whereby expenditure expanded more quickly revenues.

At first glance, this may appear to be a rather gloomy picture. There are, however, two important qualifiers to be made. First, although most indicators do point to a fall in net assets and earnings, the very complex interaction between current and capital flows, together with the effect of financial market and currency movements etc. means that a heavy rundown in earnings is not absolutely certain. Second, to the extent that foreign liabilities rise to finance investment in the UK, the fall in net assets should prove beneficial to domestic output, and at some point should even strengthen Britain's visible trade performance. From this perspective, a reduction in net foreign investment should be welcomed by those who have argued all along that Britain ought not to let the windfall earnings from North Sea oil and other capital leave the country. Furthermore, given that the balance may now redress itself through market action, the redirection of capital should be more efficient than if it were imposed by government.

The fall in real earnings on the invisible account, however, is not solely due to a turnaround in IDP earnings. Significantly, it is to be expected that net revenues will also decline on sea transport, aviation and tourism. Together, these three activities represented just over 15 percent of all invisible receipts and 20 percent of payments in 1986.[7] As a share of non-factor service trade, they accounted for 50 percent of exports and 70 percent of imports.

The deterioration of the net balance in these areas stems largely from three main factors. First, the rundown of the British merchant fleet, even if it now bottoms out, basically means that Britain will be increasingly dependent foreign carriers to ship its trade, largely out-going exports, but also in-coming imports. Second, tourism is likely to experience a widening trade deficit, not because of a poor performance by the British tourist industry, but because of greater spending overseas by British travellers. Third, given the links between tourism and air travel, this is likely to spill over onto the civil aviation account — especially as capacity constraints are likely to affect British carriers, now overwhelmingly dominated by British Airways.

The performance of "financial and other services":

In contrast to the negative evolution of transport and tourism, financial and other services are expected to display continued real growth. These is predominantly led by earnings on insurance, banking and "other services" provided within the private sector.

Despite the attention which banking in the City has received over the last years, insurance remains the largest single earner of foreign service revenues — due mainly to underwriters earnings by Lloyd's. The difficulty with forecasting the future development

246

of insurance income arises from the substantial volatility it has displayed in the past. It has therefore been assumed here that earnings of the next few years will expand slightly faster than their long term average (as international markets continue to open up). It must, however, be stressed that fluctuations which so characterize the industry greatly qualify this assumption. If the US property/casualty market goes into recession, for example, it will have an immediate impact on British earnings, quite possibly causing them to fall. On the other hand, stable world growth and the absence of exogenous shocks could mean that underwriters profits will continue to expand healthily, though almost certainly at a slower rate than was experienced between 1980 and 1986, when revenues leapt out of recession during the last two years of the period.

More stable, and hence likely to experience positive growth are the earnings on banking. To be sure, the end of the bull market means that certain sectors (especially securities business) are likely to witness less buoyant expansion than they have over the last years. At the same time, the continuing internationalization of the world banking industry, combined with the entrenchment of London as the world's third major centre make it likely that income from foreign trade will carry on growing at a robust rate.

By definition, a hard analysis and prediction of earnings on "other services" provided by British firms to overseas companies, and vice-versa, is impossible to make, and this income stream has not been covered in this report. Suffice it to say, that revenues from this amorphous category have risen during the 1980s more quickly than expenditure, and it seems likely that this will continue to be the case for the foreseeable future.

No all embracing pattern came really be distinguished for the array of activities which constitute the rest of the "financial and other services" sector. On balance, all services are expected to exhibit growth in earnings and expenditure, with the exception of services provided as part of the exploitation of the North Sea. Other financial, legal, telecommunication/postal, and film/television services are likely to exhibit relatively fast growth (of 6 percent or more). By comparison, commodity trading, consultancy, advertising, royalty transactions, and services provided to overseas students, diplomats and military personnel are likely to experience modest growth at best.

The underlying characteristics shaping the future of invisible trade:

Looking more generally at the long term determinants of invisible earnings, a number of key factors stand out. Most fundamental is the comparative performance of non-factor service trade, against IDP earnings and visible trade. Contrary to received wisdom, historical data compiled by the OECD shows that relative weight of non-factor service export revenues in all foreign income actually fell between 1965 and 1984: from 21 percent to 17 percent of the total.

This is a crucial observation, because it contradicts the frequently held notion that pure service sector trade is set for unfettered growth. Significantly, the development of non-factor service trade has therefore not matched the extension of these activities within the domestic economies of the developed world, where they account for upwards of 55 percent of GNP and employment.

The root cause for this constrained performance lies largely in the inherent nature of services. Returning to Adam Smith's remark — that services are consumed in "the very instant of their performance" — it becomes clear that their trade is immediately limited by the inability of the producer to supply the customer at a distance. A service simply cannot be wrapped up and shipped to its market in the same way that a physical product can.

With the growing sophistication of the economic process this description no longer holds true in its absolute sense. The continuing division of labour interacting with the "externalization" of many producer services, combined with emergence of high value-added services, and the development of communication techniques in the wider sense, have meant that many service sector products are increasingly transferable and marketable. The rise of Information Technology has accelerated this process. A vast number of services can now be delivered instantly through the international telecommunications network.

At the same time, the distribution of services does remain different from that of goods. Significantly, supply of distant markets (be they domestic or international) frequently involves a degree of on-site production. Indeed, at a certain stage production and distribution in service activities are essentially indistinguishable. As a result, factor or investment trade is often inherently linked to non-factor service trade. To exploit overseas markets, firms have to undertake a degree of direct investment. This means that service sector trade is much more closely linked to international investment flows, and part of the yield from such trade is recorded under IDPs.

The rise in IDP revenues in the OECD is therefore directly linked to the extended international provision of services. However, it is important not to exaggerate this phenomenon. It would be erroneous to conclude that overall service sector trade has fared much better relative to visible trade, than simply suggested by statistics on non-factor trade. The reason for this stems from the fact that foreign direct investment plays only a small part in international capital flows. The vast bulk of overseas investments are in financial instruments or arise from banking transactions. Furthermore, service activities only represent between 30 and 45 percent of direct investments in the major industrialized economies.[8] (In the UK, services accounted for just over 30 percent of FDI in the decade to 1984. Since then there has been a noticeable acceleration of investment in banking, so that the current figure is likely to be nearer 35 percent.) Even including such establishment trade, therefore, the record of service vis-à-vis visible trade remains modest.

It is possible that this will change over time. To begin with, it is unlikely that the long run shift of resources into services in the developed countries has come to an end. Granted, private consumption patterns within these economies suggest that the reorientation of consumer demand towards services is restricted. Crucially, households are purchasing manufactured goods so that they can carry out a growing number of services in the home, therefore reducing market demand. Nevertheless, the share of services in the value-added of industrial products, together with an erosion of the distinction between the software and the hardware for many consumer and producer items, suggest services will continue to expand their share of the economy. Though, it may level-off at some absolute level.

The rising weight of services alone should lead to an expansion of trade. This will likely be enhanced by the further application of Information Technology to services, and greater direct investment in foreign markets. The more intensive use of technology — apart from raising productivity levels within services — should also help to make service sector products more sophisticated. In particular, is should make it easier to customize products for specific markets and clients. This would enable services to overcome cultural factors which oft act as impediments to trade.

Similarly, technology should facilitate the development of service sector trade by expanding the scope for transnational distribution. It should strengthen the linkage between non-factor trade and establishment trade, as communication between parent companies and their overseas affiliates improves, both qualitatively and quantitatively.

Greater access to foreign markets through direct investment is, therefore, likely to become increasingly important in all forms of service sector trade. Consequently, the issue of international liberalization and the erosion of national protectionist legislation is of increasing importance trade. In particular, services are especially prone to non-tariff barriers. Deliberate exclusion of foreign producers through restricted licensing, the acceptance of domestic professional qualifications alone, government procurement policies and subsidies, as well as controls on capital movements all distort international supply when they do not prohibit it outright.

With the launch of the "Uruguay round" in September 1986, services were finally brought on to the GATT agenda. Under strong pressure from the industrialized world, led by the US, the developing nation members of GATT admitted service sector trade into international negotiations for the first time. It is as yet difficult to tell what the final results of this move will be. By nature, multinational negotiations tend to be protracted. Furthermore, given that the issue of sovereignty becomes exceedingly sensitive in areas like banking and insurance, a conclusive agreement is likely to be some way off.

Yet, even if the international market were to be opened up radically, it remains questionable to what extent Britain will benefit above and beyond its main competitors. Historical data by the OECD suggests that Britain's relative performance in service sector trade has not been impressive. Between 1965 and 1984, the UK share in all non-factor service earnings generated by the OECD fell from 13 to 10 percent. Admittedly, this contraction was predominantly led by the decline of Britain's sea transport revenues. However, even in the catch-all category of financial and other services — in which it is widely assumed that UK has a comparative advantage — the record has been poor, with Britain's percentage share falling by 3 percent during this period.[9]

It is probable that crude earnings figures distort Britain's real achievement. Notably, the aggregate trade statistics given by the OECD are in current dollars. As the pound was overvalued against the US currency at the beginning of the period (ie. before the 1967 depreciation), and undervalued in 1984 (ie. the last year of the dollars meteoric rise in the early 1980s), it is likely that real earnings were first overestimated and subsequently underestimated. Yet, even with such distortions taken into account, the performance is far from unambiguously good.

Similarly, it must be questioned to what degree the UK will succeed against future competition. The United States clearly plays the dominant role in the international trade in services, both in direct and establishment trade. American producers are strong in nearly all the industries examined here, right through from conservative banking to more creative advertising, film and television.

In addition to this source of (traditional, anglo-saxon) competition, is the growing pressure exerted by newcomers on the international scene. Most important has been the rise of Japanese finance. Catapulted into world leadership by a strong domestic economy, huge trade surpluses and an appreciating currency, Japanese banks especially are making marked inroads into the world industry. At the same time, competition to producers in the industrialized world is mounting as parts of the developing world experience rapid economic advancement. With the growing sophistication of the Newly Industrializing Countries, in particular, the international supply of services like sea transport and construction is undergoing a fundamental geographical diffusion. This is a process which is bound to continue, if not accelerate, and will probably squeeze the relative performance of the industrialized world (including Britain).

Thus, from Britain's point of view, the European Community's drive to a single market by 1992 is perhaps likely to offer the most important opportunities in the foreseeable future. Whether or not all the barriers will have come down by the end of 1992 matters less than the fact that there can now be little doubt that the 1990s will witness a fundamental restructuring of the provision of services within the EC. Companies in all commercial activities are already gearing themselves to the single market. In services, perhaps even more than industry, this movement will likely manifest itself in an increasing desire to forge pan-European links with producers in other member countries.

For Britain, 1992 is most likely to favour banking and insurance services. The huge concentration of activity in London, means that the UK has significant comparative advantages in size. Furthermore, the presence of foreign competitors in the British market, indeed the fusion of international and domestic business which was brought about by the Big Bang, should also give Britain a qualitative advantage over many of its European rivals who have greatly shielded their domestic producers from such international competition.

Notes and references:

1.   see A.P. Thirlwall's trade constraint to growth discussed in Chapter I: Introduction.
2.   Financial Times, 26 May, 1988.
3.   OECD, *Economic Outlook*, June 1988. These figures are calculated on the dollar forecasts given by the OECD in 1988 of $25 3/4 billion and $30 1/4 billion for 1989. The latter have been converted into sterling by the author, using OECD exchange rate predictions of £0.5394 and £0.5335 to $1.00 for 1988 and 1989 respectively.
4.   The dollar figures for the current account deficit are $10 1/2 billion in 1988 and $14 billion in 1989.
5.   Financial Times, 28 June 1988.
6.   It should be noted that these predictions were made on figures given in the 1987 CSO "Pink Book", which have been subsequently revised, as shown. In particular, the new estimates for financial and other services, as well as private sector IDPs, are higher.
7.   These figures are based on the 1987 Pink Book, and may be somewhat different for more recent government statistics.
8.   D. de Laubier, La percée des services dans les investissements internationaux, Economie Prospective Internationale, for the Centre d'Etudes Prospectives et d'Informations Internationales (CEPII), to be printed in the 3rd quarter 1988.
9.   OECD, *Balances of Payments of OECD Countries*, 1986.